Trusting Trade and the Private Sector
for Food Security in Southeast Asia

Trusting Trade and the Private Sector for Food Security in Southeast Asia

Hamid R. Alavi
with
Aira Htenas, Ron Kopicki, Andrew W. Shepherd, and Ramon Clarete

THE WORLD BANK
Washington, D.C.

1 2 3 4 14 13 12 11

This volume is a product of the staff of The World Bank with external contributions. The findings, interpretations, and conclusions expressed in this volume do not necessarily reflect the views of The World Bank, its Board of Executive Directors, or the governments they represent.

The World Bank does not guarantee the accuracy of the data included in this work. The boundaries, colors, denominations, and other information shown on any map in this work do not imply any judgment on the part of The World Bank concerning the legal status of any territory or the endorsement or acceptance of such boundaries.

ISBN: 978-0-8213-8626-2
eISBN: 978-0-8213-8648-4
DOI: 10.1596/978-0-8213-8626-2

Library of Congress Cataloging-in-Publication Data have been requested.

Cover photo: Panos Photos.
Cover design: Naylor Design, Inc.

The background paper of Dr. Ramon Clarete, "Policy Reforms and Regional Cooperation for Improved Food Security in ASEAN," was prepared for the Asian Development Bank under a consultancy in May 2009. The views expressed in this paper are those of the author and do not necessarily reflect the views and policies of the Asian Development Bank or its Board of Governors or the governments they represent.

The views expressed in this publication are those of the authors and do not necessarily reflect the views of the Food and Agriculture Organization of the United Nations.

Contents

Figures

Tables

Preface

This study was initiated and led by the World Bank and strongly supported by the members of the Association of Southeast Asian Nations (ASEAN). It specifically concerns certain ASEAN policy objectives outlined in the ASEAN Integrated Food Security (AIFS) framework and in the Strategic Plan of Action on Food Security in the ASEAN Region (SPA-FS) 2009–2013, (http://www.aseansec.org/22338.pdf/), in which the heads of member states pledged to embrace food security as a matter of permanent and high priority.

The AIFS framework aims to provide "scope and joint pragmatic approaches for cooperation among" ASEAN member states. A key objective of SPA-FS is "to ensure long-term food security and to improve the livelihoods of farmers in the ASEAN region." In pursuing this goal, it aims to increase food production, reduce postharvest losses, promote trade-conducive market institutions, ensure food price stability, promote availability of and accessibility to agricultural inputs, and operationalize regional food emergency relief arrangements. Its initial commodity focus is on rice, maize, soybean, sugar, and cassava.

The study was conducted in close collaboration with the ASEAN Secretariat and teams from five ASEAN countries—Indonesia, Malaysia, the Philippines, Thailand, and Vietnam—as well as the Asian Development

Bank and the Food and Agriculture Organization of the United Nations. The aim of the study was to analyze the dramatic surge in food prices in 2007–08 that set back hard-won advances in poverty reduction, and to provide advice on ways to adopt new approaches—cooperative and unilateral—to the challenge of securing supplies of food that can dependably meet citizens' needs in good times and in bad.

Acknowledgments

This study is the result of the cooperation between the World Bank, the Asian Development Bank (ADB), and the Food and Agriculture Organization (FAO) of the United Nations, under the aegis of the ASEAN Secretariat (ASEC). The World Bank was responsible for the overall coordination and drafting of the report. The ADB was responsible for the sections on the role of the government and institutional framework, while the FAO covered the sections on the role of the private sector.

ASEC was the liaison between the Study Team and the teams of experts from the five countries studied—Indonesia, Malaysia, the Philippines, Thailand, and Vietnam—which were regularly consulted during the preparation of the study. An Inception Workshop held May 25–26, 2009, in Bangkok, Thailand, with the Study Team and Country Teams discussed and finalized the study's scope, agreed on its approach, and clarified the roles of participants in the study. A Discussion Workshop to review a draft of the study, held on July 19–20, 2010, in Jakarta, Indonesia, was attended by representatives of all five countries together with members of the Study Team. This final version of the report reflects the advice and direction provided in that workshop.

The Study Team was led by Hamid Alavi (team leader) and Aira Htenas from the World Bank. It included Ronald Kopicki (lead consultant); Francesco Goletti, Marcel Stallen, Bustanul Arifin, and Larry Wong, consultants to the World Bank; Andrew W. Shepherd, FAO; and Ramon Clarete from the ADB. Neil Sood, who was a junior professional associate at the World Bank at the time of the preparation of this study, provided valuable assistance and contribution to the team. The World Bank would specifically like to express its gratitude to FAO for making available the services of Andrew W. Shepherd (group leader, Market Linkage and Value Chains Group, FAO) to assist with this study.

Enrique Aldaz-Carroll, Fabrizio Bresciani, Patrick Labaste, Stephen Magiera, Wayan Reda Susila, and Marc Sadler provided guidance and valuable comments during the review process of the manuscript.

In addition to the individual authors and peer reviewers, this book benefited from the input and support of many experts, including Lourdes Adriano, John Baffes, Luc Christiaensen, John Lamb, Nancy Morgan, Marc Sadler, Iain Shuker, Rimta K. Silangit, and Robert Townsend. We would also like to thank Katsuji Matsunami, who at the time of the preparation of this study was project leader and adviser, Office of Director General, Regional and Sustainable Development Department, the ADB, for his continuous support and guidance in the implementation of the study.

Finally, the study would not have been realized without the support and guidance of Vikram Nehru, director, Poverty and Economic Management Network, and regional chief economist, East Asia and Pacific Region, World Bank; Tunc Uyanik, financial and private sector director, Financial Systems Practice and East Asia Pacific Region, World Bank; Bernard Hoekman, sector director, International Trade Department, World Bank; and Mona Haddad, sector manager, International Trade Department, World Bank.

Special thanks are extended to Rimta Silangit, World Bank liaison officer at the ASEC, who provided valuable input to the study and helped organize the inception and dissemination workshops. Thanks are also extended to Ruangrong Thongampai and Shienny S. Lie, who provided superb assistance in organizing the two events in Thailand and Indonesia, respectively.

Denise Bergeron, Patricia Katayama, Janet Sasser, and Dina Towbin of the World Bank's Office of the Publisher were instrumental in the editing and production of this book. Bruce Ross-Larson helped improve the quality of the final manuscript submitted to the World Bank's Office of the Publisher for publication.

Financial support for this work, provided by the World Bank's Multi-Donor Trust Fund for Trade and Development, is gratefully acknowledged.

Abbreviations

ACI	Agrifood Consulting International, Inc.
ADB	Asian Development Bank
AEC	ASEAN Economic Community
AFET	Agricultural Futures Exchange of Thailand
AFP	Agence France-Presse
AFSIS	ASEAN Food Security Information System
AFTA	ASEAN Free Trade Agreement
AIFS	ASEAN Integrated Food Security framework
AMAF	ASEAN Ministers of Agriculture and Forestry
AMS	ASEAN member state
AoA	Agreement on Agriculture (World Trade Organization)
ASEAN	Association of Southeast Asian Nations
ASEAN+3	10 country members of the Association of Southeast Asian Nations (ASEAN) plus China, Japan, and the Republic of Korea
ASEC	ASEAN Secretariat
ATIGA	ASEAN Trade in Goods Agreement
BAAC	Bank for Agriculture and Agricultural Cooperatives (Thailand)

BAS	Bureau of Agricultural Statistics, Department of Agriculture (the Philippines)
BERNAS	Padi Beras Nasional Bhd. (Malaysia's partner in the domestic paddy and rice industry)
BULOG	Badan Urusan Logistik (Indonesian national logistics agency)
BUMN	a state-owned enterprise (the Philippines)
CBOT	Chicago Board of Trade
CCA	Coordinating Committee on the implementation of ATIGA
CEPT	Common Effective Preferential Tariff
CIMMYT	International Maize and Wheat Improvement Center
CMLV countries	Cambodia, Myanmar, Lao People's Democratic Republic, and Vietnam
CP	Charoen Pokphand
CRS	Congressional Research Service
DOA	Department of Agriculture (Malaysia)
e-commerce	electronic commerce
ECR	Efficient Consumer Response
EDI	electronic data interchange
EU	European Union
FAO	Food and Agriculture Organization of the United Nations
FAOSTAT	FAO Statistics
FDI	foreign direct investment
FIELDS	fertilizer, irrigation/infrastructure, extension/education, loans, dryers and postharvest facilities, and seeds/genetic materials
FOB	free on board
GAP	good agricultural practices
GATT	General Agreement on Tariffs and Trade
GDP	gross domestic product
HCM City	Ho Chi Minh City (Vietnam)
ICTs	information and communication technologies
IFAD	International Fund for Agricultural Development
IFC	International Finance Corporation (World Bank Group)
IFPRI	International Food Policy Research Institute
Incoterms®	International Commercial Terms

IRRI	International Rice Research Institute
ISO	International Organization for Standardization
IWT	inland water transport
KLSE	Kuala Lumpur Stock Exchange
KUD	Kooperasi Unit Desa (rural cooperatives) (Indonesia)
LPI	Logistics Performance Index
LPN	Rice Board (Lembaga Padi dan Beras Negara) (Malaysia)
MAV	maximum access volume
MDTF-TD	Multi-Donor Trust Fund for Trade and Development
MEP	minimum export price
MFN	most-favored nation
MIER	Malaysian Institute of Economic Research
MNC	multinational corporation
MOIT	Ministry of Industry and Trade (Vietnam)
MT	metric tons
NFA	National Food Authority (the Philippines)
NMRI	National Maize Research Institute (Vietnam)
NRA	nominal rate of assistance
OPVs	open-pollinated varieties
PAFMI	Philippines Association of Feed Millers
palay	term for unmilled rice used in the Philippines
Perum BULOG	a state-owned enterprise that replaces the National Food Logistic Agency (BULOG) (the Philippines)
PPK	Persatuan Peladang Kawasan (Farmers' Association) (Malaysia)
PPPs	public-private partnerships
PUAP	Rural Agribusiness Development Program (Indonesia)
PWO	Public Warehouse Organization (Thailand)
QUEDANCOR	Quedan and Rural Credit Guarantee Corporation (the Philippines)
Raskin	Beras Miskin (Rice for the Poor Households) program (Indonesia)
SKU	stock-keeping unit
SOE	state-owned enterprise
SPA-FS	Strategic Plan of Action on Food Security in the ASEAN Region

SPS	sanitary and phytosanitary
STEs	state trading enterprises
S/U	stocks-to-use ratio
TNCs	transnational corporations
TQ	total quality management
TRI	trade reduction index
UN	United Nations
UNCTAD	United National Conference on Trade and Development
UNESCAP	United Nations Economic and Social Commission for Asia and the Pacific
USDA	United States Department of Agriculture
VFA	Vietnam Food Association
VINAFOOD1	Northern Food Corporation (Vietnam)
VINAFOOD2	Southern Food Corporation (Vietnam)
WRS	warehouse receipts system
WTO	World Trade Organization
$	All dollar amounts are U.S. dollars unless otherwise indicated.

Executive Summary

Introduction

This book challenges policy makers who oversee the rice sector in Southeast Asia to reexamine deep-rooted precepts about their responsibilities. As an essential first step, it calls on them to redefine food security. Fixating on national self-sufficiency has been costly and counterproductive. In its stead, coordination and cooperation can both improve rice production at home and structure expanding regional trade.

To enhance regional food security through quantitative and qualitative gains in rice production, policy makers cannot solely rely on government programs. They need to also enlist private investors both as entrepreneurs and as partners who can bring capital, energy, modern technology, and experienced management into sustained efforts to reduce losses and heighten efficiency in supply chains. For such investors and participants to enter vigorously into the rice sector from which they have long held back, they will need a number of incentives, among them a confidence that the regional market for rice will evolve toward a structured, liberalized market shielded from the unilateral government interventions that have distorted it in the past and continue to do so in the present.

The study's findings make it clear that current rice sector policies are not achieving their desired goals. Its examination of the 2007–08 food crisis found, in fact, that government policies and panicky responses were the primary factors behind soaring (and later diminishing) rice prices.

Those policies vary, but they share a common premise: food security depends, first of all, on self-sufficiency in rice. That premise has driven government intervention for decades, and unpredictable government intervention, in turn, has been a significant factor in making the rice sector too risky to attract significant private investment.

Rice is a thinly traded commodity, a reality that also heightens risk, but the volatility of rice prices stems as well from misguided government responses to both real and—in 2007–08—only apparent shortages. In such circumstances, private entrepreneurs naturally limit their involvement in order to minimize risk.

Although rice and maize are very different commodities, the study takes time to examine the ways that domestic and foreign private companies have modernized maize supply chains in the ASEAN region. In theory, such firms could bring their focus on efficiency and capacity for innovation to the growing, processing, and marketing of rice. In practice, they stay on the sidelines of the rice industry. This study suggests a number of policy changes that could persuade them and other investors to reconsider.

The transition that this study urges will be difficult and, of necessity, slow to gain momentum. Nevertheless, it is already beginning. The members of the Association of Southeast Asian Nations (ASEAN) are working to liberalize trade in the region. The study is, in fact, intended to assist in implementing policy objectives outlined in the ASEAN Integrated Food Security (AIFS) framework and in the Strategic Plan of Action on Food Security in the ASEAN Region 2009–2013, in which the heads of member states pledged to embrace food security as a matter of permanent and high priority.

It is with those undertakings in mind that the authors of this book conducted their research and now present their findings and proposals for action. "A journey of a thousand miles," said Lao-Tzu, "must begin with a single step." Prompted by the food crisis of 2007–08, ASEAN is embarking on such a journey. In this book, its planners and their political superiors can find suggestions to the journey's end: secure supplies of food for growing populations with changing tastes but an abiding demand for one staple—rice.

The 2007–08 Food Crisis and Its Aftermath

When international cereal prices shot up in 2007–08, as rice prices, most notably, nearly tripled from October 2007 to April of the next year, the resulting food crisis, by World Bank estimates, drove over 130 million people into poverty. According to the Food and Agriculture Organization (FAO) of the United Nations, it also left another 75 million people malnourished (Headey 2010).

Although a number of factors played a role, the actions of ASEAN-region rice exporters set the stage for panicky buying by importers to turn a manageable supply-and-demand imbalance into a global upheaval. "The food crisis and especially the increase of the rice price was due largely to political choices," said Hafez Ghanem, assistant director-general of FAO. "In 2008, the production of rice was good; the stocks were high and consumption was stable. . . . What we saw is that the price of rice doubled in 2008, and this is explained mainly by the decision of certain countries to halt their exports."[1]

When unilateral trade restrictions imposed severe strains on the rice market in 2007–08, the spiral of responses exposed the failure of long-standing but shortsighted policies to treat rice as a modern agricultural commodity. In the case of the 2007–08 food crisis, observers initially pointed to standard factors in commodity shortages: a shortfall of production or an increase in demand or both. That familiar analysis, however, slights the deeper pressures at work.

The surge in food prices, in fact, was the result of multiple factors coming together in a "perfect storm" of concurrent conditions. Some related to the perceived tightening of demand-and-supply balances within the region; others related to the nature of the price formation process itself. Some analysts saw the 2007–08 world food price crisis as the manifestation of a long-term problem of insufficient production in the face of rising demand.[2] Others placed the crisis in the context of a larger global food crisis being driven by the weak U.S. dollar, rising fuel and fertilizer prices, increases in biofuel production, and crop failures in major agricultural production areas (drought in Australia). The two proximate but perhaps only recently acknowledged factors triggering the rice price surge, in fact, were policy decisions and buying behavior.

In other words, the dramatic escalation in rice prices in 2007–08 was not caused simply by a shortfall of production or an increase in demand. In early 2002, global prices of most commodities, including energy, agriculture, metals, and minerals, started rising after an extended period of price stability—and indeed of price decline in real terms. This upward trend intensified in early 2006 as energy prices continued to soar and the value of the U.S. dollar continued to fall. Between January 2007 and June 2008, when agricultural commodity prices reached their peak, the FAO

Food Price Index[3] rose by 63 percent, as compared with an annual rate of increase of 5 percent the year before.

Likewise, the price spike cannot be explained by a simple aggregate demand-supply imbalance. It did not reflect either below-average harvests in affected countries or rising demand or declining global supply. World milled rice production had been increasing steadily since the early 2000s. Production even registered an increase of 3.5 percent between 2005–06 and 2007–08.

All major Asian rice producers experienced good harvests in 2008, and record-high crop production was forecast for 2009. Indeed, global year-end milled rice stocks increased in 2007–08. None of the five ASEAN countries studied for this report registered alarmingly low stock levels. The average global rice stocks-to-use ratio for 2007–08 was 0.17, and by the end of the period was actually trending upward.

Until December 2007, the depreciating U.S. dollar did help to drive up the price of commodities like rice that are priced in U.S. dollars. However its drop did not play a major role in the 2008 rice price spike. Exporters in countries with stronger local currencies demanded higher dollar-denominated prices to offset their costs. By the same token, buyers in countries with appreciating currencies were able to pay higher prices at the margin. However, while Thailand's currency, the baht, appreciated 14.3 percent in 2007, contributing to the rise in rice prices, it depreciated 4.6 percent from December 2007 to April 2008, during the period when prices spiraled.[4]

Up to 2007 as well, rising oil prices did contribute to the increase in rice prices. In the absence of government intervention, higher oil prices increase production costs affected by rising fertilizer and agrochemicals prices, irrigation pumping costs, harvesting, drying, milling, and international and domestic transport costs. That upward pressure (estimated to explain around 20 percent of the rise in other grain prices like wheat and corn between 2002 and 2007) diminished at the end of 2007.

The severity of the crisis made clear the urgent need in Southeast Asia to examine and reform policies that underlay not only the immediate calamity but also the potential for a recurrence. Unfortunately, a number of postcrisis government interventions seem simply attempts to recycle the past,[5] harking back to the role of Green Revolution production technology when, along with continuing technological progress, what is required is a food supply-chain revolution. The introduction of new disease-resistant seeds and complementary investments in fertilizer, irrigation, and infrastructure did bring significantly improved crop yields in wheat, maize, and rice during the 1960s and 1970s. Those policies, focusing on internal markets, fostered large productivity gains, but the solutions of the past need to be complemented by policies to address the challenges of the present.

An example of giving priority to production is the Malaysian government's effort to increase rice yield from 2.47 to 4.48 tons per hectare by targeting specific groups of farmers, identifying Sabah and Sarawak as new frontiers for increased rice production (Arshad 2009). Also, in April 2008, the Philippine government launched its FIELDS program (fertilizer, irrigation/infrastructure, extension/education, loans, dryers and postharvest facilities, and seeds/genetic materials), which is designed to enhance the country's rice production so that, within two years, at least 98 percent of national rice consumption can be provided from local sources. Indonesia is aiming even higher, devoting public resources to increase rice production in order to attain full rice self-sufficiency (McCulloch and Timmer 2008). Even Brunei Darussalam, which is able to fill its rice requirement quite affordably from trade, launched a rice hybrid development program in September 2009.

Such subsidized yield improvements, plus any arable land expansions, will entail a considerable opportunity cost in terms of product shifts and income diversification at the farm level. At the precise time when rice sectors need to develop to the next phase of competitive capability, such government policies are pulling them backward. The renewed efforts to channel public resources into increasing local production, thereby sourcing more of their respective rice requirements internally, miss new opportunities to meet domestic demand through greater regional trade and private sector engagement.

Learning the Right Lessons

One clear message of the 2007–08 crisis is that trade is vital for ensuring regional food security. The point is worth underlining:

Agricultural trade, when structured so that the individuals and enterprises involved can operate profitably, helps countries respond quickly and efficiently to supply shocks within their own economies.

Equally important, trade can help stabilize prices by creating incentives for private merchandisers and processors to protect their own trading positions, without governments providing tacit or explicit guarantees.

Uncontroversial as those maxims are, they have yet to gain wide operational acceptance in Southeast Asia. The resistance is rooted in the place of rice as a cultural touchstone and a politicized commodity. Nearly sacrosanct, long-established patterns of rice production and processing have been hard to change. Historically, moreover, rice exports have not figured in much ASEAN thinking.

Trade in rice among them in 2008 added up to only about 3.5 million tons out of nearly 101 million tons produced. In world markets, as well, rice is very thinly traded, accounting globally for less than 30 million of the 420 million tons produced in 2008. Since nearly half of all exports that year came from Thailand (10 million tons) and Vietnam (over 4.6 million tons), it is understandable that the rice trade and its potential for expansion have held little interest for most of their fellow ASEAN members.

This study holds, however, that the experience of the 2007–08 food crisis should move issues of regional rice trade to a far higher place on the policy agenda. For that trade to grow, ASEAN governments will need to adopt measures that reduce supply-chain losses, improve supply response times, gain savings in farm-to-market costs, and shrink postharvest inventory losses.

Supply-Chain Weaknesses

Simplified and expanded trade is a critical element of the recommended shift in rice sector policies. In the ASEAN region, as noted above, trade generally involves no more than 7 percent of total rice production. In such a limited market, it is admittedly not easy to see convincing reasons why rice exporters and importers should enter into binding rice trade agreements.

Those reasons, however, exist. They can be found, quite concretely, in the rice supply-chain inefficiencies that translate into significant annual losses of rice. A reduction of postharvest physical losses by 5 percent (from nearly 14 percent to 9 percent) would create 4.3 million tons of rice equivalent for the five countries under study. This volume is more than the entire intra-ASEAN rice trade: 3.5 million tons in 2008. If that wastage could be significantly reduced, the amounts available for regional trade, to begin with, would grow in proportion. At the same time, it should be added, the savings would at least slow and possibly reverse the growth of budgetary outlays going to subsidize the rice sector and the heavy losses of state enterprises that have long controlled it.

Where rice is harvested and threshed by hand, dried in the sun, milled by low-capacity, outdated machinery, and stored so poorly that pests and even rain can attack the grain, it is hardly surprising that up to 15 percent of the crop is lost. When, moreover, rice is moved over bad roads by inefficient trucks or by sea in small vessels and through clogged ports, inadequate logistics can raise its price to consumers by 20–25 percent. Many—sometimes all—of those weaknesses feature, though to varying degrees of severity, in the supply chains of the five ASEAN countries studied for this book, with Thailand's supply chains more efficient than the four other countries.

The various failings in rice sector supply chains stem in large part from the age-old ways that rice has been grown, processed, and transported. Those inefficient patterns, moreover, are reinforced by policies that see food security narrowly in terms of self-sufficiency. Changing that perspective is crucial to the difficult tasks involved in overcoming venerable customs and inadequate infrastructure.

Rice supply chains remain reservoirs of marginally productive farmers, processors, and loosely associated ancillary service providers whose internal business processes remain independent and uncoordinated. Millions of actors are involved in national rice supply chains in ASEAN countries. Even in a country like Malaysia, with an official population of rice farmers numbering 130,000, the actual number of rice farming households probably is closer to 1 million.

Milling: Among ASEAN countries, average milling yields or recovery rates are generally well below their theoretical yields of 71–73 percent.[6] In the Philippines and Indonesia, milling yields are 63 percent; in small-scale, village-level mills, yields are even lower (57 percent). These low yields are related to the small scale of operations and sometimes result, as well, from poor-quality paddy that is processed, which, in turn, mainly results from bad drying. Poorly calibrated, maintained, and operated mill equipment aggravates this situation. Few mills have the means to measure moisture of paddy or to adjust the degree of milling that they affect.

Many of the problems identified in milling are similar in all five countries (with perhaps limited relevance to Malaysia and Thailand, where the number of mills is small) and include the following: (a) millers do not monitor grain moisture during storage and milling; (b) poor paddy cleaning results in high levels of foreign matter and cracked kernels in the paddy; (c) poor paddy separation results in low separation efficiency; (d) rubber milling rolls are used beyond their design life, and they are not interchanged or refaced; (e) milling stones are not refaced on a regular basis; (f) overmilling causes damage during the polishing process; and (g) evaluation tools, such as a moisture meter and milling degree meter for quality evaluation, are lacking.

The milling sector is in transition, with a large number of small and medium-size mills that cater to the domestic market and a few large mills, which cater to the export market, being gradually consolidated into fewer, larger mills. In Indonesia, the Philippines, and Vietnam, milling technology is often outdated, resulting in high levels of broken rice. In these same settings, millers are fundamentally constrained by a lack of capital to invest in new equipment. In Vietnam, preferential credit arrangements provided for state-owned mills hamper the ability of the private sector to compete. The awarding of government-to-government contracts to state-owned mills also prevents private mills from expanding their export base.

Quality Losses: The ability of private traders to compete both domestically and internationally is related in part to the quality of the rice they are able to offer. Concern has been expressed throughout ASEAN regarding what is generally perceived as worsening quality for its rice. Quality problems frequently originate at the production and postharvest levels of farm-to-market chains. They can be the result of factors such as the seed used, the harvesting and threshing techniques, and the drying practices noted earlier.

Excessive stockholding can also cause a loss of quality. Rice has a limited economic life after it is milled, of about six months to one year. Rice supply chains in the region contain multiple small-scale stock points, and rice requires a long time to move through chains from farm-to-retail outlets for final sale. Government direct interventions in rice chains result in additional excessive stock building, as in Thailand, and in Indonesia and Malaysia, where stock buildups are used to ensure a reliable food supply. In Vietnam, government stock building has been used to ensure the economic viability of the largest state-owned trading companies.

That said, the private sector must also accept some of the blame for quality problems in the region. Small-scale mills typically offer no premiums to suppliers for high-quality paddy and thus create no incentives for farmers to invest in improved quality. In Malaysia, the government has actually institutionalized this flat-price approach in several states where the "flat-rate deduction system" has become entrenched. Mills are effectively required to pay the same price to all farmers, regardless of quality.

Formal quality standards for either paddy or rice have not been adopted and enforced by the private trade anywhere in the region. Consumers seeking higher-quality rice tend to use price as the main indicator of quality since no formal certification exists. The presence of numerous actors in the paddy-rice chains in Indonesia, the Philippines, and Vietnam may make standards difficult to enforce. On the other hand, it is not surprising that the private sectors of Malaysia and Thailand have taken steps on their own to develop appropriate standards.

Infrastructure: To differing degrees, ASEAN government policies related to infrastructure push up transport costs and, hence, consumer prices. Regulations affecting interisland shipment in the Philippines and between provinces and islands in Indonesia, for example, keep transportation prices high. In Malaysia, impediments to the interstate movement of paddy constrain consolidation in the milling industry. The lack of incentives to realize economies of scale in the rice business limits the volumes of shipment, storage, and processing lots to sizes that are less than optimally efficient in most of the study countries.

Logistics costs associated with moving rice and maize among ASEAN countries account for 20–25 percent of the total price to consumers in the importing country. The capacity and quality of supply-chain infrastructure affect these costs and vary widely among the five study countries. Thailand generally fares better in terms of logistics infrastructure quality than Vietnam, in the southern portion of which, where much rice originates, infrastructure deficiencies impede exports.

Domestic infrastructure obstacles to efficient food chain operations are most severe in Indonesia and the Philippines. Both road and shipping constraints adversely affect movements of paddy to millers and rice to distributors and consumers. The infrastructure quality in Malaysia is generally good, with the exception of food supplies to Sabah and Sarawak.

Improvements need to be made in the countries with the lowest Logistics Performance Index, in particular in Indonesia and the Philippines (road network, interisland shipping, and customs) and Vietnam (port facilities). Poor internal logistics in Indonesia and the Philippines are partly related to the nature of these two countries as archipelagos and their difficult topography. However, congested ports and poor road conditions in such major rice-producing areas as Java also hamper performance.

The major logistics bottlenecks that inhibit regional food trade are in the ports, including the ports of one exporting country (Vietnam) and two importing countries (Indonesia and the Philippines). The waiting times in these ports (including loading, offloading, and clearance) represent about 45 percent of the time needed to move the grains from farmers in the exporting country to consumers in the importing country. Such bottlenecks result in delays that add extra costs for loading and offloading, waiting times for berths to be available, documentation clearance, and shipping itself.

Private Sector Investment: The enabling environment in the region is generally weak for rice-chain development. It is not conducive either to the private sector's testing of new supply-chain structures or to private investment in supply-chain infrastructure. Backward linkages to small-scale farm producers are particularly weak and in need of innovative approaches to strengthen them in commercially sustainable ways.

If rice supply chains in the five ASEAN nations studied are to gain in efficiency, curb losses, and produce enough quality grain of diverse varieties to build a strong base for the growth of open regional trade, they will need new milling equipment, more modern storage technology and facilities, and more reliable transport. All of those necessary improvements will require financing, which is less likely to come from government programs than, under the right conditions, from private investors.

In all the countries studied, larger companies report having fewer problems in obtaining short-term credit to cover operating costs than smaller ones. Such companies as mini- and local millers face greater problems in accessing finance than larger ones. Normally paying cash for their purchases from farmers or paddy traders, they have the advantage of providing immediate payment and of being able, as well, to respond with agility to local conditions. Still, they often must wait 30 days or more for payment from their own customers, after milling has been completed and shipments made.

Such a pattern of financing, however, weakens efforts to strengthen supply chains and can be counterproductive. In Vietnam, for instance, private companies expressed concern that state-owned enterprises enjoy preferential access to loans over private firms. In Indonesia, Malaysia, and Thailand, well-established private companies are generally able to secure loans from their banks, either solely on the basis of their reputations or, in the case of Indonesia and Thailand, by committing stocks held in their own warehouses as collateral. In the Philippines, however, private companies in the rice trading and milling business have recently experienced difficulty in obtaining working capital loans.

Small-scale millers and traders in the Philippines, for example, reportedly prefer to borrow working capital from moneylenders, despite higher interest rates, because these transactions avoid complicated paperwork (Dawe and others 2008).

As for the kind of investment capital needed to create or upgrade fixed assets, many companies prefer to use their own cash rather than bank loans for supply-chain infrastructure investments, arguing that returns do not compensate for the rates of interest that banks charge. In practice, that tendency limits the growth of fixed assets and poses a significant constraint to rice supply-chain development and consolidation. It reflects, in part, the risk that banks perceive to exist with long-term investment in the sector, as well as the low margins that prevail.

The fact is that the milling and processing sectors in most of the countries included in this study are not generating sufficient returns to invest in modern milling equipment or adequate storage. One result (and cause) of those weaknesses is the absence of large-scale modern food firms either in domestic rice markets or in regional trade.

At most, only a very few companies can be found that operate end-to-end, connecting farming, milling, exporting, or retailing within the control of a single organization. The vertically integrated food companies that come closest to this ideal are multinational supermarket chains, which, although they do not farm, mill, or export themselves, procure the food products they sell within the same region. Multinational grain trading companies, which buy and sell grains globally within their own proprietary networks, do not participate in ASEAN rice markets.

Maize: A Model? It may not be wishful thinking to imagine private companies bringing their energy and focus on efficiency into the ASEAN rice sector. As discussed in this study, it seems that they have to some degree succeeded in doing this in the maize sector, where, unlike with the situation of rice, government intervention has been very limited, the feed companies that purchase the crops are large and often multinational, and demand has grown markedly along with rising global and regional demand for poultry, livestock, and fish products.

None of those conditions obtain in the rice sector, but both maize and rice supply chains begin with small-scale farmers, and both have somewhat similar concerns with inadequate infrastructure, processing, and even storage. Another crucial distinction is that the market in which private maize-trading firms have to tackle such problems is relatively unified (whereas the rice market is fragmented) and is relatively free of government interference in the form of price supports, price setting, or trade restrictions.

More progress has been made in achieving economies of scale and of specialization in the maize sector than in the rice sector. Different development trajectories can be clearly discerned for both, with many strong backward and forward links developing in the maize sector, greater emphasis on coordination in the achievement of chain-optimizing results, faster adoption of appropriate technologies, and much more rapid growth.

The relatively low level of government intervention goes hand in hand with the vigor of the private sector. That relationship also reflects the fact that the maize market within the region is primarily related to the livestock sector[7] and is thus not politically sensitive.

The Impacts of Government Intervention

Just when ASEAN countries' rice sectors need to develop—in the aftermath of the 2007–08 crisis—government policies in some cases are pulling them backward. Instead of facilitating trade and investment and regional supply-chain formation, Malaysia, Indonesia, and the Philippines, in particular, have chosen a more costly path to food security, one that holds no guarantee of leading to its desired destination: reduced price volatility and enhanced productivity at the farm level.

A basic shortcoming in traditional public policies is that typically they are neither conceived nor assessed from the perspective of their impacts on farm-to-market chains. Rather, they are designed piecemeal to meet the specific tactical objectives that governments pursue in their quests for national food security.[8]

High Costs: Some of the negative side effects are financial. The Philippines' food security program, for example, has become financially unsustainable.[9] Its overhead alone requires a fiscal subsidy of about 1.5 billion pesos a year, and the effective cost of its rice subsidy activities more than tripled from 2007 to 2008 to reach 68.5 billion pesos. Its monopoly hold over imports meant that its plan to bring 2.5 million to 3.0 million metric tons of rice into the country in 2010 would create an inventory financing requirement of $1.5 billion to 1.8 billion.

During the food crisis, the government of Thailand also concentrated rice stocks in its hands, a plus for the public sector when international prices were high, as in the first half of 2008. However, when prices fell sharply over the next six months, the government was forced to absorb losses as the value of its rice inventory fell. Responding to petitions from rice farmers, moreover, the government raised the minimum prices it paid (Forssell 2009). ·

In Indonesia, where Badan Urusan Logistik (BULOG) policies did spare consumers from a price shock that would have greatly harmed the poor during the April–August 2008 price hike, government programs entailed longer-term costs. Domestic rice prices were much higher—$232 a ton higher on average—than international ones in the 2005–07 period. A recent World Bank public expenditure review (Armas, Gomez Osorio, and Moreno-Dodson 2010) also found that while public spending on overall agricultural development increased by 12 percent per year in real terms from 2001 to 2009, agricultural productivity remained relatively flat. The flow of public investment in Indonesia was strong; the apparent weakness lay in the kinds of investments the government chose to make.

Programmed Interventions: Public programs affect market performance both in targeted and expected ways and in collateral and unexpected ways. Among such interventions in rice markets, the primary ones come as (a) technology choices; (b) land use choices; (c) subsidies or price supports; (d) directed credits for farm inputs; (e) controls over domestic market prices; (f) stockpile management; (g) import controls; (h) direct procurement and internal distribution; and (i) food safety and quality controls.

Most food security programs serve two or more objectives, which are sometimes countervailing and mutually contradictory. Most are designed to move toward rice self-sufficiency, despite the fact that the path selected for achieving this objective often represents the more costly option. Some program elements require that others be adopted to ensure the effectiveness of the original one or to overcome unforeseen problems resulting from its implementation. Import restricting measures, for example, are frequently used to protect local producers from foreign competition. In turn, these have prompted policy makers to undertake complementary expenditures to stabilize producer and consumer prices and to ensure that rice supply is always available to the poor, independent of prevailing market conditions.

Parastatals versus Private Initiative: Governments in the region that accord wide-ranging regulatory support to parastatals (and, in Malaysia, to the privatized successor) do not provide a "level playing field" for domestic markets (Rashid, Gulati, and Cummings 2008). It is worth briefly recalling examples of such interventions during the 2007–08 food crisis:

- Establishment of what was effectively a minimum farmer price in Thailand that significantly exceeded prevailing market prices and the government's consequent reluctance to release accumulated stocks for export at a loss
- Setting of minimum buying prices in Vietnam, backed up by minimum export prices and export licensing, together with favorable interest rates applied to state bodies
- Sale of rice by the parastatal in the Philippines at prices that the private sector found uncompetitive
- Interstate restrictions on the movement of paddy and rice in Malaysia

Such policies skew competition in favor of state enterprises, including those involving state trading enterprises (STEs), or parastatals. In many policy contexts, these have been created as implementation instruments, using direct modes of intervention instead of establishing incentives and regulations that would enable private companies to do the job.

There are at least two factors that persuade governments to use parastatals to advance their agenda of rice self-sufficiency. First, governments perceive the private sector as likely to squeeze earnings from rice farmers if left alone. The farmers, for instance, may need to sell their output during harvest seasons when prices are low or may have pledged their output to lenders in exchange for production loans or multipurpose credit lines.

Second, using public corporations is administratively convenient. This is particularly the case when governments must account to legislatures for the financial resources used to support overall food security programs.

Significantly as well, the use of import restrictions to encourage local rice production usually requires two further sets of public outlays: one for price stabilization and one for consumer rice subsidies for the poor. Public investment in national buffer stocks has had to be increased to offset the increased volatility of rice prices and to ensure economic access to rice for entitled populations. In countries such as Indonesia and the Philippines, where a significant share of the population lives below the poverty line, price stabilization activities have been commingled with a targeted consumer rice subsidy to compensate for the adverse effects of import restrictions on consumers.

Costly as they are, government policies and programs for ensuring food security have led to a still more adverse consequence: the crowding out of private sector investment in rice-related businesses and the consequent missed chances to supplement public investment with private investment, lost opportunities for sector development, and the perpetual postponement of the transition from nontradable to globally tradable product status.

Moreover, private investors face a strong deterrent when they are forced to compete with public sector counterparts, which also enjoy power to regulate the food business and to set the rules for local buying. As a result, a self-perpetuating cycle compels regional governments to believe that they must make yearly commitments of budgetary resources for food security.

The Example of Maize

In the maize sector mentioned briefly above, where private firms compete with public entities, the playing field is more nearly level. As a result, efficiencies in maize production and trading have made the sector a notable success story.

Rapid Growth: Not a staple in traditional Asian diets, (yellow) maize has become popular thanks to booming regional demand for livestock and poultry feed and energizing private sector investment. Beyond supplying important help in disseminating hybrid seeds and know-how to maize farmers, governments have kept interventions to a minimum. Private companies, national and foreign, have been the agents transforming the maize business by financing and managing modern, integrated supply chains.

Total maize output in the four producing countries (Malaysia is not a producer) expanded by 45 percent in the first decade of this century, compared to average annual growth rates of roughly 33 percent from the 1960s through the 1990s. Production more than doubled in Vietnam, where maize imports skyrocketed 14-fold (admittedly from very low beginnings and still only one seventh of production) as the country's meat, poultry, and aquaculture exports swelled.

Private Sector Presence: In all the study countries, growth also mirrored rising domestic demand for pork, beef, fish, and chicken. Homegrown consumer appetites, to cite one example, were strong enough in Indonesia that use of chicken feed—one fourth of it coming from maize—increased at an annual rate of 8.3 percent between 2005 and 2009. In Malaysia, which imports most of the maize processed by about 70 animal feed companies, including U.S. and Thai multinational corporations (MNCs), industry sales grew at an annual 14 percent rate from 2004 to 2009.

Vietnam's domestic consumption of meat and fish has increased greatly. Of the firms operating approximately 180 animal feed mills in Vietnam, 15 large MNCs together produce approximately 50 percent of the animal feed consumed in the country. So much new investment has entered the feed industry over the past three years that some participants are concerned that the industry may have overbuilt.

Domestic production in Thailand actually declined slightly over the decade as imports expanded more than fourfold to meet the needs of an industry with $4.5 billion in sales in 2008. One of the government's stated agri-industry development objectives is to make Thailand the center for the animal feed industry in Asia and the Pacific. Two giant Thai firms, Charoen Pokphand (CP) and Betagro, are integrated backward and forward as chicken and pork farm franchisors and food retailers, with some 4 million tons of processing capacity shared almost equally between them.

CP entered the animal feed business from the seed distribution business in the 1970s and now maintains a market presence all over the region. It has animal feed operations in India and Singapore; animal feed and livestock farming operations in Malaysia and Vietnam; and animal feed, livestock farming, shrimp farming, and integrated broiler operations in Indonesia. CP has also integrated forward into the food retailing business and has a subsidiary that is the largest convenience store operator in Thailand, with 4,030 stores. In addition, CP operates 79 Lotus Super Center supermarkets in China.

In the Philippines, as well, foreign companies are prominent among the top 10 (out of 70) animal feed businesses. The largest companies involved in the industry are San Miguel Corporation, the Philippines' largest corporation, with animal feed operations that account for 25 percent of production capacity. Among its competitors are Cargill Philippines (14 percent), Swift Foods (13 percent), General Milling Corporation (12 percent), and Vitarich (11 percent).

Representing fully 54 percent of the 6 million tons used for animal feed in the Philippines, maize has gained strategic importance for the government because of the larger, faster-growing, and higher value-generating livestock industry that it supports. More involved in the sector than their regional counterparts, Philippine authorities plan to offer enhanced incentives for private investment in aquaculture, poultry product processing, dairy, and other forms of meat production. By fostering long-term partnerships between chain integrators and farm-level organizations, the program would encourage processing facilities and distribution channel investments.

That level of public intervention in the maize industry is somewhat unusual in the region. According to data issued by the U.S. Department of Agriculture, no ASEAN country has undertaken domestic spending on maize above 5 percent of the value of production. Not only do Asian maize farmers generally have little political influence, but the need for market intervention in the sector, such as price supports, is also limited. Maize prices have been relatively stable and generally increasing, reflecting the increasing value of maize in the region to the rapidly growing livestock sectors.

Weak Links: Although many grain collectors in Thailand contract with farmers for their maize crop, that stabilizing practice is not widespread in the other producing countries studied. In vertically integrated supply chains, some large feed companies manage their own commercial farming operations and even sell hybrid seed and fertilizer to farmers while marketing poultry and meat products.

At the lowest production level, however, the technology that could reduce physical and quality losses in the drying process and in protecting stored maize from insect and rodent attacks has not reached most smallholder farms. As a result, at a conservative estimate, the region may be losing 15 percent of the value of maize production.[10]

These losses result in lower returns to farmers, higher prices for consumers, and greater pressure on the environment because of lower production efficiencies. In this respect, if few others, ASEAN maize and rice supply share similar problems.

Summary of Conclusions

It may be tempting to think that by patterning itself on the model of the maize industry, the region's rice sector could attract new private firms or the same private firms that have brought to maize such crucial advances as modern storage technologies, effective risk management, and economies of scale and specialization. But given the political and dietary importance of rice, governments in the region still need to implement policies that protect farmers and keep rice prices stable and affordable. At the same time, it is necessary to provide incentives for private traders to manage inventories of tradable rice effectively and to invest in technology and farm business models that hold out the best prospect of improving productivity and thus increasing future rice supply.

To begin the needed transition in rice sector policies, priorities must change. At a fundamental level, governments in the region must switch their policy focus from producing rice to supporting efforts by the private sector to procure, process, and trade it efficiently—from raising output to strengthening the supply chains in which as much as 15 percent of the harvested grain now goes to waste.

Successful market development in the rice industry in Southeast Asia, as in other fields all over the world, depends basically on the willingness of individual entrepreneurs to invest in new business models and thus to improve the efficiency with which markets serve consumers. Therefore, when formulating food security policies, ASEAN governments need to give greater attention to the incentives or obstacles their policies create for private initiative. The goal should be to stimulate private sector investments in supply-chain modernization so as to increase production of farm outputs generated from enhanced input use, add value to basic farm commodities, and provide efficient distribution services to link farmers and consumers.

In the case of regional rice market development, this will entail a strenuous uphill effort. Moreover, instead of intervening directly in rice markets, governments in the region can develop ways to offer incentives and create regulatory systems to stimulate private sector activities. While a 180-degree turn from direct to indirect policy interventions in rice markets is arguably the best direction for future policy, it would seem unrealistic to expect this revolution in the short term.

Encouraging Supply-Chain Partnerships: Another feasible early reform could address the lack of accurate information that farmers and small millers, among others, need when deciding whether to sell their product or—if they can—to hold it back from the market for a time. By insisting on standard and transparent contractual arrangements along the supply chain, reformed public procurement policies could make it easier for supply chain participants to share risks specific to small-farm agriculture.

Currently, most small rice farmers have trouble supplying grain in a consistent and standardized manner. They lack up-to-date technology and capital to finance inputs and technology improvement. In return for entering price and delivery agreements under contract farming arrangements, they could gain both credit to use in upgrading their operations and the promise of reliable payment in often volatile markets. Grain collectors and processors, in turn, could improve supply reliability by working more closely with farmers and reduce their risk exposure by building similar partnerships with distributors or directly with wholesalers, perhaps even retailers, who are willing to forgo price-arbitraging freedom for reliable supply.

To expand such private sector opportunities, governments have a variety of options. Start-up programs could include education and training for local farmers, better-targeted government-led extension services, and efforts to develop product standards and certification procedures. Financial aid and model contracts[11] might help jump-start experimentation. Matchmaking services might even aid in connecting actors in supply chains with one another. Policies that support the spread of farmer organizations could lead to collective bargaining agreements with large, chain-linked buyers.

Among the latter, once such an environment begins to function, foreign investors such as the MNCs active in the maize sector could help local industries to develop modern supply-chain management discipline. Over the past two decades in many developing countries, private companies have developed new technologies and methods for managing the flow of food products from farms to markets. Increasingly adopted as practical operational methods through which chains function the world over, both supermarket chains and processors and traders have been particularly adept in applying supply-chain management methods to the flow of food staples.

Public Sector Policy Reform: As far as the general environment for doing business in the five study countries is concerned, private firms cite few difficulties that they believe cannot be remedied. A more widespread and deeper concern that keeps them on the sidelines of the rice sector is the range of interventionist government policies they face.

Each of the five study countries continues to deploy a wide array of protective mechanisms that distort national and regional rice markets. Among them, since 2009, programs designed to increase national self-sufficiency in rice have moved to the forefront and have become quite costly in both budgetary and real terms. Reversing this trend is the way forward with respect to improving the investment environment in the rice sector.

Traditional mechanisms designed into food security programs may no longer be appropriate for achieving their stated objectives. For instance, access to input credits and to fertilizer are no longer the primary constraints that prevent farmers in the region from improving their incomes, diversifying their livelihood options, or accumulating productive agricultural assets rapidly. Government expenditures need to shift from supplying what are essentially private goods at discounted prices to providing public goods and to solving the coordination and information asymmetry problems that the private sector cannot effectively address on its own.

Parastatals are inherently inefficient—despite their mandate to operate as commercial entities and to remain financially independent. They do not pursue profit maximization objectives, and their management is frequently unable to make them financially self-sustaining. Exacerbating this condition, parastatals frequently capture economic rents, exert monopoly rights, and deploy anticompetitive tactics that put private companies at a disadvantage. In these ways, as well, they distort underlying markets and discourage private investment. While in some countries, like China, less distorting income support payments programs have replaced programs that support rice market prices, most of the countries included in this study continue to intervene directly in the rice market.

In Indonesia, the Philippines, and Vietnam, private sector involvement in rice trading is restricted by the involvement of government bodies. Evidence, however, suggests that public procurement and government-managed distribution systems can be extremely costly, inefficient, and, indeed, ultimately ineffective in stabilizing prices. Poor targeting and inefficient distribution are particularly conspicuous in the rice procurement systems that continue to operate in Indonesia and the Philippines. While social protection programs may be laudable from a social security perspective and imperative from a political perspective, governments in the region need to weigh the costs of inefficient business as usual against the benefits of adopting alternative, less costly methods to attain the same goals.

In Vietnam, private exporters face considerable uncertainties and cannot maximize export returns, while millers find the obligation to stock beyond their immediate requirements a costly undertaking. In Thailand, government intervention in the market pushed up prices and withdrew rice supplies that could have earned export revenue. At the end of 2009, it appeared that revisions to the Thai government's market intervention policy were causing confusion and involving the Bank for Agriculture and Agricultural Cooperatives in noncommercial activities.[12]

Problems with the export management policy of Vietnam similarly remained unresolved.

Reducing Postharvest Losses, Upgrading Quality: One of the major factors affecting food availability and hence food prices and their fluctuations is the level of physical losses such as those that occur during rice harvesting and as a result of poor threshing, drying, and milling. Government policies that have led to excessive long-term storage have also had the ironic effect of increasing physical losses for rice in several of the countries studied.

Significant efforts and millions of dollars have been allocated to programs to reduce losses at the farmer level—in many cases, with limited success. Part of the reason may be that interventions have tended to concentrate on farmers rather than on the entire chain. Further efforts in this area are essential, but such efforts should adopt a value chain approach and work closely with the private sector to identify improvements that private partners judge workable and sustainable. Such improvements could include improved drying by mills, as well as introduction of more efficient milling equipment to overcome the existing low conversion rates in several other countries.

While countries have programs to promote improved quality, much more could be done by adopting a coherent, multistakeholder approach. Mills, for instance, could buy more wet paddy, thus reducing the need for on-farm drying and concomitant postharvest losses and quality deterioration. This requires mills to invest in mechanical drying equipment, as some have already done in some of the study countries and as, with some additional incentives, others might do as well.

More an area for extension services, the slow spread of contract farming could be accelerated through government technical assistance programs that helped farmers and millers to understand contracts and that developed quality certification standards for the parties to fulfill. The long-term potential for such developments, however, is currently constrained by arbitrary policy interventions that can jeopardize contract viability.

Bank Finance for Supply Chains: Working capital for the rice chain is mainly provided by banks to large companies, by large companies to smaller ones, and, on occasion, by small companies and traders to farmers. In some countries, large companies are able to obtain loans on the basis of their own stocks without the need for formal warehouse receipts. Availability of operating capital is not considered a significant constraint by these larger companies, but it seems to limit the options of smaller mills and village-level paddy collectors.

Fixed investments in the rice sector are usually funded by company and family resources. Both small and large operators seem to use banks rarely for investment capital, with industry sources suggesting that returns are insufficient to pay existing interest rates. Lack of finance also appears to be a major factor constraining some consolidation of the rice milling sector, in particular, the reportedly 100,000-plus mills in Indonesia and the approximately 300,000 in Vietnam. The fragmented and small-scale nature of rice milling leads to high costs and consequent inefficiency. Moreover, lack of investment in milling can be considered a significant cause of high postharvest losses and poor product quality.

The general view of those contacted for this research was that banks do not understand the needs of the agribusiness sector. At the same time, companies need to understand banks' need to make loans only for viable investments. Steps should be taken to bring banks and private sector representatives together to promote greater understanding.

Warehousing: Storing rice or maize against warehouse receipts opens up two possibilities. First, depositors could approach banks to obtain loans using the warehouse receipt as collateral. Second, the use of warehouse receipts permits the operation of commodity exchanges that are able to trade the receipts. Both possibilities require reliable, certified, and insured warehouses, as well as a reliable system of grading that removes the need for visual inspection.

To be viable, inventory credit must be carried out in an environment in which, under normal circumstances, seasonal price movements are greater than the cost of interest, storage, and any transport (Coulter and Shepherd 1995). Otherwise, there would be little incentive for mills to store; if they needed additional paddy, they could simply go out and buy it on the market. For mills, the attractiveness of inventory credit could be jeopardized if they were required to incur storage and transport costs to store paddy away from their own premises.

In general, smaller companies seek to rotate their capital as quickly as possible and thus may have limited interest in long-term stockholding. Nevertheless, the scope for promotion of commercial inventory credit would appear to merit further, more detailed investigation. Such arrangements may assist more efficient mills in building up necessary stocks to permit greater capacity utilization.

Commodity and Futures Exchanges: Commodity exchanges require agreed standards in order to operate, unless they function on the basis of visual inspection of samples. These standards do not currently exist in the ASEAN rice trade at a national level. Although various grades are used in domestic markets, usually based on the percentage of *brokens*, these have not yet reached the required level of sophistication. It is noteworthy, for example, that government tenders in Thailand are based on visual inspection and not on agreed-upon grades.

There have been some very tentative discussions among the rice and maize private sectors regarding the possible establishment of futures exchanges within the region. Trading in rice has been conducted by the Agricultural Futures Exchange of Thailand, although the exchange has tended to adapt its procedures to fit in with government policy implementation. In general, as far as rice is concerned, enthusiasm for the idea appears extremely limited among established rice companies.

It should be noted that the lack of enthusiasm of the private sector may reflect an element of self-interest in that it is clearly not in the interest of companies to support measures that may attract new competitors. The Singapore Mercantile Exchange has announced plans to open a regional rice exchange in the near future, and its experience needs to be closely monitored.

ATIGA and Rice Trade Reforms: Progress toward structured regional trade might open the way for commodity exchanges. Since the issuance of the AIFS framework in 2008 and the further successful adoption of the ASEAN Trade in Goods Agreement (ATIGA) in 2009, the probability of affecting regional food policy reforms has greatly improved. With that said, it remains clear that rice deficit countries within the region would prefer to hang tenaciously onto their long-held goal of rice self-sufficiency.

The agreement encompasses the key provisions of the ASEAN Free Trade Agreement (AFTA) on tariff liberalization, as well as its related rules on origin, nontariff measures, trade facilitation, customs, standards, technical regulations and conformity assessment procedures, sanitary and phytosanitary measures, and trade remedies. ATIGA enters into force with the deposit by member states of their respective instruments of ratifications with the secretary-general of ASEAN. The process is envisioned "not [to] take more than one hundred and eighty (180) days after the signing of this Agreement."

Structuring Regional Trade: Even without the ATIGA formal framework, ASEAN states can move ahead with new structures for regional trade. A particularly attractive leverage point involves rice procurement policies and practices that are used by public sector entities to import food grains. Policy makers should be willing to explore the benefits of harmonizing these procurement practices and in the process setting regional rules for grain trading.

To make that sort of ambitious new approach possible, regional governments would need to establish workable standards for several important aspects, including (a) rice quality standards and controls; (b) technical capabilities of asset managers, warehouse personnel, and intermediary handlers; (c) liabilities of buyers and sellers under standard negotiable bills of sale; (d) clarity with respect to custodial responsibilities through the entire chain; (e) standard arrangements for the reassignment of ownership rights for products moving in transit; (f) standard securitized interests for third parties providing trade finance; and (g) carrier and port handling liability under standard bills of lading. Any such set of commercial rules would need to be updated and revised from time to time together with the private sector to reflect changes in technology and best business practices.

To this end, the National Food Authority (NFA) in the Philippines and BULOG in Indonesia might be tasked under ASEAN with formulating regionwide, rule-based procurement practices. These practices would include (a) setting standards for rice grades and quality levels; (b) establishing module lot sizes consistent with efficient transport and storage capacities within the region; (c) establishing trading terms consistent with International Commercial Terms (Incoterms®);[13] (d) defining the liabilities and responsibilities of all trading partners under negotiable contracts of sale; (e) establishing standard custodial responsibilities for third-party warehouse personnel and transporters; and (f) enabling third-party financial institutions to create secure interests in inventories that they have financed.

Policy makers weighing the potential of such a trade structure will, however, have to acknowledge the remaining bias in the region against full integration of individual national rice markets into either global or regional markets. An underlying assumption—which prevailing policies make self-fulfilling—is that the world rice market is not a dependable source of food supply because of its relatively small size and price volatility. However, good evidence exists that full liberalization of regional rice markets would allow ASEAN countries to realize benefits that would dwarf any costs associated with perpetuating existing policies.

Grains Tariff and Related Reforms: A key test of progress toward trade reform will be the action member states take to eliminate duties on all imported goods originating in ASEAN by 2010 for Brunei Darussalam, Indonesia, Malaysia, the Philippines, Singapore, and Thailand (the ASEAN 6), and by 2015–18 for Cambodia, Lao People's Democratic Republic, Myanmar, and Vietnam. For rice and maize, import duties are to be reduced to 0–5 percent from the respective rates that will prevail at the time the agreement enters into force.

The new rates, referred to under the treaty as Common Effective Preferential Tariff (CEPT) rate levels, are legally binding. Although member states have committed not to increase their import duties above CEPT, Indonesia, Myanmar, and the Philippines have placed rice on their respective sensitive or highly sensitive lists and have "opted out" of the tariff reform. Indonesia has agreed to impose a 25 percent import duty as its final AFTA rate. Myanmar has until 2015 to adjust its import duty on rice. After its bilateral negotiation with Thailand, the Philippines will be imposing a preferential tariff rate of 35 percent on rice, with a possible earmarking of its imports from Thailand and Vietnam.

The result of continuing protectionist policies for rice is that apparently final AFTA rates on rice imports originating in ASEAN are far from those that might be expected in a free trade area. For instance, Malaysia, which has not nominated rice as a sensitive commodity, has committed to a final AFTA rate of 20 percent, down from its most-favored nation rate of 40 percent.[14] The importation of rice will apparently continue for some time to be significantly restricted by high tariffs.

However, tariffs are only one part of the problem. The continuing dominant role of parastatals in rice trading is another.

Independent of ATIGA compliance, NFA's continued import monopoly complements the Philippine government's continuing restriction on private importation of rice to very limited quantities. Thailand's and Vietnam's demands to secure a larger annual volume commitment from the Philippines would perpetuate the same arrangement that has kept the flow of rice trade in the region as low as it has been to date because such arrangements would inevitably be government-to-government. Trade would have better prospects if the private sector on both sides of the market were legally enabled to participate.[15]

To end NFA's exclusive rice importing privileges, however, the government of the Philippines would have to ask permission from its congress to amend the NFA charter. From the perspective of political viability, this would be difficult to accomplish not only in the short but even in the medium term. Legislative changes required to alter the NFA charter are in limbo, although in July 2010 the issues of overimportation and rotting rice stocks in NFA warehouses did encourage discussions on NFA reform.[16]

Rather than holding the entire ATIGA hostage because of this impasse, one possible step forward is for the Philippines to commit itself to amending the NFA charter within a workable but specifically defined time period.[17]

Without private sector dynamism, the sector will remain unreliable, inefficient, and a drain on many governments' budgets. Progressively limiting the participation of STEs in regional food staple markets is a reform on which ASEAN member states can agree as an overdue invitation to private sector participation in specific, supply-chain development in the region.

Roles for ASEAN and for Multilateral Donors

Interviews, discussions, and correspondence conducted during the course of this study have made it clear that the private sector believes that external interventions are required to restructure the ASEAN region rice sector in order to reduce the risks that deter private involvement and, through new commitments of private capital, improve competitiveness and productivity. There also appears to be general agreement among private companies that the regional market for rice needs to be reengineered into a more effective instrument to enhance growth and competitiveness. Regional trade policy, moreover, needs to focus more on allowing different economies to discover and exploit their unique sources of competitive advantage and less on increasing market access by surrendering national economic autonomy.

The private sector, however, lacks an effective starting point from which to influence policy reform in this new direction. What is missing is an institutional platform for advocates and advocacy of change. The private sector also lacks the requisite expertise in regional trade reform policy and the necessary capabilities to improve coordination among disparate governments, parastatal organizations, and various interest groups.

Arguably, the kind of fundamental industrial restructuring that this book envisions rarely takes place without a significant level of commitment from outside the industries and markets being restructured. To meet the challenge of reforming the regional rice sector, governments will need to correct deficiencies in the flow of business information, the coordination of businesses processes, and the setting of public policy.

Although the kinds of interventions required in each of these three areas differ in basic ways, a role exists in each for ASEAN as an organization and for development partners like the World Bank, the Asian Development Bank (ADB), and FAO.

A reasonable place to start on a multiparty initiative would be an open commercial learning process with the ongoing involvement of the private sector. In such a setting, commercial experiments could be deliberately undertaken, results studied, and findings regarding the creation of investor value disseminated to private sector stakeholders. The objective of the experiments would be to enhance productivity and competitiveness with new business processes, new control systems, and new technologies. The emphasis would be at the level of discrete business processes and technologies appropriate to them in farm-to-market chains, and not on rice sector reform per se. One example is specialized third-party logistics management services. Another is a regional commodity exchange.

Among various possible sponsors of eventual public-private partnerships, ASEAN can serve as the coordinator and primary focal point for regional lending activities and as the primary disseminator of information concerning business process innovation among member countries. Individual ASEAN member countries can serve as sponsors of rice sector reform councils that bring together qualified and interested agribusinesses, technology providers, and providers of ancillary services to identify useful commercial experiments, evaluate their merits, and manage information dissemination once experiments have been completed. Multilateral development institutions like the World Bank and ADB can serve as sources of financing, and, together with FAO, as architects of project design and implementation.

If coordinated investments made in one activity within a farm to market chain they can result in significant productivity gains in subsequent activities. A second set of activities involves coordinating the activities of rice sector participants in order to capture the synergies which can be realized through improved efficiency, precision, and adaptability among synchronized chain processes. To modernize the ASEAN rice sector will require expertise which is currently missing within the industry's private sector, including expertise in industrial cluster development, process engineering which leads to enhanced competitiveness, and in all of the specialized ancillary services, and specialized managerial skills required to support a vibrant sector.

Again, ASEAN can serve as the coordinator and primary focal point for this effort and as a facilitator for new business combinations that cross borders within the region. As suggested, individual member countries can sponsor rice sector reform councils composed of interested agribusinesses, academics, technology providers, and providers of ancillary services.

Conclusion: ASEAN has already begun a parallel set of efforts intended to focus on correcting policy weaknesses and creating an enabling business environment. This study is part of that process. The response that ASEAN and its member countries make to its conclusions and recommendations can signal a new beginning for efforts to remove policy obstacles to increased private sector participation and investment in regional rice markets.

Notes

1. "If every country continues to take decisions to protect its own population, and doesn't look further than the short-term," added Mr. Ghanem, "the result is often that everyone loses." "Government Decisions Fueled 2008 Food Crisis, FAO's Ghanem Says." *Bloomberg News,* May 23, 2011. http://www.bloomberg .com/news/2011-05-23.

2. The International Rice Research Institute has advocated the view that the global rice crisis was the result of insufficient production. The International Food Policy Research Institute (IFPRI) has identified "major policy failures" at the core of the food price crisis and has flagged the distortive effect of promoting biofuels on the grains markets (AFP 2008).

3. The FAO Food Price Index consists of the average of six commodity group price indexes (cereals, dairy, meat, oils and fats, and sugar) weighted with the average export shares of each of the groups for 2002–04: in all, 55 commodity quotations are included in the overall index.

4. Timmer's (2008) statistical analysis of the relationships between rice prices and exchange rates, stocks, financial speculation, and other grain prices supports the conclusions in this section.

5. Most ASEAN member states believe that there is significant scope to enhance rice productivity, despite the fact that comparative advantage in rice in ASEAN follows more from natural levels of farmland endowment than from the use of different agricultural technologies. Evidence comes from the fact that yields in major rice-producing countries within ASEAN do not differ greatly. Thailand and Vietnam have the edge over the other countries because they have larger irrigated land areas and smaller populations compared to Indonesia and the Philippines. In pursuit of efficiency gains in rice production, care needs to be taken that these gains are not offset by public resource commitments associated with the policies applied to attain them.

6. In practical terms, it is possible to obtain 68–70 percent from a good variety of paddy with high-quality equipment (FAO 1999).

7. Yellow maize is a primary feedstock for animal products. Human consumption of white maize in the region is marginal.

8. Information used here comes mainly from FAO and IFPRI. A good literature on country-specific policies and practices can be found in Rokotoarisoa (2006); Dorosh (2008); McCulloch (2008); McCulloch and Timmer (2008); Rosner and McCulloch (2008); and Simatupang and Timmer (2008).

9. Please note that the Philippines moved to a system of conditional cash transfers at the beginning of 2011 and, as a result, the NFA is no longer responsible for subsidized distribution.

10. FAO 1999.

11. See FAO's Contract Farming Resource Centre: http://www.fao.org/ag/ags/contract-farming/en/.

12. Please note that since this report was completed, Thailand's new rice policy has proposed to buy unmilled rice at higher-than-market prices.

13. "The Incoterms® rules are an internationally recognized standard and are used worldwide in international and domestic contracts for the sale of goods." http://www.iccwbo.org/incoterms/.

14. According to World Trade Organization (WTO) agreements, WTO members cannot treat their trading partners differently. This principle is known as most-favored nation treatment. http://www.wto.org/english/thewto_e/whatis_e/tif_e/fact2_e.htm.

15. As of October 2011, NFA is permitting private sector imports. They have to be organized through tenders to NFA, however, and within quantity limits set by the government.

16. For more on the issues, see "Philippines to Review Rice Import Program amid Excessive Supply," *Commodity News for Tomorrow*, July 27, 2010, and relevant articles under http://www.riceonline.com/home.shtml.

17. Adding to the complexity of the issue is the fact that while the president may lower the high import duty on rice in the context of AFTA, the congress can always restore it. Avoiding confrontation with the legislative body, previous presidents resorted to tax expenditures for the NFA, and occasionally for the few private sector importers that the NFA authorized to participate.

References and Other Sources

AFP (Agence France-Presse). 2008. "Biofuels Frenzy Fuels Global Food Crisis: Exports." May 1. Washington, DC: AFP. http://afp.google.com/article/ALeqM5jnrykdFN0nv92dF_OkNy5K1wHFQA.

Armas, Enrique Blanca, Camilo Gomez Osorio, and Blanca Moreno-Dodson. 2010. "Agriculture Public Spending and Growth: The Example of Indonesia." *Economic Premise* 9 (April), Poverty Reduction and Economic Management Network, World Bank, Washington, DC.

Arshad, Fatimah M. 2009. "Public Policy Responses to the Food Security Challenges in East Asia: The Case of Malaysia." Presentation at the First EAP Regional Agribusiness Trade and Investment Conference, "Agro-enterprise without Borders," Singapore, July 30–31.

Bloomberg News. 2011. "Government Decisions Fueled 2008 Food Crisis, FAO's Ghanem Says." May 23. http://www.bloomberg.com/news/2011-05-23.

Commodity News for Tomorrow. 2010. "Philippines to Review Rice Import Program amid Excessive Supply." July 27.

Coulter, Jonathan, and Andrew W. Shepherd. 1995. "Inventory Credit: An Approach to Developing Agricultural Markets." FAO Agricultural Services Bulletin 120, Rome. http://www.fao.org/docrep/v7470e/v7470e00.htm.

Dawe, David C., Piedad F. Moya, Cheryll B. Casiwan, and Jesusa M. Cabling. 2008. "Rice Marketing Systems in the Philippines and Thailand: Do Large Numbers of Competitive Traders Ensure Good Performance?" *Food Policy* 33: 455–63.

Dorosh, Paul. 2008. "Food Price Stabilisation and Food Security: International Experience." *Bulletin of Indonesian Economic Studies* 44 (1): 93–114.

FAO (Food and Agriculture Organization of the United Nations). 1999. "Compendium on Post-harvest Operations—Rice." http://www.fao.org/inpho/content/compend/text/ch10-01.htm.

———. Contract Farming Resource Centre. http://www.fao.org/ag/ags/contract-farming/en/.

Forssell, Sara. 2009. "Rice Policy in Thailand: Policy Making and Recent Developments." Minor Field Study 189, Department of Economics, University of Lund, Lund, Sweden.

Headey, Derek. 2011. "Rethinking the Global Food Crisis: The Role of Trade Shocks." *Food Policy* 36: 136–46.

Incoterms®. 2010. By the International Chamber of Commerce. http://www.iccwbo.org/incoterms/.

McCulloch, Neil. 2008. "Rice Prices and Poverty in Indonesia." *Bulletin of Indonesian Economic Studies* 44 (1): 45–63.

McCulloch, Neil, and C. Peter Timmer. 2008. "Rice Policy in Indonesia." *Bulletin of Indonesian Economic Studies* 44 (1): 33–44.

Rashid, Shahidur, Ashok Gulati, and Ralph Cummings Jr. 2008. "Grains Marketing Parastatals in Asia: Why Do They Have to Change Now?" In *From Parastatals to Private Trade: Lessons from Asian Agriculture,* ed. A. Gulati, S.

Rashid, and R. Cummings Jr., chapter 2. Baltimore: International Food Policy Research Institute and Johns Hopkins University Press.

Rokotoarisoa, Manitra A. 2006. "Policy Distortions in the Segmented Rice Market." Markets, Trade, and Institutions Division Discussion Paper 94, International Food Policy Research Institute, Washington, DC.

Rosner, L. Peter, and Neil McCulloch. 2008. "A Note on Rice Production, Consumption, and Import Data in Indonesia." *Bulletin of Indonesian Economic Studies* 44 (1): 81–89.

Simatupang, Pantjar, and C. Peter Timmer. 2008. "Indonesian Rice Production: Policies and Realities." *Bulletin of Indonesian Economic Studies* 44 (1): 65–79.

Timmer, C. Peter. 2008. "Causes of High Food Prices." Asian Development Bank Economics Working Paper Series 128, Asian Development Bank, Manila.

WTO (World Trade Organization). Principles of the Trading System. http://www.wto.org/english/thewto_e/whatis_e/tif_e/fact2_e.htm.

CHAPTER 1

Moving from Food Crisis to Food Security in Southeast Asia

Remember, the storm is a good opportunity for the pine and the cypress to show their strength and their stability.

— Ho Chi Minh

Introduction

After crisis, fresh resolve; out of calamity, momentum for change; from the lessons of loss, a new foundation for progress. This study of the dramatic food price surges in 2007–08 proceeds from those equations.

It finds that long-standing agricultural policies and trade restrictions set the stage for limitations imposed by exporters to trigger panicky buying, thereby turning a manageable supply-and-demand imbalance into a global upheaval that, as a senior international expert recently observed, "could have been avoided. ... Bad government policies have been a reason for volatility."

"The food crisis and especially the increase of the rice price was due largely to political choices," said Hafez Ghanem, assistant director-general of the Food and Agriculture Organization (FAO) of the United Nations. "In 2008, the production of rice was good; the stocks were high and consumption was stable. ... What we saw is that the price of rice doubled in

2008, and this is explained mainly by the decision of certain countries to halt their exports."[1]

Behind the rice sector policies, in particular, and the damaging immediate responses lies the perception, deeply embedded in the Asian culture and political psyche, that food security is best defined as self-sufficiency, especially in rice. That definition, understandable in an era of frequent famine and erratic maritime transport, is badly outdated. Establishing a new definition of food security, the study argues, is the essential first step to effective policy making in the production, processing, marketing, and trading of rice in Southeast Asia.

Simplified and expanded trade is a critical element of the recommended shift in rice sector policies. Globally and in the Association of Southeast Asian Nations (ASEAN) region, however, trade has historically been thin, rarely involving more than 7 percent of total rice production. In such a limited market, it is admittedly not easy to see convincing reasons that rice exporters and importers should enter into binding rice trade agreements.

Those reasons, however, exist. They can be found, quite concretely, in the rice supply-chain inefficiencies that translate into significant annual losses of rice. A reduction of postharvest physical losses by 5 percent (from 14 percent to 9 percent) would create 4.3 million tons of rice equivalent for the five countries. This volume is more than the entire intra-ASEAN rice trade, which was 3.5 million tons in 2008. If that wastage could be significantly reduced, the amounts available for regional trade, to begin with, would grow in proportion. At the same time, it should be added, the savings would at least slow and possibly reverse the growth of budgetary outlays going to subsidize the rice sector and the heavy debts of state enterprises that have long controlled it.

The study describes in some detail the policies and practices of rice-importing countries—and the unavoidable consequences of the narrow focus on self-sufficiency—that lead to such losses. Rethinking old patterns of thought and performance opens the way for two sorts of productive transformation. The first affects the existing operations of farmers, millers, processors, warehouse personnel, and intermediaries at various stages along the supply chain. The second, in some senses a catalyst for the first, is the rapid expansion of private investment and competition in rice supply chains, where, until now, government involvement has severely limited private investment.

It is not wishful thinking to imagine private companies bringing their energy and focus on efficiency into the ASEAN rice sector. To the contrary, the reasonable expectation of such a change is firmly based in the performance of local and international private investors in the record of maize production in the region.

Despite apparent fundamental differences,[2] maize and rice may share a common future in ASEAN countries, with the former serving policy makers as something of a model for reforming policies that have long governed the latter. With that prospect in mind, this study, while focusing on the rice sector, offers evidence at various points of the economic expansion of maize and analyses of the factors that have encouraged its growth.

The transition that the study urges will be difficult and, of necessity, slow to gain momentum. Nevertheless, it is already beginning. The heads of ASEAN member states (AMSs), for example, signed at the 14th ASEAN Summit (February 2009) in Bangkok, Thailand, the ASEAN Trade in Goods Agreement (ATIGA) to "achieve free flow of goods in ASEAN as one of the principal means to establish a single market and production base for the deeper economic integration of the region towards the realisation of the ASEAN Economic Community (AEC) by 2015."[3] The agreement codifies all trade-related agreements within ASEAN for the purpose of facilitating private sector business transactions with a clear articulation of the region's free trade rules, made more accessible, transparent, predictable, and certain.

Additionally, the Asian Development Bank has work under way to assist ASEAN in understanding the challenges its members face in moving toward more open trade in the region, among them measures that would enhance the region's capability to cope with supply shocks, avoid extreme price volatility of rice, and restore confidence in rice trade. Further, the U.S. Agency for International Development has been helping agriculture and forestry ministers explore the potential of the private sector in strengthening regional food security. (Chapter 5 of this volume discusses these supporting initiatives in detail.)

"A journey of a thousand miles," said Lao-Tzu, "must begin with a single step." Driven by the food crisis of 2007–08, ASEAN is embarking on such a journey. In this book, its planners and their political superiors can find directions to the journey's end: secure supplies of food for growing populations with changing tastes but an abiding demand for one staple—rice.

Background

When international cereal prices shot up in 2007–08, as rice prices, most notably, nearly tripled from October 2007 to April of the next year, the resulting food crisis, by World Bank estimates, drove over 130 million people into poverty. According to FAO, it also left another 75 million people malnourished (Headey 2010).

The severity of the crisis made clear the urgent need in Southeast Asia to examine and reform policies that underlay not only the immediate calamity but also the potential for a recurrence. This study examines the experiences of Indonesia, Malaysia, the Philippines, Thailand, and Vietnam in rice production, processing, marketing, and trading to illustrate the impact of those policies. It recommends ways to insure against severe shortages in the future by encouraging both eased regional trade in rice and widened private sector involvement in modernizing rice supply chains. Table 1.1 describes the place of rice in those nations' agriculture.

Impossible to quantify but nevertheless essential to understanding the societal considerations at work in shaping agricultural policies is the historical and abiding role of rice in traditional Asian culture and values. Seen as "a perpetual symbol of fecundity," rice "in ancient Siam was well known to be the gift of the perennially fruitful womb of the goddess Mae Phosop." Some Indonesian paddies were "themselves considered sacred." For "tribal Filipinos … rice is the crop of greatest concern … the most

Table 1.1   Indicators of the Importance of Rice in Agriculture, Selected ASEAN Countries

Country	Share of agricultural sector in GDP (%)[a]	Share of agricultural sector in labor force (%)[a]	Share of rice in cropped area (%)[b]	Share of rice in agricultural exports and imports (%)[c]	Number of rice farmers (million)[d]
Indonesia	13.7	43.7	78.49	2.89	12.00
Malaysia	7.4	20.3	11.41	0.78	0.13
Philippines	18.1	36.1	86.73	20.78	4.44
Thailand	8.9	41.6	36.20	36.62	9.10
Vietnam	17.5	55.7	56.38	42.96	10.00

Sources: Authors' calculations based on the following sources:
a. ASEAN 2009.
b. FAOSTAT 2008.
c. The share of rice in agricultural exports (for exporters like Thailand and Vietnam) is from the value of exports of rice and the value of total agricultural exports (ASEAN 2009). The share of rice in agricultural imports (for importers like Indonesia, Malaysia, and the Philippines) is from the value of imports of rice and the value of total agricultural imports (ASEAN 2009). For Indonesia, Ismet (2009). For Malaysia, Wang (2009). For Thailand, Isvilanonda (2009). For Vietnam, ACI (2010). For the Philippines, ACI (2010).
d. For Indonesia, Ismet (2009). For Malaysia, Wang (2009). For Thailand, Isvilanonda (2009). For Vietnam, Census of Agricultural Statistics (2006), General Statistics Office, Hanoi. For the Philippines, ACI (2010).
Note: GDP = gross domestic product.

highly valued real food. In most ritual offerings, curing rites, and for major feasts it is an essential for which there is no substitute."[4]

In modern times, rice is a "political commodity" (ACI 2010). For ASEAN authorities, and not for them alone, the reliability of rice supplies and prices amounts to a critical test of their abilities to provide their citizens with *food security*. As a formal matter, all AMSs have adopted the World Food Summit 1996 statement that "food security exists when all people, at all times, have physical, social and economic access to sufficient, safe and nutritious food to meet their dietary needs and food preferences for an active and healthy life" (World Food Summit 1996). (In addition to the five countries on which this study concentrates, ASEAN includes Brunei Darussalam, Cambodia, Lao People's Democratic Republic, Myanmar, and Singapore.) Attaining that broad, multifaceted goal requires a complex approach that depends not only on the availability of a variety of foods but also on measurements of access, use, nutrition, and stability. Too often, however, responsible ASEAN officials take a narrower view of food security, identifying it as an issue of rice availability and, more explicitly, of self-sufficiency within their respective borders.

Rear-View Mirror Responses

Specifically, a number of postcrisis government interventions seem simply attempts to recycle the past,[5] harking back to the role of Green Revolution production technology. Rather, along with continuing technological progress, what is required is a food supply-chain revolution. The introduction of new disease-resistant seeds and complementary investments in fertilizer, irrigation, and infrastructure did bring significantly improved crop yields in wheat, maize, and rice during the 1960s and 1970s. Those policies, focusing on internal markets, fostered large productivity gains, but the solutions of the past need to be complemented by policies to address the challenges of the present.

An example of giving priority to production is the Malaysian government's effort to increase rice yield from 2.47 to 4.48 tons per hectare by targeting specific groups of farmers, identifying Sabah and Sarawak as new frontiers for increased rice production (Arshad 2009). Also, in April 2008, the Philippine government launched its FIELDS program (fertilizer, irrigation/infrastructure, extension/education, loans, dryers and post-harvest facilities, and seeds/genetic materials), which is designed to enhance the country's rice production so that, within two years, at least 98 percent of national rice consumption can be provided from local sources. Indonesia is aiming even higher, devoting public resources to increase rice production in order to attain full rice self-sufficiency (McCulloch and Timmer 2008). Even Brunei Darussalam, which is able to fill its rice requirement quite affordably from trade, launched a rice hybrid development program in September 2009.

Such subsidized yield improvements, plus any arable land expansions, will entail a considerable opportunity cost in terms of product shifts and income diversification at the farm level. At the precise time when rice sectors need to move toward the next phase of competitive capability, such government policies are pulling them backward. The renewed efforts to channel public resources into increasing local production, thereby sourcing more of their respective rice requirements internally, miss new opportunities to meet domestic demand through greater regional trade and private sector engagement.

This study stresses the gains to be realized from adding those ingredients to the mix of policies that in many cases now skew ASEAN supply chains. The challenge it lays out is to move rice, in particular, efficiently and quickly—in just enough quantities to match demand and in a manner that can adapt to evolving consumer preferences and shifting market conditions—from where production is abundant to where processors and consumers demand reliable supply. When unilateral trade restrictions imposed severe strains on the rice market in 2007–08, the spiral of responses exposed the failure of long-standing but shortsighted policies to treat rice as a modern agricultural commodity.

The Crisis of 2007–08 in Context

To prescribe remedies, it is essential to identify the illness and its causes accurately. In the case of the 2007–08 food crisis, observers initially pointed to standard factors in commodity shortages: a shortfall of production or an increase in demand or both. That familiar analysis, however, slights the deeper pressures at work.

The surge in rice prices, in fact, was the result of multiple factors coming together in a "perfect storm" of concurrent conditions. Some related to the perceived tightening of demand-and-supply balances within the region; others related to the nature of the price formation process itself. Some analysts saw the 2007–08 world rice price crisis as the manifestation of a long-term problem of insufficient production in the face of rising demand.[6] Others placed the rice crisis in the context of a larger global food crisis being driven by the weak U.S. dollar, rising fuel and fertilizer prices, increases in biofuel production, and crop failures in major agricultural production areas (drought in Australia). The two proximate but perhaps only recently acknowledged factors triggering the rice price surge, in fact, were policy decisions and buying behavior.

The dramatic escalation in rice prices in 2007–08 was not caused simply by a shortfall of production or an increase in demand. In early 2002, global prices of most commodities, including energy, agriculture, metals, and minerals, started rising after an extended period of price stability— and indeed of price decline in real terms (figure 1.1). This upward trend intensified in early 2006 as energy prices continued to soar and the value of the U.S. dollar continued to fall. Between January 2007 and June 2008, when agricultural commodity prices reached their peak, the FAO Food Price Index[7] rose by 63 percent, as compared with an annual rate increase of 5 percent the year before (figure 1.1).

During this same period, international prices of traditional food staples rose even faster. More specifically, prices for rice and maize increased by 141 and 74 percent, respectively (figure 1.2). World maize production actually increased during the decade preceding the crisis, with the exception of a small decline of 2.25 percent between 2004–05 and 2005–06.[8] Moreover, although world maize stocks decreased from the highs set in 2000–01, global stocks-to-use ratios (S/Us) remained at levels that should have comforted markets in 2007–08.[9] Clearly, the inventory levels that prevailed in 2007–08 were adequate to cover demand and did not by themselves justify even the relatively modest increases in maize prices.

Figure 1.1   Food and Agriculture Organization of the United Nations (FAO) Food Price Index, 2002–10

2002–04 = 100

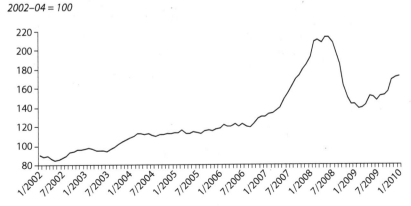

Source: FAO 2010.

Figure 1.2   Rice and Maize Prices, 2002–09

US$/metric ton

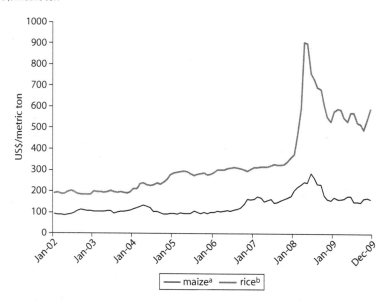

Source: Authors' calculations based on United States Department of Agriculture (USDA) data.
a. Price for Yellow No. 2.
b. Price for Thai White Rice 5% broken.

The rapid run-up in rice prices likewise cannot be explained by a simple aggregate demand-supply imbalance. It did not reflect either below-average harvests in affected countries or rising demand or declining global supply. World milled rice production has been increasing steadily since the early 2000s. Production even registered an increase of 3.5 percent between 2005–06 and 2007–08.

All major Asian rice producers experienced good harvests in 2008, and record-high crop production was forecast for 2009. Indeed, global year-end milled rice stocks increased in 2007–08 (annex table 1A.1). None of the five ASEAN countries studied for this report registered alarmingly low stock levels. The average global rice S/U for 2007–08 was 0.17, and by the end of the period it was actually trending upward.

Until December 2007, the depreciating U.S. dollar did help to drive up the price of commodities like rice that are priced in U.S. dollars. However, its drop did not play a major role in the 2008 rice price spike. Exporters in countries with stronger local currencies demanded higher dollar-denominated prices to offset their costs. By the same token, buyers in countries with appreciating currencies were able to pay higher prices at the margin. However, while Thailand's currency, the baht, appreciated 14.3 percent in 2007, contributing to the rise in rice prices, it depreciated 4.6 percent from December 2007 to April 2008, during the period when prices spiraled.[10]

Up to 2007 as well, rising oil prices did contribute to the increase in rice prices. In the absence of government intervention, higher oil prices increase production costs affected by rising fertilizer and agrochemicals prices, irrigation pumping costs, harvesting, drying, milling, and international and domestic transport costs. That upward pressure (estimated to explain around 20 percent of the rise in other grain prices like wheat and corn between 2002 and 2007), diminished at the end of 2007. It cannot explain the rice price spike relative to other grains in early 2008. Nor did financial speculation play more than a small role in rice markets, since futures markets for rice, unlike those for wheat and corn, are very thinly traded (Timmer 2009).

Finally, biofuel production only influenced the price of rice indirectly and not enough to explain the escalating prices. The impact of biofuel use on rice prices is indirect because rice is not used for biofuel production and its land is not easily switched to biofuel crops.

India Sparks the Crisis

Within an enabling context to which many of the previously noted factors may have contributed, India, the world's second largest exporter, triggered the crisis with its October 2007 decision to restrict rice exports. That action set off an uncoordinated chain reaction in policies and procurement practices, generating further trade restrictions and tendering behavior that can be seen in retrospect as the prime causes of the price upheaval.

The Indian government, which then accounted for 16 percent of world rice exports, acted out of fear that a dramatic increase in international wheat prices would lead to food inflation, as wheat is a major food staple in India. Facing an election in 2009 and having been criticized for the previous year's wheat imports, India cut back its international purchases by 5 million tons. It compensated, though, by banning exports of nonbasmati rice. The restriction was initially carried out by establishing a minimum export price well above the prevailing market price, effectively blocking any new export contracts.

India's action created a snowball effect. It put pressure on other rice exporters to take preemptive trade policy measures to secure access to rice supplies. As international rice prices then rose, food price inflation reached alarming levels in rice-importing and rice-exporting countries, threatening to undermine living standards and putting pressure on governments to safeguard domestic supplies. In its response, Vietnam—the world's third largest rice exporter—stopped accepting new export orders in early 2008 because the Southern Food Corporation, the state-owned rice exporter, attempted to lock in contracts with the National Food Authority in the Philippines without having secured sufficient supplies in the Vietnam market to cover its export position.

Fearful that rapidly inflating regional rice prices would infect domestic markets, the Vietnamese government simply shut down exports. India then banned all nonbasmati rice exports on April 1, 2008. Together, India and Vietnam accounted for 34 percent of all world trade in 2009. Other rice exporters, including Brazil, Cambodia, China, Egypt, and Pakistan, had all taken measures to restrict rice exports from the end of 2007 to the first part of 2008. Although senior government officials in Thailand's Ministry of Commerce fueled speculative pressure by raising the possibility of rice export restrictions, Thailand subsequently announced that it would not restrict rice exports.

Figure 1.3 illustrates the cumulative impact of export restrictions and large public tenders and other undisciplined buying decisions in a tight global rice market. It shows that the restrictions on rice exports and panic buying created the opposite of the intended effect in local markets where such supposedly protective measures were adopted. Domestic rice prices in India, the Philippines, and Vietnam rose quickly.

Box 1.1 summarizes the contrasting experiences of the Philippines and Indonesia, illustrating the short-term costs of panic buying in the former and the longer-term costs and risks of seeking price stabilization through managed trade in the latter.

Each country, looking after its own interests, took steps that seemed responsible and responsive to the safeguarding of its own domestic food security. However, what made logical sense at the level of individual countries had the opposite effect at the regional level. By sparking a global panic, these separate actions actually caused domestic rice prices to rise even faster. This outcome made it quite clear that no country could solve the global rice crisis on its own. Individual, uncoordinated actions are the equivalent of shooting oneself in the foot.

That truism applied as well during the more recent (June 2010–early 2011) rapid rise in global food prices, with the World Bank Food Price Index hovering around its 2008 peak by early April 2011.[11] This most

Figure 1.3   World Market Rice Price, 2004–08 (Thai 100B Export Price)
US$/ton

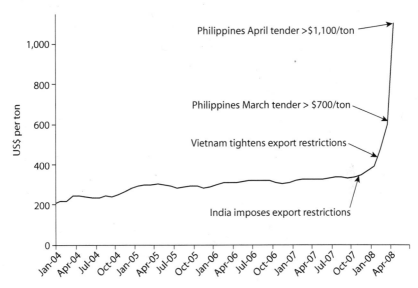

Source: World Bank. 2010. *Boom, Bust and Up Again? Evolution, Drivers and Impact of Commodity Prices: Implications for Indonesia.* Washington, DC: World Bank. http://go.worldbank.org/YY1OOD9UB0.
Note: Thai 100B is a medium grade of rice.

recent rise in prices differs from the 2007–08 crisis in two respects: rice prices have not climbed; the cost of other staples—maize, wheat, soybeans, and sugar—has risen significantly.[12]

The rise in maize prices is attributed to a variety of factors, including continuing low global stocks, especially in the United States, the world's largest exporter, compounded by weak production due to drought in Argentina and the United States; uncertainty over the size of the import demand from China in 2011 and of the maize output in the United States; high global energy prices, which have accelerated demand for biofuel; and high sugar prices, which have had a similar impact on demand for corn-based sweeteners.[13] On the other hand, global rice prices in February 2011 did not differ from those registered a year earlier, and the benchmark price is roughly 32 percent below the peak during the 2007–08 price surge.[14] Among the reasons cited for this trend are satisfactory agricultural production in major exporters, like Thailand and Vietnam, and high global stocks (reportedly the highest since 2002–03).

Box 1.1

The Costs of Losing Control and of Keeping It

The Philippines' Experience: In the last months of the food crisis, March and April 2008, the Philippine government panicked. Despite the fact that rice stocks in March were slightly higher than in March 2007 and increased again in April, the Philippines National Food Authority (NFA) went into the world market seeking to import first 500,000 tons of rice. The March tender garnered offers of only 300,000 tons at an average price of around $710 a ton—almost half again the prevailing level in February. On April 17, when the NFA sought new offers, prices skyrocketed to more than $1,100 per ton and only 309,000 tons were offered.

The surging prices turned millions of households, farmers, traders, and some governments into hoarders, sparking a sudden surge in "precautionary" demand for rice by small traders and consumers—not "speculative" demand from outside investors. The result of the NFA's moves was to change a gradual rise in rice prices from 2002 to 2007 into such an explosion that, over just four months, the price of regular milled rice in Manila increased by 50 percent with serious impact on the welfare of the poor.

The experience of the Philippines in 2008 demonstrated that, in spite of a considerable effort and enormous public revenues injected into NFA to achieve rice price stabilization, misguided procurement policies and poor market timing on the part of NFA's management aggravated rather than reduced the price spike. The price run-up could have been avoided if the NFA had used alternative procurement methods: using direct contract with different suppliers instead of public tenders, allowing private traders to import so as to increase stocks more rapidly and moderate the price surge, and letting public stocks adjust more slowly, thus achieving the same food security objectives without provoking panic.

Indonesia's Experience: In marked contrast to the Philippines and other ASEAN countries, Indonesia, where rice is the main staple for 95 percent of the population, held rice prices relatively stable. Concerned that, given its large size and the thinness of the world rice market, it cannot ensure food security through trade, Indonesia has long pursued a course of extensive (and expensive) government intervention in rice production and distribution.

Indonesia was able to avoid either a surge or a subsequent sharp fall because (a) for the first time in more than 25 years, the country achieved rice self-sufficiency in 2008, and (b) the Indonesian national logistics agency, Badan Urusan Logistik (BULOG), was able to effectively isolate the domestic market

(continued next page)

Box 1.1 *(continued)*

from international markets, precluding both imports and exports in the crisis months.

Understandably, this performance, heralded as a major success for the government, provided a strong rationale for continued support to BULOG. In particular, the two largest BULOG programs were expanded: the paddy and rice procurement to establish a floor price for paddy, and the Raskin (Rice for the Poor Households) program that distributes subsidized rice to some 19 million poor households.

BULOG policies did spare Indonesian consumers from a price shock that would have caused great harm to the poor during the April–August 2008 price hike. This positive impact, though, carried longer-term costs. For example, from 2005 until the end of 2007, domestic prices were much higher—$232 higher on average—than international ones.

Although Indonesia imported almost 7 million tons of rice in 1999 with little effect on world prices, for most of its recent history, it has relied on managed trade to fill the gap between supply and demand. During the 2007–08 crisis, Indonesia had the good fortune to avoid any major shortfall in domestic production. Had harvests failed, the price spike in the world markets probably would have been even more severe.

Source: ACI 2010.

Learning the Right Lessons

One clear message of the 2007–08 crisis is that trade is vital for ensuring regional food security. The point is worth underlining:

Agricultural trade, when structured so that the individuals and enterprises involved can operate profitably, helps countries respond quickly and efficiently to supply shocks within their own economies.

Equally important, trade can help stabilize prices by creating incentives for private merchandisers and processors to protect their own trading positions, without governments providing tacit or explicit guarantees.

Uncontroversial as those maxims are, they have yet to gain wide operational acceptance in Southeast Asia. The resistance is rooted in the place of rice as a cultural touchstone and, as noted earlier, a political commodity. Nearly sacrosanct, long-established patterns of rice production and processing have been hard to change. Historically, moreover, rice exports have not figured in much ASEAN thinking. Trade in rice among them in 2008 added up to only about 3.5 million tons out of nearly 101 million tons produced. In world markets, as well, rice is very thinly traded, accounting globally for less than 30 million of the 420 million tons produced in 2008. Since nearly half of all exports that year came from Thailand (10 million tons) and Vietnam (over 4.6 million tons), it is understandable that the rice trade and its potential for expansion have held little interest for most of their fellow ASEAN members.

This study holds, however, that the experience of the 2007–08 food crisis should move issues of regional rice trade to a far higher place on the policy agenda. For that trade to grow, ASEAN governments will need to adopt measures that reduce supply-chain losses, improve supply response times, gain savings in farm-to-market costs, and shrink postharvest inventory losses. Moving toward those goals, it must be clearly said, will require consumers, at the end of the line, to pay more for rice than they have normally.

For regional food systems to adjust efficiently and quickly to longer-term equilibrium levels, regional markets will have to increase their efficiency. That progress, though, will come, in particular, as they gain the ability to set gradually increasing prices at levels that ensure the rapid adoption of new, more productive technologies.

Deepening and strengthening regional markets and defining a profitable role for the private sector in these markets are not only components of a sound policy for short-term price stabilization but also prerequisites for smoothing the way to a new higher price equilibrium. Only at this higher price equilibrium will it be possible for new production practices and patterns to supplant the old ones by applying advanced agricultural technologies widely and productively.

Ensuring that food security is maintained and improved through regional trade entails making supply chains strong enough to produce more rapid and efficient supply responses. The challenges are complex. This study, which is aimed at helping ASEAN nations in a period of rapid economic transformation to make radical, if gradual, changes in agrarian structure, does not underestimate the difficulties to be overcome. It argues, however, that to begin that journey, first steps are as feasible as they are urgent.

After the statistical annex appended to this chapter, chapter 2 discusses the impact, often negative, of various public policies on the rice sector; chapter 3 details the workings and inefficiencies of rice sector supply chains; chapter 4 focuses on the role of private investors in the rice sector and options for enlarging it; and chapter 5 lays out conclusions about weaknesses in the rice sector and proposals to remedy them by revising government policies, encouraging greater private sector involvement at all stages of rice supply chains, and following through on ASEAN's stated goals for liberalized regional food trade. It concludes with a 17-point Agenda for Action based on principles agreed upon at the Discussion Workshop on July 19–20, 2010, in Jakarta, Indonesia.

A second part of the study includes background profiles of agricultural and trade practices in each country, followed by an appendix discussing the maize sector in the five study countries.

Annex: Commodity Tables

Table 1A.1 Milled Rice Production, Exports, Imports, Consumption, and Stocks, Selected East and Southeast Asian Countries, 1960s–2010

1,000 MT (metric tons)

a. Milled rice production

Country/ country group	1960s	1970s	1980s	1990s	2000–01	2001–02	2002–03	2003–04	2004–05	2005–06	2006–07	2007–08	2008–09	2009–10
Indonesia	10,412	15,223	26,020	31,572	32,960	32,960	33,411	35,024	34,830	34,959	35,300	37,000	38,300	37,600
Malaysia	800	1,223	1,141	1,272	1,410	1,350	1,418	1,470	1,415	1,440	1,385	1,475	1,530	1,575
Philippines	2,718	3,968	5,491	6,727	8,135	8,450	8,450	9,200	9,425	9,821	9,775	10,479	10,753	10,400
Thailand	7,242	9,605	12,599	14,040	17,057	17,499	17,198	18,011	17,360	18,200	18,250	19,300	19,400	20,000
Vietnam	5,930	6,977	10,336	16,978	20,473	21,036	21,527	22,082	22,716	22,772	22,922	24,375	24,430	23,795
ASEAN[a]	29,186	38,500	57,566	73,375	83,895	85,282	85,863	90,181	89,892	92,504	93,178	98,593	100,734	99,901
World	173,967	233,758	308,297	371,903	399,470	400,168	378,946	392,504	401,714	418,443	420,669	433,421	445,772	432,091

a. ASEAN includes Brunei Darussalam, Cambodia, Indonesia, Lao People's Democratic Republic, Malaysia, the Philippines, Thailand, and Vietnam (excludes Myanmar and Singapore).

b. Milled rice exports

Country/ country group	1960s	1970s	1980s	1990s	2000–01	2001–02	2002–03	2003–04	2004–05	2005–06	2006–07	2007–08	2008–09	2009–10
Indonesia	—	1	92	69	—	—	—	—	50	—	—	—	10	—
Malaysia	8	2	1	0.10	—	13	—	13	—	—	13	3	1	2
Philippines	17	32	35	—	—	—	—	—	—	—	—	—	—	—
Thailand	1,420	1,825	4,233	5,459	7,521	7,245	7,552	10,137	7,274	7,376	9,557	10,011	8,500	10,000
Vietnam	72	5	373	2,720	3,528	3,245	3,795	4,295	5,174	4,705	4,522	4,649	5,300	5,500
ASEAN[a]	1,901	1,905	4,737	8,254	11,049	10,503	11,357	14,745	12,698	12,431	14,542	15,163	15,111	16,302
World	7,348	9,115	11,974	19,239	24,120	26,882	23,678	27,418	28,295	29,690	31,459	31,093	27,934	29,662

a. ASEAN includes Cambodia, Indonesia, the Philippines, Thailand, and Vietnam (excludes Brunei Darussalam, Lao People's Democratic Republic, and Myanmar).

c. Milled rice imports

Country/country group	1960s	1970s	1980s	1990s	2000–01	2001–02	2002–03	2003–04	2004–05	2005–06	2006–07	2007–08	2008–09	2009–10
Indonesia	720	1,374	311	1,787	1,500	3,500	2,750	650	500	539	2,000	350	250	300
Malaysia	388	272	318	469	596	633	480	500	700	751	886	799	1,020	830
Philippines	172	151	154	590	1,410	1,200	1,500	1,290	1,500	1,622	1,800	2,570	2,600	2,600
Thailand	—	—	0.20	0.10	—	15	—	—	2	2	3	8	300	3
Vietnam	417	536	151	11	40	40	40	300	320	350	450	300	500	500
ASEAN[a]	2,076	2,789	1,206	3,230	4,065	5,818	5,252	3,184	3,786	3,814	5,738	4,435	5,061	4,673
World	6,861	8,837	10,644	17,5544	22,092	25,938	26,338	24,973	26,114	26,388	28,175	29,206	27,144	28,311

a. ASEAN includes Brunei Darussalam, Cambodia, Indonesia, Lao People's Democratic Republic, Malaysia, the Philippines, Singapore, Thailand, and Vietnam (excludes Myanmar).

d. Milled rice consumption

Country/country group	1960s	1970s	1980s	1990s	2000–01	2001–02	2002–03	2003–04	2004–05	2005–06	2006–07	2007–08	2008–09	2009–10
Indonesia	11,084	16,472	26,120	32,983	35,877	36,382	36,500	36,000	35,850	35,739	35,900	36,350	37,090	37,400
Malaysia	1,185	1,474	1,485	1,712	1,946	2,010	2,020	2,030	2,050	2,150	2,166	2,230	2,346	2,445
Philippines	2,823	4,005	5,651	7,237	8,750	9,040	9,550	10,250	10,400	10,722	12,000	13,499	13,650	13,785
Thailand	5,730	7,780	8,321	8,583	9,250	9,400	9,460	9,470	9,480	9,544	9,780	9,600	10,292	9,600
Vietnam	6,274	7,508	10,114	14,177	16,932	17,966	17,447	13,230	17,595	18,392	18,775	19,400	19,150	19,150
ASEAN[a]	29,175	39,155	53,940	67,843	77,134	79,215	79,308	80,518	80,087	82,059	84,316	87,001	88,440	88,546
World	172,465	230,718	300,287	367,977	393,778	413,027	406,328	412,189	407,202	412,541	418,275	426,242	434,704	435,490

a. ASEAN includes Brunei Darussalam, Cambodia, Indonesia, Lao People's Democratic Republic, Malaysia, the Philippines, Singapore, Thailand, and Vietnam (excludes Myanmar).

(continued next page)

Table 1A.1 *(continued)*

e. Milled rice stocks (ending)

Country/country group	1960s	1970s	1980s	1990s	2000–01	2001–02	2002–03	2003–04	2004–05	2005–06	2006–07	2007–08	2008–09	2009–10
Indonesia	220	1,175	3,434	4,226	4,605	4,683	4,344	4,018	3,448	3,207	4,607	5,607	7,057	7,557
Malaysia	228	225	230	355	485	445	323	250	315	356	448	439	642	600
Philippines	544	914	1,232	1,566	2,797	3,407	3,807	4,047	4,572	5,293	4,868	4,418	4,121	3,336
Thailand	845	1,369	1,764	894	2,247	3,116	3,302	1,706	2,312	3,594	2,510	2,207	3,115	3,523
Vietnam	—	—	—	327	978	843	1,163	1,025	1,292	1,317	1,392	2,018	1,998	1,643
ASEAN[a]	1,836	3,731	6,663	7,368	11,112	12,494	12,944	11,046	11,939	13,767	13,825	14,689	16,933	16,659
World	17,393	37,167	85,543	125,622	146,714	132,911	103,189	81,059	73,390	75,990	75,100	80,392	90,670	85,920

a. ASEAN includes Indonesia, Malaysia, the Philippines, Singapore (1970–81), Thailand, and Vietnam (excludes Brunei Darussalam, Cambodia, Lao People's Democratic Republic, and Myanmar).

Source: United States Department of Agriculture (USDA) data for Indonesia, Malaysia, the Philippines, Thailand, and Vietnam; Authors' calculations using USDA data for ASEAN and world.

Note: — = not available. The 10 country members of the Association of Southeast Asian Nations plus China, Japan, and the Republic of Korea (ASEAN+3) hold 76 percent of stocks (ending) world-wide; the 10-member ASEAN holds just 19 percent; China, Japan, and the Republic of Korea hold 56.4 percent of global (ending) stocks.

Table 1A.2 Maize Production, Exports, Imports, Total Consumption, and Stocks, Selected East and Southeast Asian Countries, 1960s–2010

1,000 MT (metric tons)

a. Maize production

Country/country group	1960s	1970s	1980s	1990s	2000–01	2001–02	2002–03	2003–04	2004–05	2005–06	2006–07	2007–08	2008–09	2009–10
Indonesia	2,802	3,064	4,644	5,790	5,900	6,000	6,100	6,350	7,200	6,800	7,850	8,500	8,700	9,000
Malaysia	8	11	25	43	65	68	70	72	72	75	80	90	95	100
Philippines	1,459	2,538	3,757	4,538	4,508	4,505	4,430	4,900	5,050	5,884	6,231	7,277	6,846	6,850
Thailand	1,027	2,371	4,000	3,700	4,700	4,500	4,250	4,100	4,210	4,000	3,800	3,850	4,200	4,250
Vietnam	36	208	557	1,184	2,005	2,112	2,313	2,800	3,757	3,818	4,251	4,600	4,530	4,800
ASEAN[a]	5,485	8,272	13,037	15,315	17,335	17,371	17,312	18,536	20,546	20,825	22,589	24,697	24,771	25,400
World	230,734	338,681	436,446	544,302	591,382	601,216	602,954	626,798	714,919	698,786	712,380	791,871	791,917	789,730

a. ASEAN includes Cambodia, Indonesia, the Philippines, Thailand, and Vietnam (excludes Brunei Darussalam, Lao People's Democratic Republic, Myanmar, and Singapore).

b. Maize exports

Country/country group	1960s	1970s	1980s	1990s	2000–01	2001–02	2002–03	2003–04	2004–05	2005–06	2006–07	2007–08	2008–09	2009–10
Indonesia	47	106	64	114	90	19	19	41	46	42	79	91	100	100
Malaysia	3	1	0.10	7	223	129	211	33	8	12	14	43	10	10
Philippines	—	—	—	2	—	—	—	—	—	—	—	—	2	—
Thailand	997	1,887	2,370	254	288	285	284	658	459	117	349	488	647	750
Vietnam	2	—	30	34	98	17	1	43	41	1	1	1	10	—
ASEAN[a]	1,154	2,103	2,571	414	702	459	515	975	757	347	693	873	1,069	1,110
World	24,245	50,883	64,603	65,072	76,851	74,666	76,714	77,279	77,645	80,951	93,956	98,609	79,947	84,077

a. ASEAN includes Cambodia, Indonesia, the Philippines, Singapore, Thailand, and Vietnam (excludes Brunei Darussalam, Lao People's Democratic Republic, and Myanmar).

(continued next page)

Table 1A.2 *(continued)*

c. Maize imports

Country/country group	1960s	1970s	1980s	1990s	2000–01	2001–02	2002–03	2003–04	2004–05	2005–06	2006–07	2007–08	2008–09	2009–10
Indonesia	—	35	67	748	1,280	1,149	1,633	1,436	541	1,443	1,069	294	250	100
Malaysia	102	327	1,070	2,089	2,588	2,425	2,408	2,401	2,406	2,517	2,363	3,181	2,000	2,600
Philippines	11	106	224	217	246	243	102	52	157	321	163	58	400	400
Thailand	—	—	—	194	122	5	126	26	126	121	100	250	500	500
Vietnam	41	78	33	51	50	122	311	204	206	475	650	500	900	700
ASEAN[a]	196	782	1,802	3,406	4,338	4,031	4,722	4,151	3,440	4,889	4,367	4,362	4,075	4,325
World	22,802	48,843	64,121	63,904	74,947	71,468	75,813	76,591	75,697	80,426	90,287	98,348	80,248	81,874

a. ASEAN includes Cambodia, Indonesia, Malaysia, the Philippines, Singapore, Thailand, and Vietnam (excludes Brunei Darussalam, Lao People's Democratic Republic, and Myanmar).

d. Maize total consumption

Country/country group	1960s	1970s	1980s	1990s	2000–01	2001–02	2002–03	2003–04	2004–05	2005–06	2006–07	2007–08	2008–09	2009–10
Indonesia	2,755	2,993	4,630	6,366	7,300	7,300	7,500	7,800	7,800	8,300	8,100	8,500	8,800	9,100
Malaysia	106	325	1,094	2,123	2,420	2,440	2,250	2,300	2,450	2,550	2,450	2,700	2,600	2,700
Philippines	1,423	2,681	3,930	4,723	4,900	4,700	4,650	4,950	5,150	5,800	6,550	7,150	7,300	7,400
Thailand	48	488	1,603	3,658	4,375	4,375	4,100	3,550	3,700	4,000	3,600	3,800	3,900	3,800
Vietnam	75	285	560	1,201	1,957	2,217	2,600	2,650	3,900	4,250	4,900	5,200	5,300	5,500
ASEAN[a]	4,499	6,980	12,222	18,236	21,158	21,296	21,349	21,399	23,076	24,937	25,722	27,524	28,075	28,675
World	230,799	329,633	433,853	536,862	608,279	621,750	626,398	648,030	686,350	705,397	723,935	770,968	775,988	801,064

a. ASEAN includes Cambodia, Indonesia, Malaysia, the Philippines, Singapore, Thailand, and Vietnam (excludes Brunei Darussalam, Lao People's Democratic Republic, and Myanmar).

e. Maize stocks (ending)

Country/ country group	1960s	1970s	1980s	1990s	2000–01	2001–02	2002–03	2003–04	2004–05	2005–06	2006–07	2007–08	2008–09	2009–10
Indonesia	—	—	175	507	540	370	584	529	424	325	1,055	1,263	1,318	1,218
Malaysia	7	53	136	195	160	84	101	241	261	291	270	798	283	273
Philippines	192	333	181	264	304	352	234	236	293	698	542	727	671	520
Thailand	208	101	250	277	399	244	236	154	331	335	286	98	251	451
Vietnam	—	—	—	—	—	—	23	334	356	398	398	297	417	417
ASEAN[a]	406	487	741	1,243	1,403	1,050	1,220	1,533	1,686	2,066	2,607	3,269	2,971	2,911
World	46,549	60,827	144,452	157,570	174,810	151,078	126,733	104,813	131,434	124,298	109,074	129,716	145,946	132,409

a. ASEAN includes Cambodia (2003–10), Indonesia, Malaysia, the Philippines, Singapore (only 2002–03 data recorded), Thailand, and Vietnam (excludes Brunei Darussalam, Lao People's Democratic Republic, and Myanmar).

Source: United States Department of Agriculture (USDA) data for Indonesia, Malaysia, the Philippines, Thailand, and Vietnam; Authors' calculations using USDA data for ASEAN and world.
Note: — = not available.

Notes

This study was prepared by the Study Team, drawing on preliminary studies and field research conducted by Francesco Goletti, Agrifood Consulting International, Inc. (ACI). It was based on two missions conducted by ACI to the five countries, a review of selected literature and data, and interviews with key informants. The study was conducted over a 60-day period between September 2009 and January 2010, including a first mission to Indonesia, Malaysia, the Philippines, Thailand, and Vietnam in September–October 2009 and a second mission in January 2010. Given the limited time and resources available for the study, only a few key informants could be contacted in each country, and no systematic surveys could be undertaken.

1. "If every country continues to take decisions to protect its own population, and doesn't look further than the short-term," added Mr. Ghanem, "the result is often that everyone loses." See *Bloomberg News* (2011).

2. "Rice is food, maize is feed; rice is politics; maize is business" (ACI 2010).

3. The agreement encompasses the key provisions of the ASEAN Free Trade Agreement on tariff liberalization, as well as its related rules on origin, non-tariff measures, trade facilitation, customs, standards, technical regulations and conformity assessment procedures, sanitary and phytosanitary measures, and trade remedies. ATIGA enters into force with the deposit by AMSs of their respective instruments of ratifications with the secretary-general of ASEAN (ASEAN 2009).

4. See Kahn (1985).

5. Most AMSs believe that there is significant scope for enhancing rice productivity, despite the fact that the comparative advantage in rice in ASEAN follows more from natural levels of farmland endowment than from the use of different agricultural technologies. Evidence comes from the fact that yields in major rice-producing countries within ASEAN do not differ greatly. Thailand and Vietnam have the edge over the other countries because they have larger irrigated land areas and smaller populations compared to Indonesia and the Philippines. In pursuit of efficiency gains in rice production, care needs to be taken that these gains are not offset by public resource commitments associated with the policies applied to attain them.

6. The International Rice Research Institute has advocated the view that the global rice crisis was the result of insufficient production. The International Food Policy Research Institute has identified "major policy failures" at the core of the food price crisis and has flagged the distortive effect of promoting biofuels on the grains markets. See AFP (2008).

7. The FAO Food Price Index consists of the average of six commodity group price indexes (cereals, dairy, meat, oils and fats, and sugar) weighted with the

average export shares of each of the groups for 2002–04: in all, 55 commodity quotations are included in the overall index.

8. Production in 2009–10 is also projected to have decreased, but by less than 1 percent.

9. Stocks-to-use ratio (S/U)—a convenient measure of supply-and-demand interrelationships of commodities. This ratio indicates the level of carryover stock for any given commodity as a percentage of the total use of the commodity (CRS 2005).

10. Timmer's (2008) statistical analysis of the relationships between rice prices and exchange rates, stocks, financial speculation, and other grain prices supports the conclusions in this section.

11. World Bank (2011).

12. Ivanic, Martin, and Zaman (2011).

13. World Bank (2011).

14. World Bank (2011).

References and Other Sources

ACI (Agrifood Consulting International, Inc.). 2010. "Enhancing Food Security in ASEAN: Policy Reforms, Private Investment in Food Supply Chains, and Cross-Border Trade Facilitation; Supply Chain Organization and Infrastructure." Final report prepared for the World Bank, Bethesda, MD, February 1.

AFP (Agence France-Presse). 2008. "Biofuels Frenzy Fuels Global Food Crisis: Exports." May 1. Washington, DC: AFP. http://afp.google.com/article/ALeqM5jnrykdFN0nv92dF_OkNy5K1wHFQA.

AFSIS (ASEAN Food Security Information System). Various years. http://afsis.oae.go.th/.

Arshad, Fatimah M. 2009. "Public Policy Responses to the Food Security Challenges in East Asia: The Case of Malaysia." Presentation at the First EAP Regional Agribusiness Trade and Investment Conference, "Agro-enterprise without Borders," Singapore, July 30–31.

ASEAN (Association of Southeast Asian Nations). *ASEAN Statistical Yearbook 2008*. 2008. Jakarta: ASEAN Secretariat. http://www.aseansec.org/publications/aseanstats08.pdf.

———. 2009. *ASEAN Trade in Goods Agreement*. http://www.aseansec.org/22223.pdf.

Bloomberg News. 2011. "Government Decisions Fueled 2008 Food Crisis, FAO's Ghanem Says," May 23. http://www.bloomberg.com/news/2011-05-23.

CRS (Congressional Research Service). 2005. "CRS Report for Congress; Agriculture: A Glossary of Terms, Programs, and Laws, 2005 Edition." Resources, Science, and Industry Division, the Library of Congress, Washington, DC. http://ncseonline.org/nle/crsreports/05jun/97-905.pdf.

FAO (Food and Agriculture Organization of the United Nations). 2010. http://www.fao.org/worldfoodsituation/FoodPricesIndex/en/.

FAOSTAT (statistical database of the Food and Agriculture Organization of the United Nations). Various years. http://faostat.fao.org/default.aspx.

Headey, Derek. 2011. "Rethinking the Global Food Crisis: The Role of Trade Shocks." *Food Policy* 36: 136–46.

Ismet, M. 2009. "Indonesia Rice Industry Outlook." Presented at the 14th World Rice Commerce 2009, Bali, October 8–10.

Isvilanonda, Somporn. 2009. "Dynamic of Thai Rice Production Economy." Department of Agricultural and Resource Economics, Faculty of Economics, Kasetsart University, Bangkok.

Ivanic, Maros, Will Martin, and Hassan Zaman. 2011. "Estimating the Short-Run Poverty Impacts of the 2010–11 Surge in Food Prices." World Bank Policy Research Working Paper 5633, Washington, DC.

Kahn, Ely J. 1985. *The Staffs of Life.* Boston: Little, Brown.

McCulloch, Neil, and C. Peter Timmer. 2008 "Rice Policy in Indonesia." *Bulletin of Indonesian Economic Studies* 44 (1): 33–44.

Samporn. 2009.

Timmer, C. Peter. 2008. "Causes of High Food Prices." Asian Development Bank (ADB) Economics Working Paper Series 128, Asian Development Bank, Manila.

————. 2009. *A World without Agriculture. The Structural Transformation in Historical Perspective.* Washington, DC: The American Enterprise Institute Press. http://www.asiaing.com/a-world-without-agriculture-the-structural-transformation-in-historical-perspe.html.

Wang, L. 2009. "The Roles of Private Sector in Malaysia's Rice and Maize Industry." Research report (draft) prepared for the World Bank, Washington, DC.

World Bank. 2010. *Boom, Bust and Up Again? Evolution, Drivers and Impact of Commodity Prices: Implications for Indonesia.* Washington, DC: World Bank. http://go.worldbank.org/YY1OOD9UB0.

————.2011. *Food Price Watch.* April. Washington, DC: World Bank. http://www.worldbank.org/foodcrisis/foodpricewatch/april_2011.html.

World Food Summit. 1996. http://www.fao.org/docrep/003/w3613e/w3613e00.HTM.

CHAPTER 2

Going It Alone versus Intra-ASEAN Trade Cooperation: How Public Sector Rice Policies Thwart Regional Food Security

We must all hang together, or assuredly we shall all hang separately.

—Benjamin Franklin, July 4, 1776

Introduction

Like many alarms, those that drove the tripling of rice prices in 2007–08 and provoked unilateral bans on rice exports, panic buying, and hoarding in Association of Southeast Asian Nations (ASEAN) countries now seem exaggerated, if not irrational. They had, it is clear, little or no basis in the actual state of regional rice supply and demand.

The output of milled rice by Indonesia, Malaysia, the Philippines, Thailand, and Vietnam in 2007–08 was the highest it had been in the 21st century, nearly 6 percent above the region's 2006–07 total. World production in those years rose also, though only by 3 percent. Combined Thai and Vietnamese rice exports exceeded 15 million tons in both 2007–08 and 2008–09. Average regional consumption in the period of the rice price spike was just 4 percent above the 2006–07 level, with only the Philippines recording a disproportionate increase of 13 percent.

Behind the worries, however, lay a set of long-standing and seemingly rational calculations by individual ASEAN governments that relied—then and still—on the public sector to promote food security as they defined it. The preceding chapter demonstrated that their definition may be too narrow.

This chapter shows that the policies based on it may also be misdirected and too often wasteful of government and natural resources. It suggests, as well, the potential value in greater private sector involvement and less constricted regional trade as alternatives to supply-chain policies that have, for the most part, remained unchanged in their organization for centuries. Pinpointing a total of annual postharvest losses of 10–15 percent (ACI 2010) traceable to weaknesses at almost every step of the supply chains, the analysis points the way to a new focus on competitive capability in the ASEAN rice sector.

Instead of providing fiscal incentives to rice farmers, for instance, and protecting them from competitive imports in some cases, the study points at a policy shift away from the production end of chains. Greater attention to integrated actions, it finds, can enhance quality, reduce physical loss, minimize buffer inventory accumulation, and expand cross-border trade so as to ensure that demand is matched with sufficient supply.

This chapter first deals generally with agricultural and food security policies and with their effects on supply chains and regional markets, focusing also on prevailing trade policy for rice. The chapter then discusses the modes and means that regional governments have chosen to implement their agricultural and food security policies, including farm support policies and their market effects.

The Effects of Government Policies on Supply Chains and Regional Markets

Just when ASEAN countries' rice sectors need to develop, in the aftermath of the 2007–08 crisis, government policies in some cases are pulling them backward. Instead of facilitating trade and investment and regional supply-chain formation, Indonesia, Malaysia, and the Philippines, in particular, have chosen a more costly path to food security, one that holds little guarantee of leading to its desired destination: reduced price volatility and enhanced productivity at the farm level.

A basic shortcoming in traditional public policies is that typically they are neither conceived nor assessed from the perspective of their impacts on farm-to-market chains. Rather, they are designed piecemeal to meet the specific tactical objectives that governments pursue in their quests for national food security.[1] Indeed, it makes sense to go even further and to use the term *food security programs* in lieu of the term *policies* when describing the current state of government involvement in food staple markets within the region. *Policy* implies a longer-term vision, a more systemic approach, and a greater degree of constancy in implementation than does *programs*. At least in several of the countries reviewed in this chapter, *programs* is a more appropriate term. Because of its strategic importance, rice is the subject of more programmatic interventions than any other farm crop. This circumstance makes the market for rice among the most distorted in the region—and indeed, the world.

Public programs affect market performance in both targeted and expected ways and in collateral and unexpected ways. Among such interventions in rice markets, the primary ones come as (a) technology choices; (b) land use choices; (c) subsidies and price supports; (d) directed credits for farm inputs; (e) controls over domestic market prices; (f) stockpile management; (g) import controls; (h) direct procurement and internal distribution; and (i) food safety and quality controls.

Most food security programs serve two or more objectives that are sometimes countervailing and mutually contradictory. Most are designed to move toward rice self-sufficiency, despite the fact that the path selected for achieving this objective often represents the more costly option. Some program elements require that others be adopted to ensure the effectiveness of the original one or to overcome unforeseen problems resulting from its implementation. Import restricting measures, for example, are frequently used to protect local producers from foreign competition. In turn, these have prompted policy makers to undertake complementary expenditures to stabilize producer and consumer prices or to ensure that rice supply is always available to the poor, independent of prevailing market conditions. Another example involves state trading enterprises (STEs), or parastatals. In many policy contexts, these have been created as implementation instruments, using direct modes of intervention instead of establishing incentives and regulations that would enable private companies to do the job.

For reasons unrelated to their cost-effectiveness, STEs have become privileged participants in many rice-trading activities. Their procurement practices and regulations have become the default rules under which regional rice markets operate. The Philippines' National Food Authority (NFA), the most independent and powerful of the STEs, possesses authority to regulate the nation's rice trade and thus owns the sole right to import or export rice. Its influence transcends national borders, however, by virtue of the procurement procedures it applies.

ASEAN countries' policies and programs have also significantly shaped the current structure of rice trade worldwide. The high level of distortion derived from public sector–managed procurement activities within the region, combined with the relative thinness of the trade, makes for a commercial environment prone to periodic crisis. Small changes in the balance of supply and demand can have large effects on world prices. Procurement processes that favor government-to-government negotiated sales over open, contestable, and competitive buying foster food systems that are less efficient and less competitive than they should be.

The thinness of international trade in rice is not only a result of, but also a reason for, the highly protective policies, which continue to be geared toward self-sufficiency (see box 2.1). National governments, especially those of the major rice-producing nations, are reluctant to rely on a world rice market perceived to be too unstable to provide dependable prices or reliable supplies for the relatively large volumes they need to support food security programs. Thailand, for example, as the world's largest exporter of rice and undoubtedly one of the most efficient rice producers, opposes any liberalization of the rice trade because of the government's desire to keep its rice policy option open should market conditions become unstable (Warr and Kohpaiboon 2009). It is the revealed behavior of the major exporting countries that clarifies their collective, market-distorting impact. When their own inventories reach low levels, their respective national laws prevent food security agencies from

---

Box 2.1

Distortions in Global Markets Due to the Prevalence of Protectionist Policies for Rice

Protectionist policies are not unique within ASEAN. While most ASEAN countries enforce protectionism by taxing rice imports, other high-income countries prefer to subsidize production. Subsidized price support creates correspondingly high levels of trade distortions, which translate into a great deal of economic inefficiency when rice is forced to flow from high-cost producing countries to low-cost producing countries.

Source: Authors.

doing business as usual. Unilateral, country-specific rice policies, such as India's and Vietnam's export restrictions in 2008, resulted in destabilizing prices even in world markets (see Timmer and Slayton 2009).

Not only for international trade in rice but also for agriculture as a whole, dramatic restructuring in Asia's economies, which involved a shift from agriculture toward manufacturing and services, greatly contributed to the dwindling share of agricultural products in the export market. Anderson and Martin (2009) observe that selected countries in East Asia, mostly in the ASEAN region, decreased the share of agriculture in their gross domestic products (GDPs) to less than 30 percent in the late 1960s. The biggest changes occurred in China and Indonesia, where the agricultural share of GDP plummeted to 13 percent in 2005 from close to 50 percent in the 1960s. For Asia as a whole, agriculture now constitutes only 12 percent of GDP, down from about 36 percent in the late 1960s. During that period, the shares of industry and services have risen from 27 to 38 percent and 35 to 49 percent, respectively.

The constantly declining share of agriculture to total production was complemented by the strong antitrade bias within the farm sector. Anderson and Martin (2009) found this distortion pattern by comparing the nominal rate of assistance (NRA)[2] of exportable and import-competing agricultural products of selected Asian economies from 1995 to 2004. Their study found that average NRAs in the region for import-competing agricultural products remained positive and that, over the period, the trend was upward sloping. However, average NRAs for exportables were negative before gradually approaching zero after the 1980s (see figure 2.1).

Large net importing countries have also contributed to destabilizing world rice market prices when they have attempted to procure from limited, available global supplies. When, as noted in chapter 1, the Philippines' NFA solicited unprecedentedly large tenders in the regional market in 2007–08, it sent signals to the few suppliers that could comply with its preconditions that it was committed to importing significant volumes of rice even at a high price. Subsequently, rice prices soared from the prevailing $375 price early in 2008 to record-high levels of $1,100 per metric ton free on board.

While efforts have been under way to remove distortions in the global rice market since the start of the Uruguay Round, reforms have been modest in spite of the emergence of regional trade agreements such as the ASEAN Free Trade Agreement (AFTA). Regional pacts are viewed as more effective than multilateral liberalization efforts, in the sense that they can be negotiated within a shorter period of time (box 2.2).

Figure 2.1   Nominal Rates of Assistance (NRAs) for Exportable, Import-Competing, and All Agricultural Products, Asian Focus Economies, 1955–2004
percent

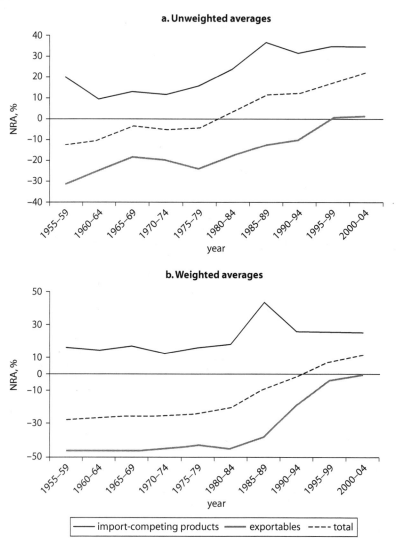

a. Unweighted averages

b. Weighted averages

—— import-competing products   —— exportables   ---- total

Sources: Anderson and Valenzuela 2008; Anderson and Martin 2009.
Note: Total NRAs may be above or below the exportable and importable averages because assistance to non-tradables and non–product-specific assistance are also included. The values used in the NRA estimates are based on the assumption that the NRAs in agriculture in China before 1981 and in India before 1965 are the same as the average NRAs in those economies in 1981–84 and 1965–69, respectively, and that the gross value of production of those economies in the missing years is the same as the average share of the value of the production of the economies in total world production in 1981–84 and 1965–69, respectively.

Box 2.2

Implications of the AFTA Agreement

Apparently not even the ASEAN Free Trade Agreement (AFTA) seems able to usher in a freer rice trade within ASEAN, increase sector competitiveness, or enhance regional supply-chain productivity. Preferential regional trade agreements like AFTA are more politically palatable to national constituencies than multilateral trade liberalization under the World Trade Organization (WTO). Neighboring countries frequently feel a deeper need to work together to solve their common problems. Regional markets being smaller than the global market, adjustment costs associated with enforcing the preferential freer trade policies should be correspondingly less for constituencies that may be giving up the protection that they currently enjoy. In the case of rice, however, the ASEAN region is most of the world market.

As of this writing, Indonesia, Malaysia, and the Philippines intend to maintain relatively high import tariff rates on rice, which currently stand at 20 percent, 25 percent, and 35 percent, respectively. The major obstacle to further liberalization is the Philippines, which has availed itself of relief available under the WTO's Agreement on Agriculture (AoA). The Philippines has not formally committed to giving up the rice import monopoly that the National Food Authority (NFA) currently enjoys. In 2012, when the NFA loses its special treatment, however, it will have to convert its import restriction to ordinary customs duties.

Source: Authors. Obtained from an interview with Ms. Allen Castro, Philippine Department of Agriculture.

Rice Trade Policies

In general, ASEAN rice policies hamper the development of efficient, low-cost, and competitive regional producers through their restrictive impact on farm-level production, processing, distribution, price formation, and international trade. The responsibility for food security accordingly falls to public sector budgets and to public sector personnel. Both formal and informal trade barriers continue to impede the development of an efficient regional market for rice. Among the formal practices are the continuing imposition by governments in East Asia of most-favored nation (MFN) tariff rates that are higher on agricultural imports than on nonagricultural imports. As table 2.1 demonstrates, the ASEAN+3 countries,[3] except for Brunei Darussalam, continue to support average agricultural

Table 2.1   Trade-Weighted Average MFN Applied Tariffs on Agricultural Merchandise of Selected East Asian Countries

percent

Countries	All goods, 2008	Agricultural goods[a]			
		2008	2005–08	2000–04	1995–99
Indonesia	3.81	6.11	5.6	4.4	4.2
Malaysia	4.76	19.89	15.5	1.6	13.0
Philippines	3.4	13.26	12.3	9.7	22.8
Thailand	4.99	15.1	—	15.1	19.7
Vietnam	14.97	24.07	24.3	30.0	45.2
Brunei Darussalam	3.69	1.78	16.8	26.4	—
Cambodia	10.9	13.9	14.8	9.7	—
Lao People's Democratic Republic	14.88	22.4	17.4	23.8	—
Myanmar	3.8	6.3	6.7	9.2	—
Singapore	0.0	0.5	3.4	0.7	0.0
China	4.4	14.8	15.0	36.5	48.3
Korea, Rep.	—	90.4	90.2	103.8	49.2
Japan	3.11	23.4	22.2	24.7	22.7

Source: World Bank, World Trade Indicators.
Note: — = not available; MFN = most-favored nation.
a. Includes preferential tariff rates.

tariffs higher than those for all imports on average. The agricultural tariff premium—that is, the gap between the average agricultural tariff and the average tariff on all goods—is highest in the case of Japan by a multiple of 7.5. Malaysia, the Philippines, and Thailand tax their respective agricultural imports at levels higher than those on all imports, by a multiple ranging from 3.0 to 4.2. China's agricultural tariffs run to 14.8 percent, compared to the 4.4 percent tariffs on all imports. Cambodia, Myanmar, the Lao People's Democratic Republic, and Vietnam (the CMLV countries) support lower premiums, ranging from 1.50 to 1.61, indicating that they have a more uniform tariff rate structure than Malaysia, the Philippines, and Thailand. The average agricultural tariff in ASEAN is 14.15 percent, 2.1 times higher than the 6.85 percent regional average tariff on all imports.

MFN tariff rates on all goods have been falling in accordance with multilateral and preferential tariff reduction obligations that countries have negotiated, with average agricultural tariffs gradually declining in East Asia, except for Indonesia and Korea. The average ASEAN agricultural tariff rate of 14.15 percent is less than the world's average tariff on agricultural imports, which is 16.74 percent.

The agricultural sector holds significant potential for further trade integration. Table 2.2 shows that, for both the world and the ASEAN region in particular, tariff peaks in agriculture in proportion to total tariff lines exceed those for all imports by multiples of 1.8 and 1.4, respectively. Still, the region has a lower share of agricultural tariffs than does the entire global trading community.

The trade-weighted average share of tariff peaks in ASEAN is 18.22 percent, compared to the world average of 38.96 percent. The same pattern is reflected in the case of the ASEAN+3 group, except for Brunei Darussalam, Malaysia, and Myanmar. These three countries have lower shares of tariff peaks in agriculture compared with all goods. Among countries with many tariff peaks in agriculture, Thailand and Vietnam top the list, with 58.72 percent and 61.27 percent, respectively (table 2.2).

As a result of the WTO's AoA, many countries now apply the tariff quota system to key agricultural imports, rather than the quantitative restrictions previously imposed. Under this system, a specified but relatively small volume of agricultural imports like those of rice and maize may be imported at very low tariffs, while unlimited amounts may be imported at higher tariff rates. These arrangements are the outcome of the tariffication process that WTO members are legally bound to follow.[4]

Table 2.2   Share to Total of MFN Tariff Lines with Rates Exceeding 15 Percent
percent

Countries	Agricultural goods	All goods
Vietnam	61.27	41.74
Thailand	58.72	23.07
Korea, Rep.	48.77	8.91
Lao People's Democratic Republic	44.65	18.81
Cambodia	34.62	20.3
Japan	34.22	8.04
China	34.04	14.54
Philippines	13.53	9.31
Malaysia	12.34	27.18
Indonesia	7.31	4.64
Myanmar	6.25	7.41
Brunei Darussalam	0.66	14.61
Singapore	0.52	0.07
World average	38.96	22.01
ASEAN (10) average	18.22	13.09

Source: World Bank, World Trade Indicators (accessed January 2010).

For example, China imposed a 1 percent tariff on half of the preferential tariff quota of 5.3 million tons of rice, which it allows to be imported by private licensed traders. The other half of the preferential quota is set aside for the exclusive importation of STEs. China's out-of-quota import tariff rate is 65 percent.

The Philippines continues to maintain a quantitative import restriction on rice, however, having availed itself twice of the special treatment provision of the AoA. The country opened a minimum access quota applicable to 240,000 tons beginning in 2004, subject to a 50 percent in-quota tariff. This special treatment expires in 2012.

Trade-restrictive policies on agriculture by most ASEAN policy makers reduced the volume of traded rice, which in turn induced relatively wide price fluctuations of rice internationally. In Asia as a whole, Anderson and Martin (2009) argue that while the region produces and consumes four fifths of the world's rice supply (compared with about one third of the world's wheat and maize), these policies resulted in only 6.9 percent of global rice production being traded internationally from 2000 to 2004.

Given the current policies of most Asian countries to insulate their domestic rice sectors from price fluctuations, it is expected that nominal rates of protection for rice are used in a way that compensates for the swings of international rice prices: high protection rates in times of low world prices and low otherwise. Empirical investigation done by Anderson and Martin (2009) supports this claim. From 1970 to 2005, a high negative correlation was present between the rice NRAs and the international rice prices: –0.59 for Southeast Asia, and –0.75 for South Asia. This pattern is evident whether the NRA is rising or falling.

Protectionist policies considerably discount the important role that trade plays in bringing stability to the world's food markets, particularly that of rice. The more countries look inward with respect to rice, the more international rice prices become unstable. Anderson and Martin (2009) argue that this may induce protectionist behavior by other countries as well. They claim that importing countries export domestic rice price volatility by varying import tariffs, while exporting countries do the same by imposing or relaxing export restrictions. They effectively impose export taxes or export controls in the name of national food security. As they vary trade policies to suit their domestic food price stabilization objectives, world prices change again in reaction, so that even larger adjustments in domestic NRAs become desirable.

The Role of State Trading Enterprises (Parastatals)

State trading enterprises (STEs) are the institutions through which ASEAN governments have chosen to regulate nearly all aspects of the rice supply chains, including international trade; to channel domestic farm support to rice producers; and to intervene in rice markets. STEs continue to provide a great deal of direct and indirect support for government policies. Not only are they direct participants in food marketing, but in many national environments they have performed double duty as regulators of entire food systems. In this latter capacity, they manage multiple aspects of government control, from the licensing of business establishments, to licensing of imports and exports, to pricing and procurement. In the course of implementing their mandates, STEs have been accorded preferential treatment by their governments over the private sector, including superior access to credit and transportation, as well as direct budgetary support (see box 2.3).

The following pages set out the country-by-country performance of STEs in the five countries studied. Generally in the name of food security, all the countries incur budgetary costs of some importance, and giving STEs the responsibility for decisions on procurement and import or export restrictions grants these bodies a significant role in shaping and sometimes distorting local and global rice markets, on occasion by setting prices that are lower than necessary for farmers and higher than would otherwise be the case for consumers.

Indonesia. From the mid-1960s until the late 1990s, the state parastatal in Indonesia, Badan Urusan Logistik (BULOG), was dominant in defending floor and ceiling prices through monopoly control over international rice trading and through domestic procurement, drawing on an unlimited line of credit from the Bank of Indonesia (Sidik 2004). It is unlikely that BULOG's distribution of subsidized rice (explained later) has any significant impact on the consumer price.

Indonesia's rice policy has been predicated on the view that food security is synonymous with self-sufficiency, together with the belief that farmers need to be supported and consumers need to be protected from high prices. BULOG's intervention in the rice market takes two forms. First, the parastatal is charged with distribution of rice to the poorest households (explained later). Second, BULOG intervenes in the market when the price to farmers for paddy goes below a certain price (Rp 2,500 per kilogram in 2009).

Box 2.3

Traditional Justifications for State Trading Enterprises

In their review of state trading enterprises (STEs) for food grains in Asia, Rashid, Gulati, and Cummings (2008) identify four possible justifications for the public sector to intervene in grain markets: (a) to compensate for a lack of market integration; (b) to mitigate risk so that technology can diffuse; (c) to stabilize prices in the face of volatile international markets; and (d) to compensate for an inability to participate in the international market. In the first case, a market failure may persist in national markets, and spatial and temporal arbitrage may not operate effectively to clear these markets for reasons associated with underdeveloped transportation and communication infrastructure. Under these circumstances, transaction costs are high and information is asymmetric. These conditions discourage farmers from participating in domestic markets. This set of circumstances surfaces most notably in times of emergency, when the private sector is not able to provide immediate relief for localized excess supply or demand and when natural calamities diminish the trade effectiveness of already weak infrastructure. Without direct STE intervention, the risk of famine in affected areas is high.

In contrast with these emergency circumstances is the more routine role of STEs in stabilizing food prices day in and day out. In many parts of the developing world, insurance markets or futures markets are underdeveloped or nonexistent. To compensate for missing market mechanisms that might be able to price and sell risk, governments build and maintain food reserves and position them strategically within their boundaries to provide needed supplies when food prices rise.

During the Green Revolution, governments realized that the success achieved through technology diffusion was itself a reason for the diffusion process to shut down. With improved yields, grain prices in local markets declined sharply, particularly during harvesttime, to levels no longer conducive for investing in fertilizer and hence in new rice production. Farmers lost incentives to continue applying the new green technologies. Even without the technology boost, rice yields are highly seasonal because of their dependence on water, with most of a country's farmers planting, harvesting, and, particularly, selling rice at the same time, thus bringing prices down sharply at harvesttime. The use of improved seeds simply aggravated the situation. STEs thus became the government instrument of preference for propping up farm prices by offering minimum prices to rice

(continued next page)

Box 2.3 *(continued)*

producers and, in the process, encouraging them to continue using improved seeds.

The fourth justification—to compensate for an inability to participate in the international market—relates to the need of individual countries to self-insure against the risk of being without food because the volume of traded rice or other cereals cannot meet their requirements at the right time. Some countries with limited foreign currency reserves are unable to source their food requirements from international trade. These conditions have prompted governments to look inward and to adopt self-sufficiency programs for their respective staple foods. In addition to delivering domestic production support to farmers, governments have also used import restrictions, some of which are implemented by granting STEs monopoly rights to import and export.

Governments in rice-consuming countries have dealt with fluctuations in rice prices by using buffer stocks during the lean months in a given year when farmers cannot grow rice because of insufficient water and buffer stocks can cushion the expected seasonal rise in rice prices. Because this phenomenon is predictable, the seasonality of rice price movements is relatively easy to address. However, certain localities may be exposed to an exceptional dry spell, which delays planting. Risks like those related to aberrations in normal weather patterns need to be anticipated because they have significant adverse effects on local and national rice prices. In countries where the rainy season is less predictable, governments must prepare for the possibility of famines.

Dorosh and Shahabuddin (2002) reviewed policy options for stabilizing food prices and highlighted the experience of Bangladesh. Until 1993, the government of Bangladesh relied exclusively on national food stocks to stabilize rice and wheat prices. After food trade was liberalized in 1993, the government allowed the private sector to import rice and wheat. As a result, Bangladesh has become more successful in stabilizing rice and wheat prices. Dorosh and Shahabuddin cite supply shortfalls in 1997–98 and 1998–99 and contrast these with more stable price behavior since. The lesson underscored in their paper is simply this: international trade, when it is effectively executed in a competitive environment, can make important contributions to national price stabilization.

Price stabilization programs may confer consumption subsidies on entire populations. This effect depends importantly on the level of rice prices that STEs seek to maintain and on how often prices are adjusted to keep up with market

(continued next page)

Box 2.3 *(continued)*

developments. In the Philippines, the idea of meeting several objectives under one program has guided policy makers trying to address the diverse problems of rice price volatility, rice access for the poor, and domestic support for rice farmers with a single program. The consequence of multi-objective food security programs not effectively constrained by hard budgets has been a drastic run-up in budgetary costs.

In the Philippines, the National Food Authority (NFA) sets official release prices for rice as part of its stabilization program. These prices are set to meet several objectives, such as ensuring that rice farmers are spared the consequence of paddy price volatility. More often than not, implied subsidies contained within price stabilization programs find their way to beneficiaries other than those initially targeted. This pattern has prompted Jha and Mehta (2008) to refer to the distribution program of the NFA as a universal one, rather than one that is well targeted at identified beneficiaries, such as the poor. Moreover, because rice release prices have not been adjusted as frequently as needed to reflect market price movements, the stabilization program has ended up providing broad rice consumption subsidies. This was a dilemma for the Philippine government in 2008, when market prices shot up from 20 pesos to nearly 40 pesos.

Sources: Rashid, Gulati, and Cummings 2008; Dorosh and Shahabuddin 2002; Goletti, Ahmed, and Chowdhury 1991; Brennan 1995; Jha and Mehta 2008.

While it does buy some paddy, BULOG intervenes primarily by buying rice (20 percent brokens) from millers (at Rp 4,600 per kilogram in 2009).[5] Given that BULOG apparently sets itself a procurement target every year and has limited resources, it is not clear how it would respond if prices fell beyond the ability of its procurement target to influence the market. In addition to buying rice, BULOG also owns 132 rice mills, each with a capacity of 3 tons an hour. This volume would appear to be excessive in light of the parastatal's current involvement in the market, although there is clearly a perceived need to ensure nation-wide coverage.

Indonesia did not suffer from the recent rises in world market prices in part because of production increases. In 2008, there was virtually no change in either the producer or consumer price for rice. When Indonesia had to import significant quantities in the past, world prices were relatively low and such imports did not have a major effect on prices. Whether events of 2008 and general indications that the downward world price trend for rice has been reversed merit a reassessment of this view remains to be seen.

Malaysia. Government announcements from time to time commit Malaysia to rice self-sufficiency. That determination was reemphasized in 2009 after the price rises of 2007–08.[6] However, its levels of self-sufficiency have fluctuated between 68 percent and 86 percent since the 1970s. The levels are much higher on Peninsular Malaysia (more than 80 percent) than in Sabah (30 percent) and Sarawak (50 percent).

The emphasis of government policy in Malaysia has historically been on rice production. From 1931, when the Rice Cultivation Committee was formed, a succession of government organizations have been devoted to rice promotion, culminating in the formation of the Padi and Rice Board, or Lembaga Padi dan Beras Negara (LPN), in 1971. In 1974, LPN was given the sole import rights for rice. In 1994, it was corporatized into Padi Beras Nasional Bhd. (BERNAS), which was to take over all commercial and social functions. In 1996, BERNAS was fully privatized (the government retained a "Golden Share"), while still being charged with social obligations such as subsidy distribution to farmers and the function of being a buyer of last resort. It was also given sole import rights for 15 years.[7]

As rice millers are required to produce 30 percent of their output at standard and premium quality, BERNAS is free to determine the price for its superior-quality rice, the profits from which are used to cross-subsidize the minimum production required in standard- and medium-quality rice. Although its responsibilities in many ways duplicate those of the NFA in the Philippines and BULOG in Indonesia, BERNAS is a private company traded on the Kuala Lumpur Stock Exchange.

The rice industry in Malaysia is heavily regulated, with the aim of assisting farmers, who are mainly poor, through subsidies and income support. There have been significant improvements in productivity, but production in many parts of Peninsular Malaysia seems to have reached a plateau because of competition for land from housing and industrial development. Given constraints on further developing the rice sector, and the fact that the nation has a large trading surplus, some have argued that the country should aim for self-reliance rather than self-sufficiency, and should aim to build up innovative sourcing and trading alliances rather than concentrate on production.

The Philippines. State intervention in agricultural production and marketing in the Philippines started when bad weather caused a drastic shortfall in staple food grain in 1962 (David, Intal, and Balisacan 2009). During the same year, the National Rice and Corn Administration was established to ensure low, stable prices for consumers and adequate price incentives for farmers. Monopoly power over importation of rice was then granted to the agency, as well as budgetary support and a credit line to undertake domestic market procurement and distribution in pursuit of maintaining price stability. The agency's power over importation was expanded in the early 1970s during the surge in world commodity prices. Renamed the National Grains Administration, it was granted tariff-free importation capability for both rice and maize. In 1981, the agency was further renamed to National Food Authority (NFA), and it also obtained import monopoly in wheat, soybean meal, soybeans, ruminant livestock, and beef.

Paddy support prices are provided under a two-tiered price mechanism, which the NFA operates. In 2002, paddy support prices were left unchanged at 9,000 pesos ($175) per ton for wet-season paddy and at 10,000 pesos ($194) per ton for dry-season paddy, with an additional 500 pesos ($10) per ton granted to members of farmer cooperatives.

The effectiveness of the government's intervention in paddy markets depends upon the volume traded, which in turn is determined by the amount of resources available for the program. After 2008 the procurement price of paddy rose to 17,000 pesos per ton, but until then the Philippines had not adjusted its procurement price because it relied on rice imports to influence the local rice market. Besides, prices that private traders paid farmers for paddy were considered reasonable, at least until fertilizer prices shot up in 2006 and 2007. Until those pressures adversely affected farm profitability, the paddy market in the Philippines had largely been determined by interplay between farmers and private traders.

By law, only the NFA is allowed to import rice in the Philippines. However, it delegates the importation of about 200,000 metric tons through auctions to hotels, restaurants, and farmer cooperatives. Accredited farmer cooperatives that wish to supplement their locally procured rice with imported rice and that have experience with importing can also obtain import permits from the NFA. The agency sets aside

100,000 tons for this purpose. A financing facility is also provided to cooperatives through the Land Bank of the Philippines.

Since 1995, when the last rice queues were observed, the NFA had managed to stabilize prices successfully by using rice imports.[8] Not even the El Niño phenomenon in 1997 and 1998 challenged the agency's capability to drive prices to levels it determined were reasonable. Private traders acknowledged its ability to intervene and successfully stabilize prices and operated with that expectation. Paddy prices likewise tracked rice prices, except for the few weeks following harvests.

In 2008, however, the market shifted against the NFA when its announced prices failed to move the market. Rice queues returned, and speculation grew as traders bet on the volume of rice imports that the NFA could secure. Essentially betting against the NFA's ability to make official prices stick, traders started to hold on to rice stocks, adding further upward pressure to local prices. Many of these traders' precautionary moves lost them money, but their initial expectations had a real market impact.

The cost of running the Philippines' food security program is exceedingly high. The NFA is provided a fiscal subsidy of about 1.5 billion pesos a year to cover its overhead.[9] The cost of its operations is financed with corporate debt, which the Department of Finance fully guarantees. At least in theory, the agency should be able to make a profit through its speculative buying and internal sales. However, the agency has been accumulating additional debt year after year with commercial banks and has continued to float long-term bonds to cover its accumulating deficit. The program has become financially unsustainable, and it requires a major rethinking in order to keep costs in line with potential profit.

As an instrument for the implementation of government food security policy, the NFA suffers from several disadvantages, which include its charter mandate, its management processes, and a lack of competition to challenge its decisions and market directions. Not all of the NFA's costs can be recovered, since the nation's rice distribution policies, which it executes, entail the distribution of subsidized rice to the poor. The NFA also holds stocks longer than private sector traders would because of its mandate to manage the country's buffer stocks. These constraints, traceable to the agency's charter, are exacerbated by its management inefficiencies, relative to the private sector, in undertaking trading operations. Thus, with all of these imports in the hands of the NFA, the government ends up paying more than the price it recovers for every ton of rice it injects into the market. The debt of the enterprise will continue to rise each year until the government makes appropriate changes both in policy and in mode of implementation.

One notable opportunity to reform the NFA involves decentralizing its rice import activities. Currently, the NFA absorbs almost the entire cost of rice imports, since it is the only entity allowed by law to import. In 2010, it announced that it would import about 2.5 million to 3.0 million metric tons. At $600 per metric ton, this amounts to the inventory financing requirement of $1.5 billion to $1.8 billion. If import activities had been decentralized, some of these costs could have been absorbed by the private sector.

Another benefit to decentralizing rice imports would come from spreading the risk of making market decisions that turn out to be incorrect. If the NFA misreads the market, the cost of rice imports can become unnecessarily high, as happened in 2008, when, according to Slayton (2009), the NFA "panicked" and disturbed the world's rice market by issuing unprecedented large rice tenders, thus pushing rice prices up. Distributed among many private traders, these imports would have been more appropriately priced to the benefit of both the country and the regional market.

Thailand. The Bank for Agriculture and Agricultural Cooperatives (BAAC), in cooperation with another government-owned company, the Public Warehouse Organization (PWO), procured paddy directly from farmers at minimum prices until 2009 through the government's paddy mortgage and pledging scheme. In 2001–02, the paddy-pledging scheme was extended to the highest-grade fragrant rice and the overall quantities targeted for intervention were substantially increased. Guaranteed prices were kept unchanged between 1999 and 2001, and they were raised marginally in 2002 (FAO 2003).

In addition to channeling farm support to rice farmers, the program enabled the government to control the country's rice export supply. By November 2009, the government had achieved a virtual export monopoly by accumulating 6 million metric tons in storage, about two thirds of Thailand's total rice exports. As explained below, the program had the unanticipated effect of passing on the government's subsidy to the world's rice consumers—or, if there were other more competitive rice suppliers like Vietnam that do not implement a similar program, of inducing financial losses for Thailand itself. This is what happened in 2009.

In the first crop of 2008, Thailand set its minimum price at 10,000 baht per metric ton and raised it to 14,000 baht in the second crop to reflect the rising world prices in the global market and to encourage more supply from farmers. According to Forssell (2009), the increase amounted to providing a subsidy of 20 percent to all farmers in Thailand. However, since market prices began to fall in the second half of 2008, the subsidy was actually higher. The recovery price associated with the minimum price of 14,000 baht was $900 per metric ton. Unfortunately for Thailand, market prices in the world fell to less than $700 in that period.

Forssell (2009) reports that export orders ceased in the second half of 2008 as importing countries waited for Vietnam's harvest to come in. In the meantime, Thailand was forced to absorb the cost of the subsidy it had provided to its rice farmers. Thailand's experience in 2008 indicates that the additional transaction costs associated with government management of large stocks can have a major impact on global trade, particularly when markets are thin. Large stocks in the hands of governments cannot move fast enough to relieve serious shortages. Public sector decision making can be slow when officials are trying to achieve multiple objectives with the stocks that they control, including efforts to recover sunk costs. In the case just cited, shortages persisted while the Thai authorities were slow to respond, before new suppliers could provide relief.

This anecdote further illustrates the lack of a level playing field on which both private and public sector entities can operate. This lack of competitive equity appears to be a general characteristic of paddy and rice domestic markets in the region. Private traders were hampered because of their limited access to a ready supply of rice. They were forced to stop procuring because they became uncompetitive relative to the government, which was buying paddy at higher prices. Many of them decided to provide milling and warehouse services to the government instead, hoping they might be able to gain advantage in tenders that government was almost certain to undertake when it later attempted to unload its stocks.

The experience likewise highlights the importance of decentralizing decision making. Decentralized decisions, as contrasted with single-government-agency decision making, enable a country to read market signals better and avoid unnecessary financial losses. For example, the Thailand government misread the market when it increased the minimum price for the second crop. It failed to anticipate that the market might go down in the second half of 2008. Had there been more private sector participation in export markets, there is a good chance that such losses might have been avoided and the world rice price crisis in 2008 might not have turned out the way that it did.

In 2009, the government of Thailand replaced the existing program with direct income support to rice farmers. However, this new program remains tied to production. It pays subsidies based on evaluations made by District Agricultural Cooperatives Boards in the local areas and based on differences between a benchmark price and the average market price paid by traders. Although the government no longer procures paddy, it also announced that if the difference is too high, it could resume past paddy procurement actions. A quality requirement also applies to the new program, which is intended to avoid the dumping of poor-quality rice. Only farmers whose rice has no more than 15 percent moisture content are eligible.

Vietnam. Since the late 1980s, Vietnam has made remarkable progress as it has converted from a closed command economy to an open market economy and integrated into the world (Athukorala, Huong, and Thanh 2009). Key to this transition has been the implementation of agricultural reforms, including the transition from collective regimes to a system in which farmers can freely make production decisions and market their produce.

Vietnam abolished quantitative restrictions on rice exports in 2001. This initiative opened up international trade to private players. Rice-exporting companies, however, were still required to preregister their export contracts. Hence, the bulk of Vietnamese rice exports remain highly regulated by the government through the Vietnam Food Association (VFA), a government body that works in close collaboration with the state-owned Northern Food Corporation (VINAFOOD1) and Southern Food Corporation (VINAFOOD2).

Vietnam's Export-Import Management Mechanism for 2001–2005[10] replaced the nation's export quota with regulation through minimum export prices (MEPs). These regulated prices are intended to ensure that sufficient rice is retained within the country to cover domestic needs. The use of MEPs and the uncertainties caused by frequent changes in them continue to distort the decisions of private traders. MEPs are supposedly set so that farmers can realize at least a 30 percent return on rice farming. It is ironic that, if they were enforced as they were designed, MEPs would actually favor Vietnam's rice consumers rather than its rice farmers because MEPs would be set above export market levels, thus increasing supply to the domestic market.

On May 1, 2005, all Vietnamese companies holding a license to trade in food or agricultural commodities were also permitted to participate in rice exporting. However, VINAFOOD maintains an effective monopoly. Exportation of rice now falls under the direction of a management team led by a deputy minister of industry and trade. Other high-level ministries that participate include the Ministry of Agriculture and Rural Development, the Ministry of Finance, the Government Office, the Ministry of Planning and Investment, and the State Bank. Through this mechanism, the government often imposes various temporary market intervention measures, such as pledging to purchase all rice in storage (at the peak of the harvest, when supply exceeds demand) in order to maintain stable prices. Another type of intervention involves the VFA, which may be directed from time to time to request enterprises to desist from exporting and stop signing further export contracts in order to stabilize domestic prices.

In the first half of 2008, a series of disruptive policy interventions took place in Vietnam (Slayton 2009). These involved first setting export targets, then reducing them, advising private exporters not to open new export contracts, banning export sales outright, and canceling or changing minimum export prices. The purpose of these regulations was to keep rice within Vietnam's borders to safeguard local supply and keep it affordable. By raising the MEP, the government effectively signaled private traders not to procure paddy, since a high MEP set above market levels deprived them of a reasonable return in the export business.

At the same time, the government, through VINAFOOD2, continued to export rice to the Philippines based on a government-to-government agreement. This government direct dealing represented a clear conflict of interest vis-à-vis the private sector. Essentially, the government-owned exporter cornered available export contracts and drove the private traders out of the market. Interestingly, local prices failed to decline in response to these initiatives undertaken in the name of food security. Indeed, by April 2008, rice prices in Ho Chi Minh City (HCM City) had doubled. Slayton suggests that when the head of the VFA projected that rice prices could reach $1,400 per ton, local traders expected further increases and increased their purchases. Unfortunately, they held those stocks longer than they should have; in the second half of 2008, these traders were caught with large volumes of rice when the price fell by half in just a matter of months. As a result of financial losses, private trading company procurement slowed down, thus pulling down farm prices.

Frequent changes in regulations introduce a fair amount of uncertainty into the domestic rice market in Vietnam. This uncertainty typically induces speculation and ultimately results in financial losses to all players. In the end, those whom regulations were intended to help also incurred significant losses. Farmers had to discount the value of their stocks in the summer harvest of 2008, and rice consumers were forced to adjust their consumption as well in response to rising prices. Private traders who changed their fundamental mode of operations in an effort to stay out in front of government maneuvers ultimately incurred losses as well.

Farm Support Policies for Rice

Trade restrictions and the interventions of STE rice programs incur costs by distorting markets and market prices. Except in Malaysia, parastatals also require budgetary support, if only for operating costs or, as in the Philippines, to finance a large and steadily mounting debt. In addition, prevailing agricultural policies in the ASEAN countries studied entail large public expenditures for farm support outlays that are incurred in acquiring rice inventories.

Rice Self-Sufficiency

As with other government interventions, farm support programs arise from commitments to self-sufficiency. Table 2.3 shows the self-sufficiency ratios of selected ASEAN states in 2008. Vietnam and Thailand, two of the

Table 2.3   Rice Self-Sufficiency Ratios of Selected ASEAN Countries, 2008

Countries	Consumption (million MT)	Self-sufficiency ratio (%)
Thailand	9,601	190
Vietnam	18,567	125
Indonesia	36,010	98
Philippines	11,556	85
Malaysia[a]	—	73

Source: Estimates from Sugden 2009, using United States Department of Agriculture (USDA) data, except for Malaysia.
Note: MT = metric tons, — = not available.
a. The information on Malaysia's self-sufficiency ratio is attributed to Deputy Agriculture and Agro-based Industries Minister Datuk Rohani Karim. See http://thestar.com.my/news/story.asp?file=/2009/2/15/nation/3272851&sec=nation.

leading rice exporters in the world, produce more rice than they require for domestic consumption. Their self-sufficiency ratios are 125 percent and 190 percent, respectively, while Indonesia, the Philippines, and Malaysia have ratios of 98 percent, 85 percent, and 73 percent, respectively.

The objective of all support programs is to increase farm yields and to ensure reasonable returns from rice farming. Major rice-producing countries in Southeast Asia, for example, set minimum price levels for public paddy procurement for the benefit of their respective rice farmers. While several nondistorting programs have been designed to enhance productivity in rice production, (see box 2.4), other subsidy programs, which are price distorting, also continue to be used in the region in both net importing and net exporting countries.

Box 2.4

Nondistorting Programs to Enhance Rice Productivity

Indonesia, a large rice-producing and rice-consuming country, continues its commitment to raising rice paddy production through intensification and the application of modern plant science. In particular, the country has embarked on expansion of areas of cultivation for rice by reclaiming land in Sumatra and Kalimantan.

Malaysia's rice sector reform is currently focused on improving efficiency through its Third National Agricultural Policy program, covering the period 1998–2010. The major objective of the program is to achieve 65 percent self-sufficiency in rice by 2010 and full self-sufficiency by 2015. To achieve this goal, the Malaysian government has provided direct technical assistance and supported research into varietal improvements using both conventional and modern biotechnologies. The program is also implementing reforms to rice supply chains through the enlargement of production units, the development of commercially viable rice farms, and a program to enhance the sector's productivity and competitiveness. In particular, the government has designated eight special zones or "granaries" in Peninsular Malaysia, where paddy production was to be enhanced by raising yields to 5.5 tons per hectare and crop intensity to 185 percent by 2010. The government also has developed an ambitious infrastructure investment program to entice the private sector to play an active role in upstream activities (such as input deliveries and mechanization services) and downstream activities (such as milling, storage, and packaging).

(continued next page)

Box 2.4 *(continued)*

Malaysia is also expanding traditional inputs and extending arable lands suitable for rice cultivation. In particular, Malaysia is reclaiming new land for large-scale paddy cultivation by the private sector in Sabah and Sarawak, in East Malaysia, and for large-scale commercial paddy production in other parts of the country.

The Philippines, in response to the rice crisis in 2008, is currently investing to make the country self-sufficient in rice in three years. The rice program includes the following interventions: (a) improvements to irrigation systems' effectiveness and efficiency through rehabilitation; (b) use of high-quality hybrid and inbred seeds; (c) integrated crop management; (d) provision of soft loans for shallow-tube wells; (e) surface water pumps; (f) agronomic research and development; and (g) delivery of extension support services for unmilled rice through a Palay-Check system.

Thailand and Vietnam, two of the world's top rice exporters, are both more than self-sufficient in rice at normal world price levels. Because of the price premium attached to its high-quality and aromatic rice exports, Thailand is able to segment the markets that it serves and to improve farmers' incomes through both enhanced efficiency and superior quality control. The thrust of the country's rice extension program rests on the distribution of high-quality seeds and improved use of pesticides. Similar to Malaysia, Thailand envisages a zoning of rice fields to avoid the mixing of varieties and to extend the development of fragrant rice in the northeast.

Source: Authors.

Net rice-importing countries tend to have higher price supports than net exporters. Without data on actual public procurement in the years 2001–04 (and acknowledging that support price levels may have changed since), it is difficult to evaluate precisely the extent of market distortions that have resulted from these incentives. Among the net importing ASEAN countries, Malaysia provided the highest price support in 2003, procuring paddy at $210 per ton. Indonesia came second, with an official procurement price of $193. The Philippines followed, setting its farm support price at $169. Rice exporter Thailand had the lowest price guarantee levels, ranging from $176 (for fragrant rice) to $132.

Net importing countries. In the case of net importing countries, including *Indonesia* and *the Philippines*, which support minimum price guarantees for paddy, other forms of price support operate. For a period of time, both countries appeared to support similar price guarantees for paddy, import restrictions, public spending to attain self-sufficiency in rice, and active market intervention through government trading companies (such as BULOG and the NFA). Both public trading companies procure paddy from rice farmers at minimum prices. However, in the 1990s, the NFA procured significantly less than BULOG: 2–3 percent of production compared to 6–7 percent, respectively (Sidik 2004).

The Philippines did not adjust the levels of its price guarantees for a long time, knowing that market prices for rice and paddy were acceptably high and provided rice farmers with a decent return. Since minimum prices offered by the NFA were marginally less attractive than market clearing prices, traders and creditors purchased nearly all the rice produced in the Philippines. The NFA's intervention shifted increasingly toward stabilizing consumer prices and providing supply for emergency purposes. By way of contrast, BULOG continued to commit large fiscal resources in paddy procurement and to lead rather than follow the market.

Other differences are worth noting. With its procurement, the NFA follows a parity rule between paddy and milled rice prices of 1:2. The NFA distributes milled rice to the market at official prices in order to stabilize them. Once it has set its official rice price, the NFA pegs its paddy price at half that price. Preceding the 2008 rice price crisis, and for a fairly long period of time, paddy prices remained low in line with low world rice prices. When fertilizer costs started to rise sharply in 2007, political pressures mounted on the NFA to recalibrate its long-standing parity. However, the parastatal's management ignored the pressures and continued to peg paddy prices at half that of milled rice prices.

BULOG, on the other hand, increased its price guarantees from Rp 1,500 per kilo to Rp 1,700 in 2004. Because of this adjustment, rice prices shot up in Indonesia to Rp 2,750 per kilo. This was higher than the imputed wholesale price for imported rice of Rp 2,200 per kilo inclusive of the tariff on imports at Rp 430 per kilo (Sidik 2004). In sum, Indonesia's subsidy policies appear more supportive of producers, while the Philippines' subsidy policies are more supportive of rice consumers.

In 2008, when international rice prices reached 40 pesos, the Philippines suffered growing financial losses by releasing rice at 25 pesos per kilo. At that time, the NFA was forced to adjust its official rice prices to 34 pesos per kilo. This meant that paddy support prices were set at 17 pesos in accordance with the price parity of 1:2. Immediately after it made the adjustment, the NFA was inundated with offers from farmers to sell, so that in 2008 it reached its second highest level of procurement of paddy in 30 years. Once again these developments had their origins in what was happening in the rice consumer market, rather than at the other end of the chain.

It is apparent, however, that not all rice farmers are able to avail themselves of the minimum prices that STEs offer. These STEs buy paddy from specific sets of local farmers for well-defined reasons, including stabilizing local paddy prices, procuring sufficient volumes of paddy to build up buffer stocks, stabilizing consumer prices, and providing emergency relief to local areas after natural disasters. Once these objectives are met, there is no need for further procurement. For instance, if market prices remain high at harvesttime and attain levels that ensure reasonable returns to rice farmers, STEs will stay out of the local market unless they need to replenish their buffer and emergency rice reserves.

Government trading companies ultimately decide to offer minimum prices to specific sets of farmers and not to others depending upon factors related primarily to the logistics costs that result from repositioning local paddy for use or sale once it is procured. The size of the harvest in any given locality and its distance to the nearest storage facility are important additional considerations when sourcing paddy.

Net exporting countries. Public procurement of paddy in exporting countries like **Thailand** and **Vietnam** is intended to increase overall production and thus increase rice exports.

In **Thailand**, the paddy pledging program, which ended in 2009, put the bulk of Thailand's rice exports in the hands of its PWO. While the PWO auctions these stocks to private exporters, the government can also use them to ensure stable and affordable local rice prices. That said, local prices in Thailand normally reflect export parity.

Minimum price guarantees for paddy have not historically been a feature of Thailand's rice policy. Indeed, for many years the government taxed the sector in favor of rice consumers. Rather than supporting rice farmers, exports were taxed and the government required traders to set aside part of their exports as a rice requirement. Warr and Kohpaiboon (2009) note that the objective of the export tax, which reached 40 percent, was to raise revenue for industrialization. Siamwalla and Setboonsarng (1991) report that the Ministry of Commerce required exporters to sell rice accumulated as part of the nation's rice reserve at below-market price levels, which indeed is the opposite of the way that current pro-farmer price supports work. These measures, in any case, phased out with the end of the government's rice export monopoly.

A policy shift under way since the 1980s resulted in the government introducing rice price guarantees as part of a reorientation in rice policy toward supporting rice farmers and encouraging greater exports. The program entailed rice farmers depositing paddy with an accredited rice mill to collateralize the loan they had previously received from the state-owned BAAC. The value of the pledged paddy was set at official prices normally above market prices. The government offered participating farmers two options: to repay or to keep the loan they received from BAAC within three months after harvest. If the borrower-farmer retained the loan, the paddy sale was completed at the official price and the government took ownership of the pledged paddy. After ordering the mill to polish the paddy, the government paid BAAC the farmer's outstanding loan balance and stored the milled rice.

One effect of the program was to concentrate rice stocks in the hands of the government, a plus for the government when international prices were high, as in the first half of 2008. However, when prices declined sharply, as they did in the second half of 2008, the government was forced to absorb losses associated with the diminished value of its rice inventory. As stakeholders in the program, rice farmers petitioned the government to extend it, thus causing the government to suffer additional losses. According to Forssell (2009), the Thai government spent 35 million baht after raising minimum prices from 10,000 baht per ton in the first half of 2008 to 14,000 baht in the second harvest of that year.

Because of these losses, the government of Thailand stopped paddy procurement in favor of an income support program that benefits less-well-off rice farmers. The (District) Agricultural Cooperatives Board in each area determines the direct income subsidy, which is computed as the difference between a calculated benchmark price and the average market price that local traders have paid. In this way, farmer beneficiaries are more precisely targeted.

In **Vietnam**, one of the world's top rice exporters, internal rice policies are designed more effectively than those of Thailand to ensure first that local populations have good access to rice at affordable prices. The government intervenes in rice markets in several unique ways. First, it regulates the use of farmland that is committed to rice cultivation and limits its use for other crops or other uses. In areas where rice productivity is low or unstable, the government, through Provincial Committees, normally permits farmers to use these lands for other uses from which they can derive higher incomes. If a rice farm exceeds 2 hectares, however, the Office of the Prime Minister must grant an alternative use permit. Normally, these permits are not granted when the rice farms are located in areas in which the government has invested in rice-specific irrigation facilities.

Second, while it allows private companies to export rice, the government regulates them to ensure that no local shortage occurs. When the country needs to keep its rice stocks for domestic consumption, the government orders traders to stop contracting for export. All export contracts must be registered in any case with the VFA, which has a mandate to advise the government on food security and related policy issues. Another pragmatic measure is the mandate that private exporters pledge a part of their respective stocks in order to stabilize rice prices.

VINAFOOD2, which is the largest state-owned company operating in southern Vietnam, where most rice is grown, undertakes most of the public procurement of paddy. The company exports directly for its own account. However, it also sells rice to private traders to complete their orders if they already have 50 percent of the contracted volume in their stores.

Rice Distribution Policies

Two key public concerns affect rice consumers: keeping rice price fluctuations down and ensuring access to those identified as deserving beneficiaries of public subsidies. The latter cover those below the poverty line (see box 2.5) or special groups within the population such as schoolchildren, as well as those suffering from natural disasters when the normal working of the market system temporarily breaks down and rice consumers in a specific locality are affected.

In 1998, before shifting to its Beras Miskin (Raskin) program, **Indonesia** implemented a general rice consumption subsidy tied to stabilizing rice prices. However, at the height of the Asian financial crisis in 1997, the government launched a subsidy program that targeted poor households, making them eligible to receive 20 kilograms of rice per month at the price of Rp 1,000, roughly 35 percent of the 2004 market price. The program is large, delivering around 2.2 million metric tons of rice to about 9 million beneficiaries. According to Sidik (2004), the subsidy amounted to Rp 4.6 trillion in 2004.

Indonesia has since adjusted its Raskin program. Based on recent data, about 19.1 million poor households are eligible to receive 15 kilograms

Box 2.5

Impacts of High Food Prices on the Poor

Among the many collateral consequences of the 2007–08 food price spiral was its heavy impact on the poor. High food prices threatened to reverse successful poverty alleviation programs under way for 20 years in the five countries studied. Price shocks in national rice markets alarmed ASEAN governments as few recent shocks have. The shocks highlighted the fact that hunger (and poverty) could increase dramatically if households with limited purchasing power were forced to decrease their food consumption levels or switch to lower-quality food. The crisis raised fundamental issues among ASEAN governments concerning the continued efficacy of legacy price stabilization mechanisms and controls.

Prices for major food staples are the major determinants of residual disposable income that poor households have to cover all nonfood household needs. The share of food expenditure for the five study countries is sizable and, as of 2006, ranged from about 15 percent in Malaysia to close to half of a household's final consumption expenditures in Indonesia (figure B2.5).[a] However, the consequences of food price rises on the poor are not completely adverse. The farm gate prices

Figure B2.5   ASEAN Countries' Food Expenditure as a Share of Final Consumption, 2002–06

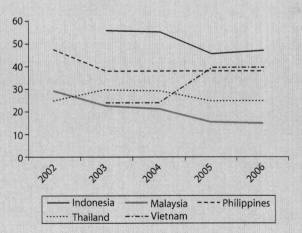

percent

Legend: Indonesia — Malaysia ---- Philippines ...... Thailand —·—· Vietnam

Source: Study Team prepared the graph using data from Economic Research Service, United States Department of Agriculture (USDA). Percent of household's final consumption expenditures.
a. In contrast, the share of food expenditure for the United States in 2006 was 5.7 percent.

(continued next page)

Box 2.5 *(continued)*

of these agricultural commodities are also major determinants of the incomes of the farmers who produce them. Policy makers of ASEAN governments are therefore faced with the classic food policy dilemma: how to benefit producers without hurting consumers (Timmer, Falcon, and Pearson 1983).

of subsidized rice. The program now accounts for 90 percent of BULOG's market operations. It is implemented through about 50,000 Raskin distribution centers located in 15 regions throughout the country. All of BULOG's regional and 105 of its subregional offices manage the Raskin program. BULOG also provides supplies to the military and in times of disaster.

BULOG reports that Raskin rice accounts for about 90 percent of its total distribution. While the distribution of rice is of some benefit to the recipients, it must be noted that the costs of the exercise are extremely high. There are 50,000 Raskin distribution points, 25 regional and 105 subregional offices. The overall benefit of supplying the poorest third or so of the population with just 10–20 percent of their needs (depending on household size) at a discount of approximately 35 percent may therefore be questioned, as this effectively reduces the household expenditure on rice by between only 3.5 percent and 7.0 percent.

Even this calculation, however, may exaggerate benefits for individual families, since local authorities can intervene in their areas to reallocate the 15 kilograms into smaller parcels to benefit a greater number of households. There are also suggestions that a significant percentage does not reach the intended beneficiaries. One earlier estimate was that 18 percent went missing, on average, although the bulk of the disappearance was accounted for by a relatively small portion of villages (Olken 2006). In the near future, the challenge will be to improve the cost-effectiveness of the program, concentrate more on assistance to people in urban areas, tighten eligibility criteria and beneficiary reporting, and ensure that the program is placed on a financially sound footing.

In *the Philippines*, the NFA pursues policies very similar to those of BULOG in the rice market (box 2.6). The NFA has a mandate to stabilize rice prices by selling the commodity directly to the general public when prices become unaffordable. This program normally comes into play during the third quarter of the year, which is considered to be the lean period for rice production. When natural calamities hit the country,

Box 2.6

Snapshot of Agricultural and Food Security Policies in the Philippines

The Philippines offers instructive lessons concerning the effectiveness and afford-ability of its policies, public institutions, and means and modes of private sector outreach. Jha and Mehta (2008) have provided some valuable insights into the operations of the National Food Authority (NFA) rice subsidy program. First, only about 16 percent of the population have availed themselves of the program, in Jha and Mehta's view because of high participation costs. Second, only about 25 percent of the poor have availed themselves of the NFA rice subsidies, while nearly half of those who were able to purchase NFA rice at its official price are nonpoor. Program leakage is higher in urban than in rural areas. Third, for every dollar that the NFA committed to rice consumption subsidy, it spent $2.21 in 2008, assuming there was no leakage of benefits (table B2.6). The NFA program, a very costly one for the Philippines, has achieved questionable results. Jha and Mehta estimate that the operational cost of the NFA rice subsidy program (price stabiliza-tion and targeted rice distribution programs) is 2.5 percent of the Philippine gross domestic product (GDP).

Table B2.6   Philippine Rice Subsidy, Cost-Benefit Calculations

Measure	Unit	2006	2007	2008
Effective NFA program cost	billion pesos	16.4	18.6	68.6
Maintenance and other operating expenses	billion pesos	6.4	1.6	4.2
Less: net profit (loss) from sales	billion pesos	−10.0	−17.0	−64.4
Consumer price subsidy = retail price of rice less the NFA rice retail price	pesos per kg	5.6	6.5	12.4
Imputed volume of NFA sales	million metric tons	1.6	1.9	2.5
Total consumer subsidy	billion pesos	8.7	12.4	31.0
Cost-benefit ratio = NFA cost/consumer subsidy		1.89	1.50	2.21
Cost-benefit ratio, assuming 50% leakage		3.77	3.01	4.42

Source: Jha and Mehta 2008, table 2.
Note: NFA = National Food Authority. The gross sales and cost of sales not only cover rice but are also a close approximation, as the bulk of NFA sales relate to rice.

A review of the "Filipino Report Card on Pro-Poor Services," based on a survey conducted by the World Bank in 2000, reached the same conclusions (World Bank

(continued next page)

Box 2.6 *(continued)*

2001). Only 15 percent of the respondents purchased NFA rice, which was both of low cost and low quality. In addition, although proportionally more poor people purchased NFA rice, their absolute number was almost the same as the middle-income and high-income people who took advantage of subsidized rice.

Clearly, the effectiveness of government procurement and distribution programs needs to be reviewed. While some developing countries (such as China) have replaced price support programs with farm income support payment programs, several ASEAN region countries continue to intervene directly in the market to regulate prices and assist farmers during times of falling rice prices. Private sector participation in marketing and trading is still limited in countries such as Indonesia, Malaysia, and the Philippines. Evidence in China and India, as presented by McCulloch and Timmer (2008), and in the Philippines (Jha and Mehta 2008) shows that public procurement and distribution systems can be extremely costly, inefficient, and of limited effectiveness in stabilizing prices.

Some proposed reforms aim to improve targeting. However, without a strong third-party audit of the implementation of these programs, they will continue to be plagued with substantial leakage and high administrative cost. While public procurement and distribution systems may appear laudable in a social security perspective, it is still worthwhile for governments to weigh the cost of the system against other public intervention that can attain the same goal.

Source: Authors' elaborations, based on World Bank 2001; McCulloch and Timmer 2008; and Jha and Mehta 2008.

seasonal low supply deteriorates even more rapidly, and the NFA is charged with ensuring that rice stocks are available to carry the country through the lean period, doing so by injecting mostly imported rice into the local market through its accredited rice retailers.

In addition, the agency implements a rice subsidy program that benefits the poor. In cooperation with the Department of Social Welfare and Development, it distributes rice at below-market prices. A third program executed by the NFA is designed to address humanitarian emergencies. The NFA implements this program in coordination with the National Disaster Coordination Committee and is expected to move rice stocks to areas hit by natural calamities, where normal market operations have ceased. Fifteen days' consumption of rice stocks are stored in various strategic distribution centers for this purpose.

Malaysia, through BERNAS, manages the country's rice stocks, which it obtains from local paddy procurement as well as from imports. However, unlike the agencies in Indonesia and the Philippines, BERNAS has no mandate to provide subsidies to the country's poor. Incorporated in 1994, the state-owned company entered into a privatization contract with the government in 1996, under which it provides a range of services. These include maintaining the nation's rice stockpile; acting as the buyer of last resort for paddy farmers; managing the Bumiputera Rice Millers Scheme, which benefits Malay Muslim rice millers; distributing paddy price subsidies to farmers on behalf of the government; and distributing and marketing rice in Malaysia. BERNAS currently controls about 24 percent of the nation's paddy market and 45 percent of the local rice market.

Ensuring that low-income households have access to rice is not a day-to-day concern for a major rice exporter like *Vietnam*. However, in 2008, concerns arose within the government that the local rice market, particularly in HCM City, might run out of supply at the same time that rice was being exported to the more lucrative overseas markets. This possibility prompted the VFA to ask its members to allocate more of their supply to the local market. A top Ministry of Industry and Trade (MOIT) official attributed concerns like this to the underlying weakness of the local rice distribution system. While recognizing that the export supply chain is working smoothly, the MOIT official believed the Vietnamese food system needs larger food companies that are better able to organize the distribution of rice and other food efficiently and quickly, while at the same time having enough credibility and local market influence to stabilize domestic price fluctuations.

A self-perpetuating policy cycle. While the propriety of setting aside public resources for the public distribution of food staples to the poor is not a controversial policy issue, other closely related issues are. For example, how public expenditure programs for stabilizing rice prices are designed, what their appropriate costs are, and how they can be designed not to undermine economic incentives in the sector are among the issues that have engaged the thoughtful attention of policy makers in all five of the study countries.

There are at least two factors that persuade governments to use parastatals to advance their agenda of rice self-sufficiency. First, governments perceive the private sector as likely to squeeze earnings from rice farmers if left alone. The farmers, for instance, may need to sell their output during harvest seasons when prices are low or may have pledged their output to lenders in exchange for production loans or multipurpose credit lines.

Second, using public corporations is administratively convenient. This is particularly the case when governments must account to legislatures for the financial resources used to support overall food security programs.

Significantly as well, the use of import restrictions to encourage local rice production usually requires two further sets of public outlays: one for price stabilization and one for consumer rice subsidies for the poor. Public investment in national buffer stocks has had to be increased to offset the increased volatility of rice prices and to ensure economic access to rice for entitled populations. In countries such as Indonesia and the Philippines, where a significant share of the population lives below the poverty line, price stabilization activities have been commingled with a targeted consumer rice subsidy to compensate for the adverse effects of import restrictions on consumers.

Costly as they are, government policies and programs for ensuring food security have been designed to strike a balance between helping producers and consumers. Policies that decoupled these two interests and dealt separately with rice affordability to consumers and livelihood assurance for farmers might have been easier to implement than prevailing policies that combine the two.

Achieving the hoped-for outcomes of these policies—stabilized prices and enhanced farm-level productivity—is uncertain, at best (box 2.7). However, a still more adverse consequence is the crowding out of private sector investment in rice-related businesses and the consequent missed chances to supplement public investment with private investment, lost opportunities for sector development, and the perpetual postponement of the transition from nontradable to globally tradable product status. Moreover, private investors face a strong deterrent when they are forced to compete with public sector counterparts, which also enjoy power to regulate the food business and to set the rules for local buying. As a result, a self-perpetuating cycle compels regional governments to believe that they must make yearly commitments of budgetary resources for food security.

The self-perpetuating cycle of thin international trade and protectionist policies inflicts collateral damage on private sector investments. Restrictive policies and policies that change frequently over time enhance risk and discourage investment in rice supply chains. These risks exacerbate those related to the already uncertain nature of rice production and

Box 2.7

Government Investment in Agriculture

The boundary line issues between public and private sector investment are cast in a revealing light in a public expenditure review recently completed in Indonesia for the World Bank (Armas, Gomez Osorio, and Moreno-Dodson 2010). It found that public expenditures on agricultural development increased significantly from 2001 to 2009, by 12 percent per year in real terms. However, over the same period, agricultural productivity remained relatively flat. Analysis presented in the budget review suggests that the cause of this failure to increase productivity is related not to the level of overall investment but to the kinds of investments that the government has been making since 2001.

Unlike earlier periods in which government support primarily focused on investment in public goods like research and development, extension, and irrigation, more recent investments have focused on providing private goods in the form of farm inputs and production subsidies through outright grants, subsidies, and other modes of delivery. These latter investments have failed to realize the positive externalities that investment in public goods brought. This analysis bolsters further recommendations regarding the need for food security policy both to avoid undercutting private sector incentives to invest in private goods and to provide support for activities that will remain uninvested or grossly underinvested if governments failed to provide support.

Source: Authors; Armas, Gomez Osorio, and Moreno-Dodson 2010.

can, indeed, lead to an unwinding cycle of continuously dwindling investment, reduced food production, and spiraling food prices.

In the case of the Philippines, which is the world's largest rice importer, the self-perpetuating policy cycle described above has a twist that involves the instrument that the government has chosen to implement its food security policies—the NFA. The NFA enjoys a monopoly in food importation, and its procurement policies essentially define an important set of market rules in the regional market. The NFA expends $1 billion to $2 billion annually to import rice into the Philippines. Other modes of achieving the government's objectives might spread this expense and the corresponding risk over a number of private sector traders.

Even exporting countries like Thailand and Vietnam, which are more than self-sufficient in rice, use parastatals in the rice business, a practice traditionally explained by the desire of government to prevent farm prices from falling so low during harvest seasons as to discourage rice farming. However, the activities of parastatals have discouraged the participation of the private sector in the export business and thus reduced the efficiency, precision, and adaptability of regional supply chains.[11]

Conclusions

The 2007–08 food price crisis and governments' subsequent response to it can usefully be thought of as a test for the legacy regional food system. The crisis opened a window of opportunity for policy makers to conduct a thoroughgoing review of the merits and demerits of the institutions, policies, and programs that affect rice markets. Clearly many of these legacy foundations did not work well during the crisis and need to be fixed.

The events that transpired in 2007–08 illustrate relatively well that regional trade plays an important price-stabilizing role and that the lack of normal trade can be destabilizing. According to Slayton (2009), government policy responses in 2007–08, such as export restrictions and panic buying, added greatly to price volatility. It was only in the second half of 2008 that prices began their descent to normal levels, once export restrictions eased up, large orders for rice were withdrawn, and added supply came onto the market from Japan's WTO rice inventory.

Though slow to take root since the crisis, reforms are clearly under way. Many of them, however, involve looking backward toward the Green Revolution, with its narrow focus on increased farm production and enhanced farm-level productivity. Fewer reforms address other links in the farm-to-market chain or technologies other than those related to plant science to reduce harvest, postharvest, and distribution channel losses and to enhance food product quality.

Fragility in food security within the region can be self-perpetuating when policies and programs like the ones described in this chapter continue to be used to support it. When self-sufficiency in rice at any cost becomes an overriding government goal, governments may inadvertently trap themselves in situations that cause them to shoulder the full cost of food security with little private sector participation.

A myopic focus on rice production and a unilateral rush to secure rice self-sufficiency can be self-defeating. Unilateral policies designed to achieve stand-alone supply self-sufficiency will only thwart the development of comparative advantage within the region, diminish trade, and increase price volatility in already thin markets. Policies that are not coordinated with the private sector, moreover, afford little opportunity to strengthen farm-to-market supply chains.

Notes

This report was prepared by the Study Team, drawing on preliminary studies and field research conducted by Ramon Clarete, professor, School of Economics, University of the Philippines. The Asian Development Bank commissioned this report in a collaborative research undertaking on food security policy for ASEAN.

1. Information used here comes mainly from the Food and Agriculture Organization (FAO) of the United Nations and the International Food Policy Research Institute. Literature on country-specific policies and practices can be found in Rokotoarisoa (2006); Dorosh (2008); McCulloch (2008); McClulloch and Timmer (2008); Rosner and McCulloch (2008); and Simatupang and Timmer (2008).

2. The NRA to producers is the percentage by which the domestic producer price is above (or, if negative, below) the border price of a like product. This measure is an estimate of direct government policy intervention (due to trade taxes, taxes, or subsidies to domestic production, for example, or government intervention in the domestic market for foreign exchange). It is net of transportation and trade margins. Anderson and Martin (2009) define NRA as the percentage by which government policies have raised the gross returns to producers above the gross returns they would have received without government intervention.

3. The group includes the 10 ASEAN member states, plus China, Japan, and Korea.

4. Under the AoA, the use of quantitative import restrictions on agricultural products is prohibited. Existing restrictions are to be converted into ordinary customs duties, unless a member avails of a right under the agreement to defer implementation of this commitment.

5. Broken rice is rice with kernels that are less than three quarters the length of the whole kernel (http://www.fao.org/WAICENT/FAOINFO/AGRICULT/AGP/AGPC/doc/riceinfo/Riceinfo.htm). The percentage of rice that is considered broken is a measure of the quality, or level of refinement, of rice. Brokens are the rice fragments produced during threshing and hulling. They are removed in the rice mill by screening at the end of processing and are usually further processed into rice flour or rice semolina.

6. Malaysia has almost always elected to be a net importer of rice, targeting about 86 percent rice self-sufficiency, according to Deputy Agriculture and Agro-based Industries Minister Datuk Rohani Karim.

7. See Athukorala and Loke (2009) for an enumeration of other specific roles of BERNAS besides importing.

8. In 1995, the government overestimated the country's local rice supply. The NFA had inadequate rice stocks as the Philippines went into the lean months for rice from June to August, and it had to ration to household representatives waiting in line at its branch offices.

9. Please note that the Philippines moved to a system of conditional cash transfers at the begining of 2011 and, as a result, the NFA is no longer responsible for subsidized distribution.

10. Decree No. 46/2001//QD-TTg.

11. Slayton (2009) points out that it was profit considerations that drove the government of Vietnam to adjust its export policies through the crisis.

References and Other Sources

ACI (Agrifood Consulting International). 2010. "Enhancing Food Security in ASEAN: Policy Reforms, Private Investment in Food Supply Chains, and Cross-Border Trade Facilitation; Supply Chain Organization and Infrastructure." Final report prepared for the World Bank, Bethesda, MD, February 1.

Anderson, Kym, and Will Martin. 2009. "Introduction and Summary." In *Distortions to Agricultural Incentives in Asia*, ed. Kym Anderson and Will Martin, chapter 1, 3–82. Washington, DC: World Bank.

Anderson, Kym, and Ernesto Valenzuela. 2008. "Estimates of Global Distortions to Agricultural Incentives, 1955 to 2007." World Bank, Washington, DC. http://www.go.worldbank.org/5XY7A7LH40.

Armas, Enrique Blanca, Camilo Gomez Osorio, and Blanca Moreno-Dodson. 2010. "Agriculture Public Spending and Growth: The Example of Indonesia." Economic Premise 9 (April), Poverty Reduction and Economic Management Network, World Bank, Washington, DC.

Athukorala, Prema-Chandra, and Wai-Heng Loke. 2009. "Malaysia." In *Distortions to Agricultural Incentives in Asia*, ed. Kym Anderson and Will Martin, chapter 5, 197–221. Washington, DC: World Bank.

Athukorala, Prema-Chandra, Pham Lan Huong, and Vo Tri Thanh. 2009. "Vietnam." In *Distortions to Agricultural Incentives in Asia*, ed. Kym Anderson and Will Martin, chapter 8, 281–302. Washington, DC: World Bank.

Brennan, D. 1995. "Policies for Stabilizing Rice Prices in Bangladesh." Final research.

Report of the Bangladesh Foodgrains Management Operations Project, Chemonics International.

David, Cristina, Ponciano Intal, and Arsenio M. Balisacan. 2009. "The Philippines." In *Distortions to Agricultural Incentives in Asia*, ed. Kym Anderson and Will Martin, 223–54. Washington, DC: World Bank.

Dorosh, Paul. 2008. "Food Price Stabilisation and Food Security: International Experience." *Bulletin of Indonesian Economic Studies* 44 (1): 93–114.

Dorosh, Paul, and Quazi Shahabuddin. 2002. "Rice Price Stabilization in Bangladesh: An Analysis of Policy Options." MSSD Discussion Paper 46, International Food Policy Research Institute, Washington, DC.

FAO (Food and Agriculture Organization of the United Nations). 1998. "Crop and Grassland Service: International Rice Commission." http://www.fao.org/WAICENT/FAOINFO/AGRICULT/AGP/AGPC/doc/riceinfo/Riceinfo.htm.

———. 2003. "Review of Basic Food Policies." Commodities and Trade Division. http://www.fao.org/es/esc/default.htm.

Forssell, Sara. 2009. "Rice Policy in Thailand: Policy Making and Recent Developments." Minor Field Study Series 189, Department of Economics, University of Lund.

Goletti, Francesco, Raisuddin Ahmed, and Nuimuddin Chowdhury. 1991. "Optimal Stock for the Public Foodgrain Distribution System in Bangladesh." Working Paper 4, Food Policy in Bangladesh, International Food Policy Research Institute, Washington, DC.

Jha, Shikha, and Aashish Mehta. 2008. "Effectiveness of Public Spending: The Case of Rice Subsidies in the Philippines." ADB Economic Working Paper Series 138, Asian Development Bank, Manila.

McCulloch, Neil. 2008. "Rice Prices and Poverty in Indonesia." *Bulletin of Indonesian Economic Studies* 44 (1): 45–63.

McCulloch, Neil, and C. Peter Timmer. 2008. "Rice Policy in Indonesia." *Bulletin of Indonesian Economic Studies* 44 (1): 33–44.

Olken, Benjamin A. 2006. "Corruption and the Costs of Redistribution: Micro Evidence from Indonesia." *Journal of Public Economics* 90: 853–70.

Rashid, Shahidur, Ashok Gulati, and Ralph Cummings Jr. 2008. "Grains Marketing Parastatals in Asia: Why Do They Have to Change Now?" In *From Parastatals to Private Trade: Lessons from Asian Agriculture*, ed. Ashok Gulati, Shahidur Rashid, and Ralph Cummings Jr., chapter 2. Baltimore: International Food Policy Research Institute and Johns Hopkins University Press.

Rokotoarisoa, Manitra A. 2006. "Policy Distortions in the Segmented Rice Market." Markets, Trade and Institutions Division Discussion Paper 94, International Food Policy Research Institute, Washington, DC.

Rosner, L. Peter, and Neil McCulloch. 2008. "A Note on Rice Production, Consumption, and Import Data in Indonesia." *Bulletin of Indonesian Economic Studies* 44 (1): 81–89.

Siamwalla, Ammar, and Suthad Setboonsarng. 1991. "Thailand." In *The Political Economy of Agricultural Pricing Policy*, ed. Anne O Krueger, Maurice Schiff, and Alberto Valdés. Washington, DC: World Bank; Baltimore: John Hopkins University Press.

Sidik, Mulyo. 2004. "Indonesia Rice Policy in View of Trade Liberalization." Paper presented at the FAO Rice Conference, Rome, February 12–13.

Simatupang, Pantjar, and C. Peter Timmer. 2008. "Indonesian Rice Production: Policies and Realities." *Bulletin of Indonesian Economic Studies* 44 (1): 65–79.

Slayton, Tom. 2009. "Rice Crisis Forensics: How Asian Governments Carelessly Set the World Rice Market on Fire." Working Paper 163, Center for Global Development, Washington, DC.

Sugden, Craig. 2009. "Responding to High Commodity Prices." *Asian-Pacific Economic Literature* 23 (1): 79–105.

The Star. 2009. "86% Self-Sufficiency in Rice Production Next Year." February 15. http://thestar.com.my/news/story.asp?file=/2009/2/15/nation/3272851&sec =nation.

Timmer, C. Peter, and Tom Slayton. 2009. "Arson Alert: Philippines Is Playing with Fire! Again!" Center for Global Development Notes, Center for Global Development, Washington, DC.

Timmer, C. Peter, Walter P. Falcon, and Scott R. Pearson. 1983. *Food Policy Analysis*. Baltimore: Johns Hopkins University Press for the World Bank.

Warr, Peter, and Achanun Kohpaiboon. 2009. "Thailand." In *Distortions to Agricultural Incentives in Asia*, ed. Kym Anderson and Will Martin. Washington, DC: World Bank.

World Bank. 2001. "Philippines: Filipino Report Card on Pro-Poor Services." Report No. 22181-PH, World Bank, Washington, DC.

CHAPTER 3

Rice Supply Chains: How They Work and Don't

We the nations and peoples of Southeast Asia, must get together and form . . . a new perspective and a new framework for our region.

—Tun Abdul Razak, August 1967

Introduction

Where rice is harvested and threshed by hand, dried in the sun, milled by low-capacity, outdated machinery, and stored so poorly that pests and even rain can attack the grain, it is hardly surprising that an estimated 10–15 percent of the crop is lost. When, moreover, rice is moved over bad roads by inefficient trucks or by sea in small vessels and through clogged ports, inadequate logistics can raise its price to consumers by 20–25 percent. Many—sometimes all—of those weaknesses feature, though to varying degrees of severity, in the supply chains of the five Association of Southeast Asian Nations (ASEAN) countries studied for this book, Thailand least of the five.

Compared to supply chains for maize discussed in the appendix, those for rice have altered very little over the centuries. Even in recent years, private firms have shied away from investments that could modernize equipment and processes, largely because government policies that put barriers in their path make the rice sector too risky a field. Maize is a newer crop in the ASEAN region and is open to private and even foreign investment. In comparison, rice is ancient and tradition bound.

The various failings in rice sector supply chains stem in large part from the age-old ways that rice has been grown, processed, and transported. Those inefficient patterns, moreover, are reinforced by policies that see food security narrowly in terms of self-sufficiency. Changing that perspective is crucial to the difficult tasks involved in overcoming venerable customs and inadequate infrastructure. The first step toward modernizing the rice sector is to find and explain the weak links in the supply chains, as this chapter does. Tackling targeted infrastructure bottlenecks may be easier. Progress in both areas can, in turn, create a more attractive environment for private investment that can both profit from efficiency gains and produce more of them.

One source of such efficiency is vertical integration of the sort that distinguishes maize supply chains from those for rice. In ASEAN's rice sector very few examples of such structures exist, and no companies can be found that operate end-to-end, connecting farming, milling, exporting, or retailing within the control of a single organization.[1] The vertically integrated food companies that come closest to this ideal are multinational supermarket chains that, although they do not farm, mill, or export themselves, procure the food products they sell within the same region. Multinational grain trading companies, which buy and sell grains globally within their own proprietary networks, do not participate in ASEAN rice markets.

At least since the 1960s, government policies in the region have concentrated on improving farm-level productivity through agricultural extension and other government initiatives. Supply-chain development has not enjoyed comparable priority. Neither government purchasing power nor investment incentives have been leveraged to strengthen rice supply chains or ease the way for private sector investment to do so.

Such inattention has hurt farmers as well as private collectors, processors, and marketers. It has meant, for example, that links between chain partners remain weak, information moves slowly and unevenly, physical losses are significant, and quality is poorly controlled and often degraded as inventories accumulate. Not only has little product differentiation occurred, but process innovation is also conspicuous by its absence within the rice sector of most economies in the region.

The forces that drive these chains "push supply" into markets, rather than having retail or overseas customers "pull supply" toward them. Prices continue to fluctuate widely, entailing high market and price risk, with relatively little investment in brand development or product quality management and little entrepreneurial activity in chains that specialize in niche products or, more generally, in management processes.

Slightly different structures have emerged for chains that serve export, import, and domestic markets. Primarily because of government involvement in the export and import ends of regional chains, greater economies of scale exist in these domains than in domestic markets. That said, the lack of competition in chains has also reduced incentives to enhance productivity, control quality, and adopt technology in a timely fashion.

This chapter first examines government policies that shape existing supply chains and measures the losses along the chains in storage, milling, and quality. It then analyzes the design of rice supply chains for domestic consumption, import, and export and closes by studying the logistics of supply chains, particularly the impediments presented by inadequate infrastructure.

Government's Impact on Supply Chains

The rationale for analyzing rice supply chains is that they show the practical effects of the policies and practices arising from the almost exclusive focus of ASEAN governments on supply-side interventions in the rice sector. That emphasis on boosting production overlooks the benefits that can come from strengthening the supply chains linking farms to consumers. As noted in chapter 1, it is the efforts of governments to achieve *food self-sufficiency* that thwart the development of efficient, responsive supply chains capable of providing regional *food security*.

The rice sector in particular has lagged behind other agribusiness sectors in attracting private investment, particularly foreign direct investment (FDI), because direct market interventions by governments create risks that the private sector judges to be too high. Even multinational corporations, which have played a significant role in boosting FDI in agriculture generally within the ASEAN region, demonstrate little interest in rice.

In other agricultural sectors, including, to some extent, maize in the ASEAN region, the supply chains that operate are integrated or synchronized arrangements involving producers, traders, processors, and buyers in ways that allow them to decide jointly what, when, and how much to produce, what food quality and safety standards to meet, and what price to expect. Participants in integrated chains depend on other chain participants to perform as they are scheduled and committed.

Such supply-chain methods, if they are strategically applied in partnership with the private sector, could greatly assist regional governments in responding to threatened food shortages. However, trade-restricting policies, price controls, national food distribution programs, and subsidies reduce incentives for private companies to invest in such methods. Moreover, most countries in the region have .attempted to implement food self-sufficiency through food agencies and state-controlled companies that seek to blend commercial and social objectives. Protected from open competition, they have retarded the development of private supply chains, introduced a variety of rent-seeking activities, exposed governments to enormous budgetary costs, and achieved only limited success in terms of food security.

A related consideration that may help to explain the slow pace of industrial restructuring in the rice sector is the very direct nature of government intervention, ranging from imposing price controls to subsidizing procurement (Rodrik 2007). An indirect approach, using incentives and light-handed regulation, can steer private sector behavior in ways that are socially beneficial. The difference is the difference between competition for markets between the public and private sectors and collaboration in markets between the two sectors.

Losses Incurred along Existing Chains

A valid measure of the success or failure of long-standing government policies is the rate of loss in rice supply chains as the crop makes its way from farmers to consumers. Estimated at 10–15 percent of production, harvest and postharvest losses result in lower returns to farmers, higher prices for consumers, and greater pressure on the environment due to lower production efficiencies (Rickman 2002). Ideally, all chain participants should apply technologies that minimize physical and quality losses between harvesting and final consumption and that complement one another for maximum effectiveness. Although many programs have been implemented over the years to achieve that ideal, ASEAN producers still lack incentives to adapt and invest in the best technologies. As a result, improvements in postharvest systems for rice have been quite modest over the past few decades and have fallen short of gains achieved in farm productivity.

A stronger private involvement in process integration and risk management along farm-to-market chains could spur much needed postharvest improvements, the kind that individual farmers cannot make by themselves. Firms operating within supply chains could, for instance, enforce mutual requirements on participants—requirements alternatively imposed on and responded to by traders, millers, processors, warehouse managers, and large retailers. With the major exception of Thailand, however, private investors have insufficient incentives under prevailing policies either to build up these reciprocal commitments or to make the necessary investments.

Whatever the actual size of postharvest losses in the ASEAN rice sector, it is clear that smallholder farmers are the most affected. What needs to happen is for mills, not farmers, to do the drying, and for that to happen, farmers need to sell immediately after harvesting. Table 3.1 estimates these losses for each of the countries included in this study.[2]

A reduction of postharvest physical losses (from 14 percent to 9 percent), while difficult to achieve in the short run, would translate into 4.3 million tons rice equivalent for the five countries.[3] This is more than the entire intra-ASEAN rice trade, which was estimated to be 3.5 million tons in 2008. In the case of the Philippines, the largest rice importer, a reduction of postharvest losses from 15 percent to 10 percent would represent almost half a million tons in saved rice imports.

Although postharvest losses occur throughout the supply chain, most losses occur during the milling process. Significant additional losses have been reported during harvesting, threshing, and drying as well in Southeast Asia. Table 3.2 presents an overview of different estimates of losses along the supply chain. Unfortunately, no consistent and reliable data exist from any single source with which to reliably determine these losses. Consequently, this table, based on a diversity of sources, is more indicative than precise.

Table 3.1   Postharvest Paddy and Rice Physical Losses in Selected ASEAN Countries

Country	Total production of paddy 2007 (million tons)	Losses as a share of total production (%)	Total losses of paddy (million tons)	Total losses in rice equivalent (million tons)[a]
Indonesia	57,157	15	8,574	5,144
Malaysia	2,277	14	319	191
Philippines	16,240	15	2,436	1,462
Thailand	30,014	13	3,902	2,341
Vietnam	35,918	14	4,921	2,952
Total	**141,606**	**14**	**20,151**	**12,091**

Sources: Authors' calculations based on ASEAN (2008) for total production of paddy for 2007 and on averages from table 3.2, where data were compiled from FAO (1999) for losses as a share of total production.
a. Calculated with an average and assumed milling efficiency of 60 percent.

Table 3.2   Postharvest Losses at Different Stages in Asian Rice Production
percent

Country	Cutting, harvest, and handling	Threshing	Drying	Milling	Storage	Handling and transport	Total
Indonesia	0.8	—	2.9	4.4	3.2	—	12.2
Vietnam	2.9	1.7	2.2	—	1.4	—	8.1
Thailand	11.3	2.3	—	—	—	—	13.6
Southeast Asia	1.0–3.0	2.0–6.0	1.0–5.0	—	2.0–6.0	2.0–10.0	10.0–37.0
Philippines	—	—	—	5.0	7.0	3.0	15.0
China	—						5.0–23.0
China	—						8.0–26.0
Vietnam	—						10.0–25.0

Source: FAO 1999.
Note: Losses that occur during on-farm storage are not included. Although there is considerable variation in the data, average postharvest loss data have been used for further calculations. Each row refers to different studies in FAO 1999. — = not available.

Delays between harvest and threshing reportedly have a significant impact on quality and on quantity losses.[4] Poor-quality drying also causes major problems. In some farming and postharvest systems in Indonesia, usually involving the use of hired labor, losses have been estimated to be as high as 20 percent, although, given the practice of gleaning by laborers' families, these losses may impact farmers more than actual food production. In systems where farmers play a more important role, often working cooperatively, losses are believed to be significantly less.

To date, mechanical drying has not been successfully introduced in any of the five ASEAN countries, and sun drying remains the most popular means of drying grain and seed in the region. Sun drying is still a common practice. Although the cheapest drying method, it causes greater grain fissuring and subsequent breakage during milling. Open-air sun drying is done on concrete floors especially constructed for drying at the village level, at centrally located communal locations, or at the side of the roads on plastic sheets. Inadequate drying and high moisture levels of rice during the wet season are the major problems related to sun drying.

Inadequate drying causes problems at all subsequent stages in the supply chain. In all five study countries, paddy is sold at suboptimal moisture levels during the wet season. Although it is common knowledge that rice should be milled and stored at a moisture percentage of 14 percent, farmers and traders do not adhere to this quality standard. Indeed, they often lack the means to measure the moisture content of rice objectively. Goletti (2009) estimates that up to 4 percent of grain in the Philippines is lost or damaged from moisture incursion during farm storage. See box 3.1.

Box 3.1

Storage Infrastructure

In addition to storage deficiencies at the farm level, further losses occur after rice has moved through the milling stage to be warehoused. Bulk rice storage in silos is not a common practice in any of the five ASEAN countries, and it is unlikely to replace warehouse storage in bags in the medium term. What is possible is to have paddy in bulk and then rice in bags and retail packs. Commercial storage in the region is usually open to atmosphere, causing moisture uptake and pest problems. However, when rice is stored in batches and provisions made for clear headways and walkways, it is relatively easy to fumigate and diseases and rot can be isolated to a number of bags or batches.

Bulk storage remains unpopular in the region and underinvested, in spite of its efficient use of space and ease for controlling pests, rodents, and birds. To be fully productive, bulk storage requires supportive processes on both the inbound and outbound sides of the storage facility. It requires a standard end-to-end infrastructure to function well, including bulk transport equipment, bagging infrastructure, and bulk intermodal handling. In other words, it requires the prior existence of supply-chain organizational structures to internalize all of the potential benefits.

Since small-scale farmers predominate at the first stage of production and in most cases generate extremely small lot sizes for sale and separate handling, bulk transport and handling is not an economic way to manage paddy collection. Several past attempts on the part of governments within the region have achieved poor results. Most of the mill-level silos introduced into Indonesia and Vietnam, for example, remain empty.

With the exception of Vietnam, commercial and state storage capacity seems to be adequate to store sufficient rice to cover the period when rice production cannot meet demand. Excluding household storage, most current storage capacity in Vietnam is under the control of state-owned enterprises. The quality of storage facilities is generally recognized to be poor. This poor quality is reflected in the relatively low cost of storage that prevails in the country. Storage prices are

(continued next page)

Box 3.1 *(continued)*

50,000 dong per ton for a storage cycle of three to six months. This represents less than $3 per ton. In Thailand, by way of contrast, the government has recently paid storage costs of 216 baht per ton for six months in old-type warehouses. Storage costs can increase to 246 baht per ton ($7–8 per ton) if the rice is stored in modern structures (Arunmas 2004).

Source: Authors.

Milling Inefficiency Losses

Among ASEAN countries, average milling yields or recovery rates are generally well below their theoretical yields of 71–73 percent.[5] In Indonesia and the Philippines, milling yields are 63 percent; in small-scale, village-level mills, yields are even lower (57 percent) (table 3.3). These low yields are related to the small scale of operations and sometimes result, as well, from the poor-quality paddy that is processed, which, in turn, mainly results from bad drying. Poorly calibrated, maintained, and operated mill equipment aggravates this situation. Few mills have the means to measure moisture of paddy or to adjust the degree of milling that they affect.

Many of the problems identified in milling are similar in all five countries (with perhaps limited relevance to Thailand and Malaysia, where the number of mills is small) and include the following: (a) millers do not monitor grain moisture during storage and milling; (b) poor paddy cleaning results in high levels of foreign matter and cracked kernels in the paddy; (c) poor paddy separation results in low separation efficiency; (d) rubber milling rolls are used beyond their design life, and they are not interchanged or refaced; (e) milling stones are not refaced on a regular basis; (f) overmilling causes damage during the polishing process; and (g) evaluation tools, such as a moisture meter and milling degree meter for quality evaluation, are lacking.

The milling sector is in transition, with a large number of small and medium-size mills that cater to the domestic market and a few large mills, which cater to the export market, being gradually consolidated into fewer, larger mills. In Indonesia, the Philippines, and Vietnam, milling technology is often outdated, resulting in high levels of broken rice. In these same settings, millers are fundamentally constrained by a lack of capital to invest in new equipment. In Vietnam, preferential credit

Table 3.3 Theoretical and Actual Rice Milling Yields, Selected ASEAN Countries

	Theoretical yield	Cambodia	Indonesia	Malaysia	Philippines	Thailand	Vietnam
Capacity (tons/hour)		1.35	0.75	—	0.73	Med[a]	1.00
Husk (%)	19	24	26	22	24	22	22
Brown rice (%)	82	76	74	78	75	78	78
Bran (%)	8	11	11	10	8	10	16
Milled rice (%)	72	65	63	68	63	68	62
Head rice (%)	55	40	46	—	38	44	44
Broken kernels (%)	17	25	17	—	27	24	18

Sources: Rickman 2002; ACI 2005; http://www.bernas.com.my/.

Note: — = not available.

a. Med refers to output from medium mills (80–100 tons per day). One possible explanation for the seemingly rather high number for Thailand is that a lot of long grain is in Thailand, making it hard to obtain head rice.

arrangements provided for state-owned mills hamper the ability of the private sector to compete. The awarding of government-to-government contracts to state-owned mills also prevents private mills from expanding their export base.

In *Vietnam*, milling takes place in two stages: dehusking into brown rice (stage 1) and milling and polishing into white rice (stage 2). This practice supports small-scale operations in the paddy-rice supply chain, particularly that of the Mekong River Delta. However, it also contributes to transport and handling losses. Dehuskers typically operate outdated and poorly maintained equipment, which exacerbates the situation. The fragmented supply-chain structure in the Mekong River Delta hampers the transformation into shorter and more modern rice chains, which have lower postharvest losses.[6]

In *the Philippines*, laboratory analysis has demonstrated that 80 percent of the rice in large retail markets fails to comply fully with grading criteria. Only 2 percent of the samples met a standard above the lowest national grade.[7] In the Philippines and *Indonesia*, there is a strong correlation between price and the degree of yellowness of the grain. Moisture meters are little used by farmers and even by mills in these two countries, partly because of their high cost.[8] Significant losses at farm level in Indonesia are exacerbated by losses during milling. The milling ratio (conversion factor) has reportedly declined significantly in recent years due to the use of aging equipment and of mobile operations. If true, this has major implications for the ability of Indonesia to feed itself, suggesting that resources may be better directed to reducing such losses rather than to increasing production of paddy that is going to be badly milled.[9]

Quality Losses

The ability of private traders to compete both domestically and internationally is related in part to the quality of the rice they are able to offer. Concern has been expressed throughout ASEAN regarding what is generally perceived as worsening quality for its rice. Quality problems frequently originate at the production and postharvest levels of farm-to-market chains. They can be the result of factors such as the seed used, the harvesting and threshing techniques, and the drying practices discussed earlier.

A significant cause of quality problems is poor drying. Government and donor attempts to address this problem have tended to work at the level of farmers, but there may be a case for working more closely with millers to explore the extent to which they could undertake the drying. In most cases mills would prefer to do their own drying.

Excessive stockholding can also cause a loss of quality. Rice has a limited economic life after it is milled, of about six months to one year. Rice supply chains in the region contain multiple small-scale stock points, and rice requires a long time to move through chains from farm-to-retail outlets for final sale. Government direct interventions in rice chains result in additional excessive stock building, as in Thailand, and in Indonesia and Malaysia, where stock buildups are used to ensure reliable food supply. In Vietnam, government stock building has been used to ensure the economic viability of the largest state-owned trading companies.

That said, the private sector must also accept some of the blame for quality problems in the region. Small-scale mills typically offer no premiums to suppliers for high-quality paddy and thus create no incentives for farmers to invest in improved quality. In Malaysia, the government has actually institutionalized this flat-price approach in several states where the "flat-rate deduction system" has become entrenched. Mills are effectively required to pay the same price to all farmers, regardless of quality.

Formal quality standards for either paddy or rice have not been adopted and enforced by the private trade anywhere in the region. Consumers seeking higher-quality rice tend to use price as the main indicator of quality since no formal certification exists. The presence of numerous actors in the paddy-rice chains in Indonesia, the Philippines, and Vietnam may make standards difficult to enforce. On the other hand, it is not surprising that the private sectors of Malaysia and Thailand have taken steps on their own to develop appropriate standards.

Organization of the Rice Sector

ASEAN paddy-rice supply channels are complex and diverse. A simple linear diagram representing flows from input providers to final consumers hides the underlying web of relationships and the presence in some areas of multiple layers of agents at different stages of the supply chain. Even basic functions such as collecting paddy and delivering it to a mill can involve several types of actors—collectors, their agents, mill agents, small millers, large millers, and state companies. Milling is often specialized according to the final destination of the products: home consumption, local rural markets, or urban markets. In Vietnam, milling is often conducted in two stages, making the supply chain even more complex.

Various factors have shaped these convoluted supply channels. A root cause is an agrarian structure characterized by millions of smallholders who often lack effective farmer organizations, have only weak infrastructure and thus require a variety of transportation modes (pickups, trucks, boats, carts, tractors),[10] and lack access to finance. (Collection agents and millers often assume this function or provide access to third-party finance as part of their interlinked merchandising services.) Typically, a large state organization (as in Indonesia or the Philippines) manages to manipulate the market by handling relatively small shares of it, or a private monopoly (as in Malaysia) exerts control, or a combination of central and provincial state enterprises (as in Vietnam) dominates the market. This very fragmented market, moreover, has to respond to the needs of millions of consumers in terms of affordability, quality, and convenience.

A full discussion of rice marketing channels needs to take into account the basic fact that a considerable amount of paddy is consumed by the households who produce it. The marketable surplus—that is, the amount of paddy that enters the supply chain—varies between 40 and 80 percent of production (table 3.4), except for Thailand, where the rice farmers consume is typically purchased in shops.

Processing marketable rice varies according to whether it is destined for domestic consumption or export, and the corresponding supply chains each involve two set of activities. The first involves paddy moved from farmers to millers, and the second involves rice moved from millers to consumers or exports. State and private actors influence each segment of the supply chain, directing movement along three distinct paths: domestic consumption, exports, and imports, as analyzed below.

Table 3.4   Share of Paddy Production That Is Marketed, Exported, and Imported, Selected ASEAN Countries

percent

Country	Approximate percentage of production marketed domestically	Approximate percentage of production exported	Percentage of consumption imported (equivalent)
Indonesia	60	0	0–5
Malaysia	80	0	30
Philippines	50	0	10–15
Thailand	50	50	0
Vietnam	60	20	0

Source: Field interviews by Agrifood Consulting International, Inc. (ACI).

Supply Chains for Domestic Consumption

The paddy-rice supply chain is usually quite long, involving several intermediaries between farmers and consumers and a correspondingly large number of inventory storage points. Typically governed by the "push" of supply rather than the "pull" of demand, participants share little information because superior knowledge secures for its possessors an advantage in chain negotiations. Typically, the supply chain for domestic consumption involves numerous actors in the production, collection, milling, and retailing stages, each of which is linked to other stages of the supply chain by several coexisting channels. For example, collectors can move farmers' paddy to millers, but farmers can also go directly to millers and in some cases sell the milled product to wholesalers and retailers, thus bypassing several intermediaries.

This pathway redundancy makes the chains both competitively robust and inefficient in terms of the working capital tied up in them. The multiple stock points that frustrate efforts to complete independent buy and hold decisions up and down the chain also can swell when independent traders expect prices to increase. In this sense, they are "spongy," and the chains themselves affect price elasticity.

Supply chains for domestic consumption, usually "long" ones that include multiple independent actors, both private and government, can adopt some form of risk sharing where mixed public-private channels occur.[11] "Shorter" channels are emerging, however, through a combination of factors, including occasional contract farming between millers and farmers; direct supply by millers to retailers, including supermarkets; and involvement of farm organizations that might sell the paddy milled in their own mills to retailers. These shorter channels typically entail more "demand pull" controls, less speculative behavior, and less inventory sponginess.[12] Importantly, they engage supply-chain integrators directly in stabilizing prices as their customers prefer. They still represent a small share of total supply chains, however.

In all importing countries, domestic channels include state actors, usually a national food security agency or (in Malaysia) a private monopoly, to procure and distribute rice. Rice can be distributed either through centers serving targeted consumers, such as with the Raskin (Rice for the Poor Households, Beras Miskin) program in Indonesia, or through open market operations to stabilize prices.

Primary-production-to-mill segment. In the five countries studied, paddy-rice supply chains differ significantly. The 300,000-plus small dehusking mills in Vietnam and around 100,000 mills in Indonesia compare to around 1,000 mills in Thailand and just 231 in Malaysia. These differences in scale of operations are largely reflected throughout the chain, with the many small mills in Indonesia, the Philippines, and Vietnam being supplied by numerous small-scale intermediaries who buy from farmers. Although chain actors in Malaysia and Thailand achieve comparative economies of scale, because of higher labor costs their overall costs are not lower. Rural wages in rice cultivation (seeding to harvesting) in Thailand varied between 188 and 207 baht per day in 2007–08, equivalent to $5.50–6.10 per day. In Vietnam, equivalent wages varied between 40,000 and 60,000 dong, equivalent to $2.10–3.30.

Formal links between farmers and millers are underdeveloped. A few examples of contract farming exist, mainly for specialized varieties and qualities. Paddy is primarily a commodity sold on the spot market by farmers choosing the buyers who offer the best price. That said, there is considerable interest by the private sector in the development of improved links. Such improvement, though, carries risks where continued government involvement in price setting could encourage one or both partners to a contract to break the agreement.

Domestic-mill-to-market segment. as with farm-to-mill chains, patterns of rice marketing vary significantly among the five countries, according in large measure to the influence of modern retailing. Its relevance to rice supply-chain development is that modern retailers have refined techniques that can make the pull of demand effective in transforming traditional supply chains.[13] With this transformation come significant gains in efficiency, precision, and adaptability.

Modern retailers, including supermarkets, are playing an increasingly important role in all five countries, particularly in Malaysia and Thailand, without yet achieving a quantifiable impact on rice supply chains. One limiting factor comes from consumers' expectations about quality, which vary significantly, probably as a result of differences in purchasing power. Branded retail packages, for example, are more common in the higher-income countries; bulk rice is more common where income is lower. Countries that have numerous stages in the marketing chain between farmer and miller (notably the Philippines and Vietnam) also tend to have more stages and actors in the chain between the miller and consumer.

The growth of modern food retailing in Asia has been documented extensively (see World Bank 2007b, Nielsen Company 2008). For example, the Nielsen Company (2008) shows that modern retail in ASEAN now accounts for between 20 percent of total consumer purchases in urban centers in Vietnam to over 40 percent in Malaysia and Thailand (figure 3.1). These percentages are likely to increase further in the near future because retailers continue to expand the number of outlets in most ASEAN countries. Unfortunately, no precise data exist for the share of rice that moves through modern retail channels in the region. A reasonable assumption can be made, however, that it is increasing in line with other food products.

Modern retail outlets' penetration in food distribution is growing even though traditional markets are still the main source of food in Indonesia, the Philippines, and Vietnam (table 3.5). Malaysia and Thailand have already crossed an important threshold, with more than 50 percent of food (including fresh and dry groceries) bought in modern retail stores in urban centers.

Average-quality and low-price rice is usually not present on supermarket shelves, although some stores in the Philippines have recently tried with mixed success to target low-income consumers. Most high-quality rice products are targeted to middle- and higher-income groups. Low-income groups do not typically buy rice in supermarkets,[14] either because prices are too high or because they simply are not supermarket patrons (such as most rural households).

In the countries where supermarkets have been developing rapidly, their spread has meant that companies in a position to supply the large stores, as well as the chains of smaller convenience stores, have had to make significant adaptations, both in terms of the development of retail

Figure 3.1   Share of Trade for Modern Retail Outlets, Selected ASEAN Countries, 2003–05

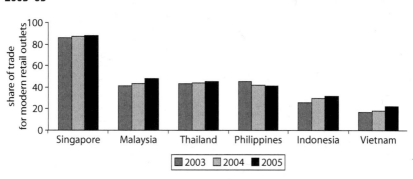

Source: Nielsen Company 2008.

Table 3.5   Penetration of Modern Retail Markets in Food Distribution, Selected Asian Countries

percent

Country	Share of modern retail outlets in food distribution
Malaysia	71.0
Thailand	53.2
Indonesia	30.4
Philippines	16.6
China	11.2
Vietnam	—

Source: http://www.businesstrendsasia.com/print.php?cat=64&art=0&page=0.
Note: — = not available.

packaging and branding and in terms of financing the transactions, given the delayed payment that supermarkets always insist upon. This is particularly the case in Malaysia and Thailand, and perhaps the Philippines—but such developments also exist in a more embryonic phase in the other two countries.

With the exception of the growth in supermarkets and convenience stores, many features of the rice market differ significantly among the five countries. The quality of rice available at retail levels tends to be higher in Malaysia and Thailand, at least when measured by the percentage of brokens. In those countries, distribution also tends to be more structured and consolidated, with a relatively small number of firms involved in wholesale distribution compared to the other countries. Given the reluctance of supermarkets to deal with many small suppliers, such consolidation is likely to occur as supermarkets elsewhere take on an increasingly important role as retailers of rice. Arguably, the most significant set of developments, however, involve multinational chains like Carrefour, which are beginning to purchase food items, including rice, regionally and, in the process, creating economies of scale and specialization in the relationships they are developing with suppliers.

Exporters' Supply Chains

With a few minor exceptions, rice exports are limited to those from Thailand and Vietnam,[15] the bulk of whose exports go outside the region. Important markets include Africa and the Gulf countries. Some Latin American countries have in the past banned Asian rice imports through sanitary and phytosanitary (SPS) measures, although those actions may have been primarily protectionist measures, as U.S. exports were similarly affected (USDA 1999). Within ASEAN, Malaysia is a deficit country that buys from Thailand and increasingly from Vietnam, a trend that has recently led to complaints by consumers about the quality of rice available.

Exporters send orders back to their suppliers (typically millers) either directly or through brokers, specifying clearly defined standards, volumes, prices, and delivery times. The export channels tolerate relatively less variability in quality when compared to domestic channels, and they do not generally value features such as geographic origin, freshness, and texture to the degree that discriminating domestic consumers do.

The two major exporters (Thailand and Vietnam) differ considerably in terms of private sector involvement. While Thailand's rice exports are handled primarily by private firms, in Vietnam state organizations are the dominant players in terms of volume and power. In Vietnam a number of millers also export directly or via state-owned enterprises (SOEs) such as VINAFOOD1 and VINAFOOD2 (Northern and Southern Food Corporations). Even in Thailand, however, the state plays a major role through the Public Warehouse Organization, the main agency responsible for storing paddy and rice stocks that are released to exporters upon auction.

Export chains are distinct from those that serve domestic markets. For example, millers engaged in providing supplies for exporters usually take no part in domestic distribution. In Thailand, the export industry is reportedly becoming increasingly concentrated, with the top 25 companies accounting for around 90 percent of sales.[16] The largest companies all have the capacity to export more than 500,000 tons per year. Many exporters have facilities just north of Bangkok, on the Chao Phraya River.

Because the large exporters are located close to export facilities rather than to producers, they tend to rely on other companies to collect and mill the rice they export. However, some express a preference to expand their own milling facilities for reasons of quality control. For the most part, rice is exported in bulk or bag, but several companies also market retail packs and branded rice overseas, including "Hom Mali" and organic rice.

The Thai Rice Exporters Association had 187 members as of July 2009, although many of them export only small quantities, and there is considerable turnover of membership. Some smaller mills are also beginning to export directly. Established exporters report that the millers' children have studied overseas and have learned foreign languages, and thus are keen to carry out overseas transactions. However, many smaller exporters ran into difficulties in 2008–09 when they were unable to secure sufficient rice to honor their export commitments. Small mills tend to lack necessary market information to trade effectively and do not have the social capital that has been built up by larger businesses.

Companies such as SGS and Crown Agents do surveying of export consignments, but there has also been a growth in Thai surveying companies in recent years. Surveyors check for quality and weight and carry out fumigation. The government plays an inspection role only in the case of aromatic rice, which it certifies as true "Hom Mali," although some industry spokespersons argue that it is difficult to conduct reliable tests.

Thailand has recently become an export conduit for rice grown in surrounding countries. Production figures in 2008–09 were slightly swollen by unofficial imports of paddy from Cambodia and Myanmar that were sold through official channels as if Thai farmers had produced them. Some official imports from Cambodia are permitted under a Thai government scheme that promotes contract farming in that country. That said, unofficial trade remained more attractive to Cambodian exporters, since they could benefit from the inflated Thai government intervention prices.

In **Vietnam**, where SOEs monopolized the rice export trade until 2002, the private sector still accounts for only an estimated 10 percent of exports (Goletti 2009), and VINAFOOD2 accounts for 50 percent of the total. Unlike in Thailand, there is virtually no branding of rice for export.

VINAFOOD1 operates in the north of the country, while VINAFOOD2 operates in the south. It trades on its own account and subcontracts private companies to provide rice for export. Private companies are able to conclude export contracts, but these are subject to approval by the Vietnam Food Association; where possible, the companies therefore prefer to subcontract to VINAFOOD2. While Thailand exports a range of qualities of rice and gives private firms a large role in exporting, Vietnam's exports tend to be of lower quality and are mainly carried out by the state sector.

The private sectors of both countries faced problems in 2008–09. In Thailand, state intervention in the market limited supplies available for export, while in Vietnam, "stop-go" approval for private sector exports created major difficulties.[17] Such government involvement seems to be the major problem faced by the private sector.

There are no regionwide trade standards for rice, but at present traders do not consider this a problem. Although application of SPS regulations may affect trade with some countries outside the region, there is no evidence of such problems within ASEAN.

Importers' Supply Chains

Among the five study countries, Malaysia and the Philippines are constant importers, whereas increases in Indonesia's production reduced imports to negligible quantities in the last few years, with the exception of 2006–07, when the country imported 2 million tons.

Throughout the ASEAN region, import channels are more tightly organized than export channels and are dominated by national agencies, with the private sector limited to small quantities of special types of rice such as basmati and jasmine. Over the past 10 years, the national agencies (or privatized national agency, in the case of Malaysia) have been responsible for importing between 1 and 10 percent of domestic rice consumption in Indonesia, 10 and 15 percent in the Philippines, and 20 and 35 percent in Malaysia. The private sector in the Philippines makes nominal imports amounting to 200,000 tons per year, compared to the National Food Authority's (NFA's) average of over 1.5 million tons per year in 2000–08. Most of the imports by the national agencies tend to be of lower quality, with high percentages of broken grain, and are often conducted on a government-to-government basis.

There are also some unofficial imports into Indonesia and the Philippines from Malaysia and Singapore. Unofficial paddy imports from Cambodia, the Lao People's Democratic Republic, and Myanmar to Thailand can also be significant. Such illegal arbitrage opportunities depend on a combination of prevailing government pricing policies and world market trends.

In **Malaysia**, official imports amounted to 0.750 million tons of rice in 2007. In the late 1990s, BERNAS (Padi Beras Nasional Bhd.) established joint ventures with rice exporters in Pakistan and Thailand to guarantee supplies of particular varieties or qualities. There are some unofficial imports across the Thai border (although probably not recently, given the high prices in Thailand) and unofficial transshipments to both Indonesia and the Philippines. Per capita consumption of rice in Malaysia is estimated at 79 kilograms, less than in other countries covered in this study, largely because wealthier Malaysian consumers are able to move away from dependence on the staple food.

In **the Philippines**, where only the parastatal NFA is allowed to import rice, it permits the importation of about 200,000 metric tons by farmer cooperatives. This is often specialized varieties used for the hotel or restaurant trade. Financed by the Land Bank of the Philippines, accredited farmer cooperatives—which are ready to supplement their locally procured rice with imported rice and have the experience of importing—can obtain permits from NFA against the tons set aside for this purpose. In many cases, coops act surreptitiously as agents for private companies.

In *Indonesia*, the state parastatal, BULOG (Badan Urusan Logistik), was dominant in defending floor and ceiling prices from the mid-1960s to the late 1990s. This was done through monopoly control over international rice trading and through domestic procurement, drawing on an unlimited line of credit from the Bank of Indonesia (Timmer 2008). In the late 1990s, imports by the private sector were permitted, but they were then halted again in 2003. More recently, in 2007, BULOG imported significant quantities, and private sector imports were again permitted until June 2008. With production reportedly equaling or exceeding consumption in 2009, and with BULOG's warehouses reportedly well stocked,[18] the only imports permitted in 2009 were specialty rice, such as sticky rice, a variety for diabetics, and rice types needed for Indian and Japanese restaurants.

Smuggling, made possible by a lengthy coastline and corruption at the smaller ports, has been occurring in Indonesia for many years. These days, smuggled rice is believed to come primarily from Vietnam through Singapore and Malaysia, reaching Sumatra on small boats that have a capacity of around 100 tons.[19] In 2009, however, smuggling must have been minimal because Vietnamese free on board prices of rice with 15 percent brokens were around $450 a ton and the selling price of comparable rice by Indonesia's millers was around $520 a ton, providing little margin for smugglers.

Supply-Chain Logistics: The Role of Infrastructure

For rice, as for many other commodities, the quality and capacity of logistics infrastructure—including roads, ports, railways, and multimodal transfer facilities—greatly affect supply-chain efficiency, precision, and adaptability. Those attributes determine the time and costs of food delivery to consumers and the efficiency and adaptability of food supply chains. Indirectly, infrastructure also lowers the risk of complementary private sector investment in productive assets and hence makes such investment more likely to occur. Potential investors consider efficient logistics and adequate supportive infrastructure as important criteria when they decide where and when to commit their funds (World Bank 2007a). When comparing Thailand and Indonesia, for example, it becomes immediately obvious that the excellent road system in Thailand

and its superior ports are two reasons why companies prefer to invest there, in spite of the availability of cheaper labor and substantial natural resources in Indonesia.

Table 3.6 benchmarks the five study countries against one another in terms of indicators within the aggregate Logistics Performance Index (LPI) developed by the World Bank, as well as a number of subordinate indexes, each of which feeds into the development of the composite LPI. These comparisons suggest that the five study countries can be separated meaningfully into three transport infrastructure classes: high performers (Thailand and Malaysia) and low performers (Indonesia and Vietnam), with the Philippines falling in between.

Vietnam's and Indonesia's low scores on the LPI metric relate to insufficient and poorly maintained rural roads, inadequate port facilities, and railway systems not suitable for the transport of International Organization for Standardization containers. In Indonesia, most rice is moved overland. Hence a poorly maintained road network with insufficient capacity translates directly into higher transport costs (Asia Foundation 2008). In *Vietnam*, major investments are required to improve all aspects of the nation's transport infrastructure (Meyrick and Associates 2006). However, poor infrastructure does not have as dire an impact on the nation's rice and maize value chains as might be expected because rice and paddy are mostly transported by boat throughout the Mekong River Delta. Products moving through export chains do not incur major infrastructure hurdles until they arrive in the ports of Can Tho or Ho Chi Minh City for movement beyond.

These scores are mirrored in an assessment of the logistics infrastructure in Indonesia, Malaysia, the Philippines, Thailand, and Vietnam, and the Philippines conducted by Agrifood Consulting International, Inc. (ACI) for the purposes of this study. Results are reported in table 3.7.

Effects of Infrastructure Policies on Supply Chains

To differing degrees, ASEAN government policies related to infrastructure push up transport costs and, hence, consumer prices. Regulations affecting interisland shipment in the Philippines and between provinces and islands in Indonesia, for example, keep transportation prices high. In Malaysia, impediments to the interstate movement of paddy constrain consolidation in the milling industry. The lack of incentives to realize economies of scale in the rice business limits the volumes of shipment, storage, and processing lots to sizes that are less than optimally efficient in most of the study countries.

Table 3.6 Logistics Performance Index, Selected ASEAN Countries

International LPI rank	Country	LPI	Customs	Infrastructure	International shipments	Logistics competence	Cargo tracking and tracing	Timeliness
29	Malaysia	3.44	3.11	3.50	3.50	3.34	3.32	3.86
35	Thailand	3.29	3.02	3.16	3.27	3.16	3.41	3.73
44	Philippines	3.14	2.67	2.57	3.40	2.95	3.29	3.83
53	Vietnam	2.96	2.68	2.56	3.04	2.89	3.10	3.44
75	Indonesia	2.76	2.43	2.54	2.82	2.47	2.77	3.46

Source: World Bank LPI Ranking (http://info.worldbank.org/etools/tradesurvey/mode1b.asp).
Note: Countries appear in descending order of their overall LPI score. The LPI scores are from 1 to 5, with 1 being the worst performance for the given dimension.
LPI = Logistics Performance Index (World Bank).

Table 3.7 Quality of Logistics Infrastructure for Rice and Maize, Selected ASEAN Countries

Country	Roads	Ports	IWT	Airports	Railways	ICT
Indonesia	Fair/poor	Fair	Fair/poor	Fair	Fair/poor	Poor
Malaysia	Good	Fair/good	Fair	Good/fair	Good	Good
Philippines	Fair/poor	Fair/poor	Fair/poor	Fair	Poor	Poor
Thailand	Good/fair	Good	Fair	Good/fair	Fair/poor	Good
Vietnam	Fair	Fair/poor	Fair/good	Fair	Poor	Poor

Source: Authors' compilations based on industry data and Agrifood Consulting International, Inc. (ACI) interviews with key informants.
Note: IWT = inland water transport; ICT = information and communication technology.

A report on the cost of moving goods in Indonesia prepared by the Asia Foundation (2008) finds that domestic logistics costs are higher in Indonesia than in Malaysia, Thailand, or Vietnam. Topography, poor maintenance of infrastructure, local government fees, illegal charges, and poor cargo security all affect the high cost of moving commodities in Indonesia and explain the wide differentials in rice prices among different regions and between producing and consuming areas.

Some regional governments are more mindful of the importance of logistics efficiency to economic development than others. Thailand, for example, has set up a Logistics Agency and has ambitious plans for logistics efficiency improvement (Keretho 2009). To date, however, the agency's lack of funds has slowed implementation of its plans. Indonesia is in the process of finalizing its blueprint for logistics improvement. The Department of Agriculture and the Department of Transport in the Philippines are currently implementing a Grain Highways Program to link farmers with markets through improved feeder roads, which will connect them to the national highway system. Considerable improvements and cost reduction could also be obtained by harmonizing and simplifying customs and inspection processes at ports.[20] In Indonesia and Vietnam, investments in connector roads and port facilities are required to alleviate bottlenecks that currently lead to delays and increase costs. In spite of the excellent road infrastructure in Thailand, additional cost savings could be realized through the use of railways to transport commodities from major producing and milling areas to the main ports or, at least, to the main exporters close to Bangkok.

Professional competence in logistics management has a direct and significant effect on the quality of distribution and the efficiency of supply chains. Varying widely throughout the region, it is generally high in

Malaysia and Thailand as compared with Indonesia, the Philippines, and Vietnam. Due to the relatively high level of industrialization, Bangkok has become an important trade and services hub in the region. Thailand has attracted a range of modern international retailers; they, in turn, have attracted a range of third-party logistics service providers. These developments have pushed the whole transport and distribution sector to a much higher level, and the rice sector benefits from this improvement. Indonesia is at the lower end of the spectrum of specialized competence in logistics management, followed by the Philippines.

Port infrastructure. Port handling facilities and handling operations create inefficiencies in food supply chains in Indonesia, the Philippines, and Vietnam. Port facility limitations on the demand side of regional chains have knock-on consequences for more efficient ports within the region. It is this knock-on effect that has adversely affected food security throughout the region in recent years.

For example, the port of Laem Chabang in eastern **Thailand** is constrained not by its own capabilities but by the facility limitations of counterpart ports in Indonesia and the Philippines. In both those countries, importers prefer to receive break bulk shipments in 50-kilogram lots, instead of either container-load lots or full-vessel loads of 15,000–30,000 tons of bulk, flowable rice.

Together with Bangkok and Koh Si Chang, Laem Chabang specializes in rice exports. All three ports are forced to handle break bulk cargoes for which they were not designed, in lieu of bulk and containerized shipments for which they were designed. For this reason, both their throughput capacity and berth retention time are compromised. Thai ports are more efficient than the ships they are loading. Ports can load 3,000–4,000 tons a day, but the ships' cranes can often handle only 1,500 tons.

Exporters in Bangkok would prefer to sell (and to ship) in larger lot sizes. Not only are per ton transport charges less for larger lots, but so too are insurance, port handling, and customs clearance costs. However, cargo capacity limitations in the Port of Manila for container vessels translate into delays exceeding 14 days and entail that the designated cargo owner absorb vessel demurrage charges of $15,000–25,000 per day. Other smaller ports in both **Indonesia** and **the Philippines** have only limited capacity to handle containers, and none to handle bulk cargoes. Box 3.2 illustrates the impact of shipping costs on Vietnamese rice exports to the Philippines.

Box 3.2

Logistics Costs along an Export-Import Supply Chain

Using the example of a shipment of rice that originates from Vietnam's Mekong Delta and reaches the retail market in Metro Manila, this box shows that shipping and port costs account for about 25 percent of the final price to Filipino consumers, the next largest element of total costs after those of production (see table B3.8).

Cutting those logistics costs by half at both the source and destination could potentially reduce shipping costs by 12.5 percent and the final price to consumers in Manila by about 8 percent. This reduction of price would benefit consumers in the Philippines, without any loss to farmers in Vietnam.

**Table B3.8   Costs, Margins, and Prices for Rice Imported
by the Philippines from Vietnam**
US¢/kilogram

Country or transit	Actors	Input cost	Other cost	Total cost	Unit margin	Price received
Vietnam	Farmer	9.3	4.7	14.0	9.3	23.3
Vietnam	Collector	23.3	0.8	24.2	0.8	25.0
Vietnam	Miller	25.0	1.0	26.0	0.3	26.3
Vietnam	Transporter	—	0.4	0.4	0.3	0.7
Vietnam	Exporter	27.0	0.5	27.5	0.5	28.0
Shipping	Shipping company	—	5.0	33.0	0.5	5.5
Philippines	Unloading and loading	33.5	0.5	34.0	0.5	34.5
Philippines	Wholesaler	34.5	0.8	35.3	0.7	36.0
Philippines	Retailer	36.0	0.7	36.7	1.2	37.9

Source: Agrifood Consulting International, Inc. (ACI) interviews with key informants in Vietnam and the Philippines.
Note: — = not applicable.

Conclusions

Rice supply chains remain reservoirs of marginally productive farmers, processors, and loosely associated, ancillary service providers whose internal business processes remain independent and uncoordinated. Millions of actors are involved in national rice supply chains in ASEAN countries.

Even in a country like Malaysia, with an official population of rice farmers numbering 130,000, the actual number of rice-farming households probably is closer to 1 million.

This situation is changing, but only slowly. As the economic transformation from agrarian to industrial societies proceeds in all ASEAN countries, more off-farm employment is being created; as a result, collateral competitive forces are at work in labor, land, and other factors of production. As these competitive effects play out and as the farming population declines, the number of agents likely to be available at various stages of supply chains and productivity is likely to rise. Other exogenous factors—such as supermarkets becoming involved in rice distribution, and economies of scale created through modern logistics management—may help accelerate this transformation.

For now, however, the chains for domestic consumption are longer than chains for imports, which are controlled by national monopolies, and for exports where major parastatals are engaged primarily in only some stages of the supply chain. Still, few competitive pressures exist either to drive productivity improvement or to strengthen links in supply chains for rice.

For example, little differentiation has taken place among supply chains or among rice products within the region. Although local brands exist, few national brands for rice have succeeded. No international brands have proven successful in regional markets, except for the house brands of multinational supermarket chains.

Different varieties of rice (fragrant, glutinous, and so on) are recognized within the region and differentially valued. However, few, if any, companies have been able to market a proprietary rice brand over an entire country (such as Uncle Ben's in the United States), let alone throughout the region. Thailand has been able to establish its dominance regionally in the high-end market not by protecting domestic brands but by controlling its country-of-origin certification processes and through them enforcing rigorous, high standards for international trade.

As for supply-chain *infrastructure*, storage capacity is sufficient in four of the five countries. Vietnam is the exception, where limited capacity at several links in the chain causes rice to degrade in quality. Logistics costs associated with moving rice and maize among ASEAN countries, however, account for 20–25 percent of the total price to consumers in the importing country. The capacity and quality of supply-chain infrastructure affect these costs and vary widely among the five study countries. Thailand generally fares better in terms of logistics infrastructure quality than Vietnam, in the southern portion of which, where much rice originates, infrastructure deficiencies impede exports.

Domestic infrastructure obstacles to efficient food chain operations are most severe in Indonesia and the Philippines. Both road and shipping constraints adversely affect movements of paddy to millers and rice to distributors and consumers. The infrastructure quality in Malaysia is generally good, with the exception of food supplies to Sabah and Sarawak.

Improvements need to be made in the countries with the lowest LPI, in particular in Indonesia and the Philippines (road network, interisland shipping, and customs) and in Vietnam (port facilities). Poor internal logistics in Indonesia and the Philippines are partly related to the nature of these two countries as archipelagos and their difficult topography. However, congested ports and poor road conditions in such major rice-producing areas as Java also hamper performance.

The major logistics bottlenecks that inhibit regional food trade are in the ports, including the ports of one exporting country (Vietnam) and two importing countries (Indonesia and the Philippines). The waiting times in these ports (including loading, offloading, and clearance) represent about 45 percent of the time needed to move the grains from farmers in the exporting country to consumers in the importing country. Such bottlenecks result in delays that add extra costs for loading and offloading, waiting times for berths to be available, documentation clearance, and shipping itself.

Although improvement in infrastructure and logistics will facilitate trade among ASEAN countries and speed up the response time to food imbalances (both surpluses and deficits), an improvement in logistics will probably have small effects on regional food trade overall.

The *enabling environment* in the region is generally weak for rice and maize chain development. It is not conducive to either private sector testing of new supply-chain structures or of private investment in supply-chain infrastructure. Backward links to small-scale farm producers are particularly weak and in need of innovative approaches to strengthen them in commercially sustainable ways. The milling and processing sectors in most of the countries included in this study are not generating sufficient returns to invest in modern milling equipment or adequate storage. Consolidation within the milling sector has only just begun in two countries (Malaysia and Thailand) and has not started in the others.

Other aspects of regional food chains besides infrastructure—including the reform of prevailing institutional arrangements and the opening up of food procurement policies—pose more significant challenges to regional market integration. However, relieving specific infrastructure bottlenecks may open a path to increased private participation in regional food markets through the offer of infrastructure investment and management opportunities in return for increased involvement in regional trade.

With respect to policies for future rice chain development, rules established by governments will continue to matter greatly, including the incentives (and disincentives) created through government rice procurement programs, specific forms of government support for rice production, and programs related to public-private partnership investment in food chain infrastructure. The import procurement policies of at least one of the main parastatal buyers in the region (NFA) exacerbate infrastructure-related constraints in the ports by requiring break bulk deliveries. Streamlining export and import procedures and harmonizing customs documentation would also reduce times and costs.

Annex: Examples of Marketing Channels

Some specific Indonesian chains are presented in more detail in figure 3A.1.

In general, export supply chains are shorter and national agencies are often involved. Some specific export-oriented supply chains are presented for Thailand in table 3A.1 and figure 3A.2, and for Vietnam in figure 3A.3.

Figure 3A.1 Specific Domestic Supply Chain for Rice, Indonesia

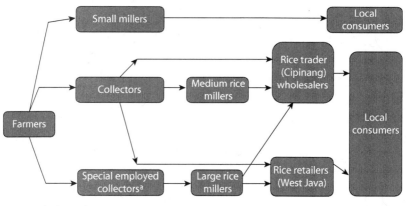

Source: Agrifood Consulting International, Inc. (ACI).
a. "Special employed collectors" buy on behalf of a miller and are, to a certain extent, employees of the mill.

Table 3A.1 Export Supply Chain, Thailand

Case A (export)	Production Farmers	Collection or trading Rice traders	(Primary) milling Rice millers	Processing or trading Exporter	Export or import National agencies
Activities and functions	Inputs Production Harvest Threshing Drying Bagging (incidental, mostly in bulk)	Transport Credit (incidental redrying) Temporary storage	Paddy storage, operational (Re)drying, mechanical Dehusking (first-stage milling) Temporary storage Bagging	Mixing (homogenizing) Polishing (second-stage milling) Bagging Export preparations Transport to port	Maritime transport Importing Offloading Transport Storage
Distinct features per link of supply chain	Depending on the area and facilities, farmers transport in bulk after drying.	Transport of rice by truck in bulk (mostly). Depending on contract, collector or miller redries in wet season.	Millers keep only a minimum operational reserve of paddy, to operate their mills optimally. Mechanical (re)drying in wet season when paddy too moist. Milling on request. Some millers operate their own trucks for delivery with exporter.	Traders and exporters mix rice from various mills (homogenized) and polished until uniform white rice. Standard 50-kg bags for export FOB. Prepare for export order as general cargo (incidentally in containers).	For export to the Philippines by NFA, Manila port can handle only general cargo (rice in bags). Import and customs clearance by private, specialized companies on behalf of NFA. Transport to NFA stores.

(continued next page)

Table 3A.1 *(continued)*

	Production	Collector or trader	Milling	Wholesaling or distribution	Sales and marketing
Case B *(domestic retail)*	*Farmers*	*Rice trader*	*Rice millers*	*Wholesalers*	*Retailers (traditional) / (modern)*
Activities and functions	Identical to export supply chain		Operational inventory Dehusking and polishing (second stage) Bagging Transport	Storage and inventory Bagging in 2- to 10-kg consumer packs Transport to distribution centers (modern retail) or directly to traditional retailers Cross-dock operations (modern retail) City distribution	Ordering per store and distribution
Distinct features per link of supply chain			For domestic markets, some millers will conduct dehusking and polishing (second stage) into white marketable rice. Transport to wholesalers (markets).	Wholesalers distribute to traditional or modern retail. Or via distribution centers, modern retail, and distribution per store in mixed trucks.	

Source: Agrifood Consulting International, Inc. (ACI).

Note: NFA = National Food Authority (the Philippines); FOB = free on board; kg = kilogram.

Figure 3A.2   Export and Domestic Supply Chains for Rice, Thailand

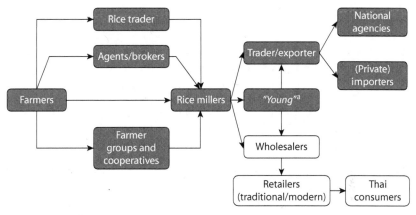

Source: Agrifood Consulting International, Inc. (ACI).
Note: Grey boxes = export; white boxes = domestic.
a. *"Young"* is the word used in Thailand for a commissioner who facilitates trade for a small fee.

Figure 3A.3   Supply Chains for Rice Exports, Vietnam

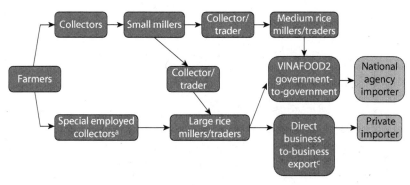

Source: Agrifood Consulting International, Inc. (ACI).
Note: VINAFOOD2 = Southern Food Corporation.
a. "Special employed collectors" buy on behalf of a miller and are, to a certain extent, employees of the mill.

Notes

This report was prepared by the Study Team, drawing on preliminary studies and field research conducted by Francesco Goletti of ACI, It was based on two missions conducted by ACI to the five countries, a review of selected literature and data, and interviews with key informants. The study was conducted over a 60-day period between September 2009 and January 2010, including a first mission to Indonesia, Malaysia, the Philippines, Thailand, and Vietnam in September–October 2009 and a second mission in January 2010. Given the limited time and resources available for the study, only a few key informants could be contacted in each country, and no systematic surveys could be undertaken. The second main source is a draft prepared by Andrew W. Shepherd, senior marketing officer, Market Linkages and Value Chains Group, the Food and Agriculture Organization (FAO) of the United Nations, Rome, as well as case studies prepared by Bustanul Arifin (Indonesia), Larry Wong (Malaysia), and ACI (Vietnam). Fieldwork was conducted in Thailand and the Philippines in July 2009 and in the remaining countries in September–October 2009. The assistance provided to Andrew Shepherd in Thailand by Juejan Tangtermthong and in Rome by Maja Rueegg is gratefully acknowledged. Comments received on earlier drafts from David Dawe of FAO and the case study authors proved very helpful.

1. When a company operates end-to-end, processes are involved that connect buyers and sellers directly.

2. Loss measurement is not an exact science, and even if losses are of the magnitude reported in table 3.1, what is important is what percent can be economically avoided. Moreover, postharvest practices vary so much within the region, within countries, and even within islands (e.g., Java, Indonesia) that it is very difficult to summarize issues. Nevertheless, an attempt has been made, in the hope that even an imperfect presentation will spark debate.

3. Authors' calculations based on data from AFSIS (2008).

4. During the three to four days between cutting and threshing, panicles (flower heads with branches that carry more flowers) are left wet in piles (more than 16–17 percent moisture), leading to discoloration—a major reason for lower market prices.

5. In practical terms, it is possible to obtain 68–70 percent from a good variety of paddy with high-quality equipment (FAO 1999).

6. The fragmented chains found in Vietnam are said to be a contributory factor to poor quality and to high postharvest losses, estimated by Goletti (2002) to be at least 9 percent. As a result of the buildup of stocks, sometimes mandated by the government, Vietnamese millers and polishers often find themselves with excessive quantities of rice that they cannot easily sell. High moisture levels mean that the rice must be remilled and polished every few months to be saleable. This double milling contributes to further losses.

7. A limited market exists in the Philippines for high-quality rice, mainly the market serviced by supermarkets. In general, the Philippines market is price sensitive and suppliers are oriented toward low prices. Incentives for good-quality postharvest treatment are limited, and as a result poor-quality rice with a short shelf life is the main product available to consumers. Much rice is marketed with 35–40 percent brokens. This percentage is much higher than in, say, Thailand, where the corresponding percentage is 5 percent. In part, the high level of brokens can be attributed to the many stages in the marketing system and frequent handlings of the bags.

8. This remains the case even though the International Rice Research Institute has developed cheap meters in collaboration with a Chinese company. Whiteness meters are used only in large mills.

9. One extreme estimate puts the conversion rate as low as 0.57, compared with a more normal rate of 0.63 and the possible rate of 0.67 or better that can be achieved with modern equipment.

10. Poor rural road conditions in many rice-growing areas require the use of sub-optimal transport for upstream links in the chain and postpone the assembly of large economic shipment lots until upstream in the chain.

11. *Risk sharing* in this context refers to the procurement rules and conditions that apply under the several food security programs that operate in the region; these were discussed in the previous chapter.

12. *"Demand pull" mechanisms* in the form of advanced purchase agreements or standing orders reduce marketing, inventory holding, and pricing risks incurred by upstream chain participants. They also facilitate the realization of logistics cost savings associated with continuous order fulfillment, and they require that less buffer inventory be held in order to satisfy more predictable orders from downstream buyers.

13. In "demand pull" chains, integrators (modern retailers, exporters with standing orders, and the like) make projections of anticipated demand and share that projection with other chain participants. Supplies then move forward on a schedule that is designed to match the projected demand. The responsibility and corresponding risk associated with forecasting either too much or too little demand reside in the first instance with the chain integrator. In "supply push" chains, no chain integrator acts to project expected demand and to manage inventory risk. Rather, responsibility for holding either too much or too little inventory is distributed throughout the chain, and imbalances between demand and supply at the demand end result.

14. 7-11 network stores may be the exception. 7-11 outlets throughout the region do stock rice products and target lower-income customers.

15. There is some repacking of imported rice in Malaysia for export sale, and some limited export of high-quality rice from Indonesia.

16. From Thai industry sources, based on interviews by Andrew Shepherd for this study.

17. Vietnam enforces minimum export prices and export licensing. Stop-go approval stems from changes in the minimum export prices.

18. According to private sector sources interviewed, there may be some doubts about the quality of rice in store, however.

19. From industry sources, based on interviews by Andrew Shepherd for this study.

20. See Hausman et al. (2009) for a discussion of modes and means for improving trade efficiency.

References and Other Sources

ACI (Agrifood Consulting International). 2005. "North East Thailand Rice Value Chain Study." Final report prepared for the National Economic and Social Development Board of Thailand and the World Bank, Bethesda, MD.

AFSIS (ASEAN Food Security Information System). 2008. http://afsis.oae.go.th/.

Arunmas, W. K. A. P. 2004. "Rice Storage Facilities to Be Upgraded." *Bangkok Post,* June 21.

ASEAN (Association for Southeast Asian Nations). 2008. *ASEAN Statistical Yearbook 2008.* http://archive.asean.org/Publication-ASEAN-SYB-2008.pdf.

Asia Foundation. 2008. *The Cost of Moving Goods. Road Transportation, Regulations and Charges in Indonesia.* Jakarta: Asia Foundation. http://asiafoundation.org/resources/pdfs/movinggoodslightenglish.pdf.

BERNAS (Padi Beras Nasional Bhd). http://www.bernas.com.my/.

FAO (Food and Agriculture Organization of the United Nations). 1999. "Compendium on Post-harvest Operations—Rice." http://www.fao.org/inpho/content/compend/text/ch10-01.htm.

Goletti, Francesco. 2002. "Rice Value Chain Study: Vietnam." Report prepared for the World Bank, Agrifood Consulting International/World Bank.

———. 2009. "Economic and Sector Analysis for Agriculture, Rural Development, and Natural Resources Management in Viet Nam in 2009 and 2010 (Phase 1)." Internal Report by Agrifood Consulting International/World Bank.

Hausman, Warren H., Hau L. Lee, Graham R. F. Napier, and Alex Thompson. 2009. "How Enterprises and Trading Partners Gain from Global Trade Management." Stanford University.

Keretho, Somnuk. 2009. "Some Steps towards Paperless Trade: Exportation of Frozen Shrimp and Rice." Paper prepared for the Expert Group Meeting, "Strengthening Partnerships for Development through Enhanced Regional Trade," Advisory Committee, National Single Window/e-Logistics Project, Ministry of Information and Communication Technology, Institute for IT Innovation, Kasetsart University, United Nations Conference Centre, Bangkok, January 21–22.

Meyrick and Associates. 2006. "Vietnam: Multimodal Transport Regulatory Review." Draft final report prepared in association with the Transport Development and Strategy Institute and Carl Broals for the World Bank and the Ministry of Transport, Vietnam. http://www.amchamvietnam.com/download/142/L2Rvd25sb2FkLzE0Mg==.

The Nielsen Company. 2008. "Retail and Shopper Trends Asia Pacific 2008." http://au.nielsen.com/site/documents/ShopperTrends08_AP_report.pdf.

Philippines–Industries–Retail. http://www.businesstrendsasia.com/print.php?cat=64&art=0&page=0.

Rickman, Joseph F. 2002. "Grain Quality from Harvest to Market." Paper presented at the Ninth JIRCAS International Symposium 2002, "Value-Addition to Agricultural Products," 94–98. http://www.jircas.affrc.go.jp/english/publication/annual/2002/98-114.pdf.

Rodrik, Dani. 2007. *One Economics, Many Recipes: Globalization, Institutions and Global Growth*. Princeton, NJ: Princeton University Press.

Timmer, C. Peter. 2008. "Postscript: The Debate over Food Security in 2006—An Update on the Role of BULOG." In *From Parastatals to Private Trade*, ed. Shahidur Rasid, Ashok Gulati, and Ralph Cummings Jr. Baltimore: IFPRI and John Hopkins University Press.

USDA (U.S. Department of Agriculture). 1999. "Upcoming World Trade Organization Negotiations: Issues for the U.S. Rice Sector, Rice Situation and Outlook." ERS/USDA, Washington, DC, November.

World Bank. 2007a. *Connecting to Compete: Trade Logistics in the Global Economy*. Washington, DC: World Bank. http://siteresources.worldbank.org/INTTLF/Resources/lpireport.pdf.

———. 2007b. "Horticultural Producers and Supermarket Development in Indonesia." Report 38543-ID, World Bank Sustainable Development Department, Rural Development Natural Resources and Environment Sector Unit, East Asia and Pacific Region, World Bank, Jakarta.

CHAPTER 4

Doing Business in Rice: Private Sector Potential

When most of the Third World was deeply suspicious of exploitation by western MNCs (multinational corporations), Singapore invited them in. They helped us grow, brought in technology and know-how, and raised productivity levels faster than any alternative strategy could.

— Lee Kuan Yew, November 2005

Introduction

A constant theme in this study is the need to improve efficiency, quality, and reliability in the business of growing, processing, marketing, importing, and exporting rice in Southeast Asia. A corollary premise is that many long-standing government policies of direct and even indirect intervention in the rice sector have become obstacles to progress. Implied but not yet argued at length is the contention that private enterprise could bring new investment and energy to the challenge.

Government policies directly affect the level of risk associated with specific private sector investments. Thus, for example, risks associated with investing in a fixed facility that requires a minimum break-even flow of farm products to operate profitably are linked directly to government policies affecting incentives, to subsidies, or to both, as well as to government procurement policies. Whether the policy environment is favorable or not, investing in agriculture is riskier than in manufacturing simply because of varying climate conditions and logistics costs that are seasonal rather than steady, as well as unreliable information flows up and down supply chains.

This chapter seeks to make the case for improving the investment environment for the Association of Southeast Asian Nations (ASEAN) rice industry. It does so with occasional references to the rapid growth and modernization of the maize sector in the region and the crucial part that private firms have played in that process. But, like the study as a whole, this chapter also recognizes that rice and maize occupy vastly different societal and political space in the five countries studied. Not a new crop—a Javanese myth has rice, maize, and the coconut palm springing to life miraculously and simultaneously (Kahn 1985)—maize goes far more often to feed animals than humans. Rice is the staple around which food security policies have been and still are built.

As long as governments put rice in that context, they will understandably also prefer to rely on their own efforts to ensure adequate, safe, affordable, dependable supplies. The more they maintain that status quo, however, the more inefficiency builds along rice supply chains and the higher are the costs to consumers or taxpayers or to both. Were more responsibility and opportunity transferred to private hands, sometimes in partnerships with government, this chapter argues, losses along the chain would diminish. The resulting increases in supply, moreover, would make it easier to meet food security goals through regional trade.

ASEAN governments welcome private enterprise, including investments by foreign firms, in many strategic areas of their economies: finance, communications, mining, and oil and gas exploration, among others. Private companies are also prominent in such agricultural areas as maize, soybeans, and oilseeds. The low level of foreign investment in regional rice supply chains, however, reflects, more than any other single factor, the high level of risk inherent in a thinly traded market[1] that is subject to frequent and unpredictable government intervention.

Just as the alarmed responses of ASEAN nations to the 2007–08 crisis dramatized such risks, the high costs incurred by governments trying to preclude real or imagined rice shortages have occasioned a serious reconsideration of long-accepted policies. As noted in chapter 1, the countries on which this study focuses formally agreed in February 2009 that they would work to "achieve free flow of goods in ASEAN as one of the principal means to establish a single market and production base for the deeper economic integration of the region... by 2015."[2] Since then, the ASEAN Ministers of Agriculture and Forestry (AMAF)

scheduled the first AMAF-Private Sector dialogue in June 2010,[3] and ASEAN has asked the World Bank to assist in developing a regional regulatory framework for food safety.

This study is meant to broaden understanding of the rice sector, and this chapter seeks to inform discussions of the private sector's presence, problems, and potential within it. The following pages look briefly at the overall business environment in the five study countries as well as at the setting for private investments in milling, marketing, and trading rice. Subsequent sections explore various actual constraints on private sector investing that could stimulate innovation and modernization of processes within rice supply chains. The chapter closes by looking at the dim prospects for advances in structuring rice trading and the to-be-realized benefits of a full and frank, public-private dialogue about the sector's flaws and needs.

Conditions for Doing Business

The degree to which a country's business environment invites or deters private investment has been shown to have a critical effect on triggering and sustaining economic growth. Broadly, not just in agriculture, many developing countries have found that consistent investments in public service delivery allow private companies to realize adequate returns on their own investments (Christy and others 2009). On the other side of the equation, corruption in all of its manifest dimensions translates into a curb on risk taking.

The conditions for doing business in the five study countries vary widely, from some of the world's most conducive for private sector investment to some of the least supportive. In the most recent World Bank survey, *Doing Business 2010*, Thailand and Malaysia stood near the top of the 183 countries surveyed in 2008–09, ranking 12 and 23, respectively.[4] While Vietnam was midway in the listing at 93, Indonesia's position was 122 and, last among the five study countries, the Philippines was 144th (see table 4.1).

With respect to "ease and cost of trading across borders," the entire set of countries fared better. On this basis, Thailand ranked 12, followed by Malaysia (35), Indonesia (45), the Philippines (68), and Vietnam (74). The conclusion that the five countries chosen for this study are relatively good trading partners is reinforced by more detailed survey findings regarding trade facilitation and cross-border transportation. In general, the five study countries appear to have open and friendly borders (figures 4.1 and 4.2).

Finally, close to a third of the executives of private companies already operating in the five study countries told joint World Bank–International

Table 4.1   Doing Business Ranking, Trading across Borders, East Asia and Pacific, 2010

Country	Overall rank	Starting a business	Construction permits	Employing workers	Registering property	Getting credit	Protecting investors	Paying taxes	Trading across borders	Enforcing contracts	Closing a business
Thailand	12	55	13	52	6	71	12	88	12	24	48
Malaysia	23	88	109	61	86	1	4	24	35	59	57
Vietnam	93	116	69	103	40	30	172	147	74	32	127
Indonesia	122	161	61	149	95	113	41	127	45	146	142
Philippines	144	162	111	115	102	127	132	135	68	118	153

Source: World Bank 2010.

Figure 4.1 Doing Business Ranking, Cost to Import/Export, Selected Southeast Asian Countries, 2010

transport cost per ISO container

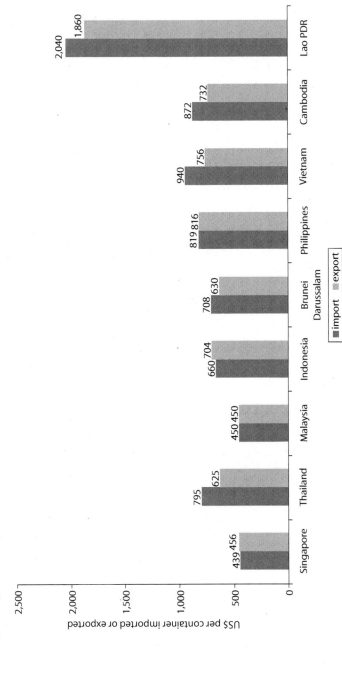

US$ per container imported or exported

■ import ■ export

Source: World Bank 2010.
Note: ISO = International Organization for Standardization; Lao PDR = Lao People's Democratic Republic.

Figure 4.2 Doing Business Ranking, Number of Documents Required to Import/Export, Selected Southeast Asian Countries, 2010

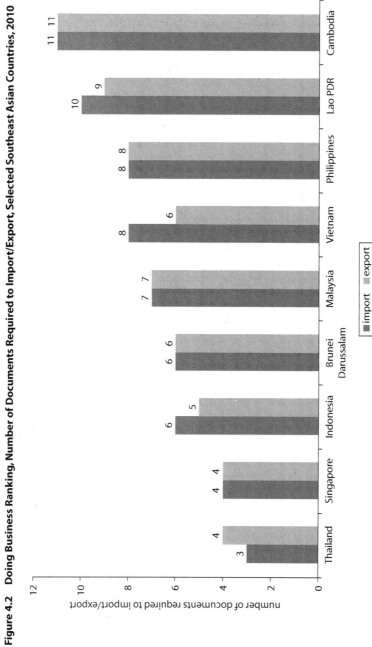

Source: World Bank 2010.
Note: Lao PDR = Lao People's Democratic Republic.

Finance Corporation Enterprise Surveys[5] that they see corruption as the most significant problem their firms have to deal with.

In four of the five countries, corruption stands out as the first or second most mentioned flaw in the business environment. Over a third of Malaysian executives, on the other hand, identified the availability of a trained workforce as their biggest single challenge, twice the proportion who identified corruption and crime constraints. Some 50 percent of Malaysian companies offer formal training to their workforces. In Thailand, the leader by most measures in ease-of-doing-business rankings, private firms put corruption, high tax rates, and poor administration at the head of the problems they listed.

Businesses surveyed in 2010 praised Vietnam's administration of its macroeconomy and its increasing openness to investment and trade, but at the same time reported continuing weaknesses in terms of infrastructure, protection of intellectual property, capacity to access foreign currencies, and administrative service quality. While Vietnam's infrastructure remained the biggest obstacle for both local and foreign enterprises, fully 67.2 percent of firms acknowledged making informal payments to public officials "to get things done." An even higher percentage of firms expected to give gifts when meeting tax officials (79 percent), and 40 percent explained that they expected to give gifts to officials in order to secure a government contract. Most of this corruption appears to be petty, however, since only 15 percent of companies surveyed identified corruption as a major constraint to their growth.

Foreign investors consider the overall business environment in Indonesia and the Philippines the least attractive among the study countries, in all of which, however, local and national investors are routinely better treated than firms from abroad. As for corruption, 42 percent of Indonesian managers surveyed in 2003 and 22 percent of their Filipino counterparts in 2009 named corruption as a major constraint. Fully 44 percent of companies surveyed in Indonesia (and 18.6 percent in the Philippines) admitted that they expected to make informal payments to public officials, and 11.2 percent (21.8 percent in the Philippines) conceded that they expected to provide gifts in meetings with tax officials.

Rice Sector Environment: Milling, Marketing, and Monopolies

Corruption, although the most often named business environment problem generally, is not a major issue in the rice sector. Nor, except for inter-island trade in the Philippine and Indonesian archipelagos, is infrastructure.

Instead, the highest barriers grow from government policies that block markets from setting prices, limit private firms' participation in cross-border trade, and give preferred status to parastatal organizations even when, as in Malaysia, they have been privatized.[6]

Thailand too, though unquestionably the most open to private investment of the five countries studied and the largest rice exporter among them, engages in practices that leave private firms on the sidelines. In 2009, for example, government-to-government export sales continued to be negotiated, leaving little scope for private exporters to win contracts except those engaging them to supply state-owned enterprises (SOEs). The biggest difficulty that private sector participants in Thailand face is that state intervention in local markets has limited supplies available for export.

Rice Milling

A summary look at conditions in the milling industry of the five study countries shows that from the one where mills are most numerous to the one with the fewest mills, government policies directly or otherwise shape the industry's organization. In many instances, those policies aim at maintaining control and stability in the sector instead of freeing market forces to promote efficiency through modernization and economies of scale through consolidation where that option exists. Such a status quo approach in effect leaves a significant number of private millers in the region to make do with outmoded equipment and to cope when government decisions, sometimes on short notice, overturn their business planning and financial outlook. The annex to chapter 1 (table 1A.1 a and d) documents the growth in both their output and in regional consumption of milled rice since the early years of the Green Revolution.

The situation of millers in **Indonesia** illustrates the practices and their effects. The 110,000 small-scale private millers generally operate antiquated, poorly maintained machinery. Moreover, it remains difficult for private firms to contract with farmers to supply specialized varieties and qualities when government-set prices can make such agreements unprofitable for one partner or another.

Vietnam's milling industry is also characterized by extremely small-scale operations, with as many as 300,000 mills handling about 36 million tons of rice a year. Most of the mills are private, but SOEs are prominent in the sector, accounting for fully 60 percent of milling value added. Buying from mostly private dehuskers, the public mills polish the dehusked rice and sell it into wholesale markets. The separation of dehusking and polishing is blamed for a significant part of the high losses that typically occur in the milling process.

Although a good deal of consolidation and ownership restructuring is under way within the sector,[7] the Vietnam Food Association (VFA) maintains control over the rice industry. It intervenes through the minimum floor prices it sets for farmers, through pressure on millers to purchase rice at times of surplus, and through its allocation of export quotas among roughly 100 large traders, many of them SOEs. As a result of government mandates, millers are frequently forced to build up stocks beyond their normal requirements. Unsold, these stocks absorb high moisture levels, with the result that the millers must absorb the costs of remilling and repolishing every few months to keep their inventories saleable.

Next in order of descending number of mills is the fragmented industry in **the Philippines**, where there are only a few large-scale processors among the estimated 10,000 private millers. Faced with competition from the National Food Authority, their firms cannot obtain sufficient rice near their factories, and even where they have invested in modern milling equipment and steam polishers,[8] they cannot operate them profitably because of overcapacity. Technologically challenged, private millers are at a competitive disadvantage in responding to changes in demand, particularly from supermarkets and other high-end food outlets that are beginning to have an impact on the national market.

The approximately 1,000 millers of **Thailand** maintain high standards in a mature and stable setting. Even they, however, suffered—one or two went bankrupt—in 2008 when, having agreed to one-month future delivery contracts, they could not find paddy at a reasonable price to cover their obligations. Prices had skyrocketed, and government intervention attracted much of the remaining supply. Learning caution from that experience, exporters consider it too risky to sell forward and now prefer to buy before they write contracts. In these circumstances, millers may have to store their own output longer than usual and at higher cost.

Finally, of the 231 mills of **Malaysia**, 40 are owned by a single company, BERNAS (Padi Beras Nasional Bhd.) which produces roughly one fifth of the country's total output. Charged also with stabilizing both rice supplies and prices and enjoying a recently renewed monopoly on importing, the former parastatal regulates the rice industry it dominates. The company has also effectively integrated backward into the provision of rice seed stock and forward into wholesale and retail sales. In this way, it has formed the most vertically integrated rice chain in the region. In any contest with smaller private millers, BERNAS can set the pace of modernization in the sector, but its size and power could also tilt the competitive table too far in its own direction.

In summary, in Indonesia, the Philippines, and Vietnam, many private firms use mostly old and sometimes outdated milling equipment. Resulting inefficiencies are high; rice quality tends to be low, as does paddy-maize conversion rates; modernization is slow. Integrated milling, dehusking, and polishing facilities in one factory (from paddy to white rice) are still scarce in ASEAN but are becoming more popular in Vietnam, whereas most Thai mills are already integrated in this way.

Marketing Rice

Public policies have little or no direct impact on the varying patterns of retail and wholesale distribution of rice in the five countries. As in the milling sector, what does matter is the degree to which those policies act indirectly to encourage or discourage the spread of modern food retailing. Although supermarkets and similar outlets are becoming increasingly common in the region, their penetration corresponds more to the presence of high-income consumers than to government support for investments in modernizing and diversifying rice supply chains so as to enable them to produce reliably high-quality rice worth packaging and branding differentially (see table 4.2).[9]

It appears from table 4.2 and other measurements that where urban incomes are low, so is the incidence of modern retailing and of such merchandising in rice markets. That said, the beneficial effects that modern retail management methods have on product differentiation, branding, product quality controls, reductions in inventory shrinkage, and loss of in-channel inventory (including damage to the packaged product, pilferage, and insect and pest infestation) are beginning to be felt in all five countries. Increasingly sophisticated consumer demand is making a difference in rice supply chains with little regard to the influence of official policies on processing and pricing.

Modern supermarket chains and convenience stores have made their deepest penetration in **Thailand**, registering a significant impact on their suppliers and generally raising the bar on supply-channel management methods. The Rice Packers Association, an industry group, negotiates with individual retail chains on behalf of its miller and packer members, while the government Quality Control Board regulates packaging, labeling, product safety, and label integrity. In merchandising in Thailand, a power struggle is already under way between packagers through their association and emerging supermarket chains.

Table 4.2 The State of Modern Rice Merchandising in the Five ASEAN Study Countries

Country	Supermarket penetration of national food markets (top five food companies, %)	Supermarket and "modern retail" penetration of rice market (%)	Modes of backward linkage from supermarkets to rice millers	Number of rice brands stocked by leading supermarket chains
Indonesia	7.8	10.0	Retail branding and own-branding by leading distributors. Branding <10% of total rice sales in Indonesia.	House brand plus 7–10 other brands. Pack size 5, 10, 20 kg.
Malaysia	15.7	60.0	House brand and branded supplies from wholesalers with own mills.	House brand plus up to 40 brands from up to 6 suppliers (each supplier has a few brands for different types of rice— calrose, basmati, fragrant, parboiled, glutinous, specialty, and local rice). Pack size 1, 2, 5, 10 kg.
Philippines	20.4	—	Branded or house brand products supplied by leading millers; in-store unbranded packing.	Convenience stores. 1–2 supermarket brands.
Thailand	31.1	45.0	Branded products from major distributors. House brand products from mills.	20+
Vietnam	20.5	—	Limited branding by VINAFOOD1.	Most rice is unbranded.

Source: Authors' compilations.
Note: VINAFOOD1 =Northern Food Corporation (Vietnam); — = not available; kg = kilogram.

In *Malaysia* too, rice merchandisers are merging and consolidating in an effort to form stable supply chains from production to consumption. Wholesalers have been buying up millers, and vice versa. Wholesalers have also been attempting to develop long-term relationships with supermarkets and hypermarkets, and a number of large trading groups have emerged—again, without government acting as a midwife to the process.

The wholesale sector of *Vietnam* is entirely in private hands. Specialist retailers, very few of which are supermarkets, purchase rice in wholesale markets and resell it in local neighborhoods or villages, typically providing as many as 20 different grades and varieties. There has not been much retail branding of rice to date. However, in the north of the country, the VINAFOOD1 (Northern Food Corporation) is beginning to supply convenience stores and supermarkets with special quality prepacked and branded rice.

Similarly, in *Indonesia*, traditional merchandising structures of cascading wholesale and retail distribution remain dominant, with millers and traders supplying wholesalers operating in large markets within the main cities. They, in turn, supply retailers and may on occasion have the capacity to move rice into areas where shortages have raised the price of rice. Considerable competitive activity exists within the supermarket sector, which department stores have recently entered and where minimarkets and discount retailers are attracting lower- to middle-income consumers from both supermarkets and traditional outlets. One market entry strategy involves the incentive offer of packaged rice products.

Retail food distribution modernization is also taking place in *the Philippines*, where supermarket chains are rapidly increasing their rice sales and, thus, their potential backward influence on the entire supply channel within the country. Still, most rice reaches consumers through local shops specializing in rice. In a setting of intense price competition, wholesalers even provide credit in the form of prepaid purchases to millers and trade credits to retailers, activity that government normally only watches from the sidelines.

While the growth in supermarkets and convenience stores is a common feature throughout the five countries, many features of national rice markets differ significantly. Quality maintenance within channels, product differentiation, and levels of supply-chain losses vary. The quality of rice available at the retail level tends to be higher in Thailand and Malaysia where distribution also tends to be more structured and consolidated, with a relatively small number of firms involved in wholesale distribution, compared to the other countries. Given the reluctance of supermarkets to deal with many small suppliers, such consolidation is likely to occur throughout the region as supermarkets gain increasing importance as retailers of rice.

Importing and Exporting Rice[10]

The private sector is excluded from importing in the Philippines, is represented by a single, former parastatal with a monopoly on imports in Malaysia, and is only provisionally allowed a marginal role in Indonesia, importing specialty rices, such as sticky rice, a variety for diabetics, and rice types needed for Indian and Japanese restaurants. Government policy in those countries does not so much interfere with would-be private importers as it denies them any influential trading role.

Private exporters in Vietnam also have limited scope, accounting for only an estimated 10 percent of total exports. The VFA, which sets minimum export prices and limits export rights under a national quota, stopped accepting registrations for rice export contracts in February 2009 and then reversed itself in May and issued new rules in October effectively reducing the number of companies that could qualify to export. Such stop-and-go export permissions marginalize private exporters. Furthermore, these exporters stop buying from millers and traders when they cannot sell rice abroad at a price higher than the VFA minimum. In such cases, their collective withdrawal from the local market creates inventory surpluses, which drive down prices and, consequently, profits for private farmers, processors, and wholesalers.

Only in Thailand's export industry are private firms operating so vigorously that the industry is reportedly becoming increasingly concentrated, with the top 25 companies accounting for around 90 percent of sales. Some large firms are said to be considering expanding their own milling facilities to ensure quality control. At the same time, some smaller mills are beginning to export directly, apparently because the owners' children, having studied and learned foreign languages abroad, are keen to carry out overseas transactions. All exporters, though, still face some risk that the government, which hinted at but did not impose export restrictions in 2008–09 and continued in 2009 to negotiate government-to-government export deals, could interfere with trade more dramatically in a future crisis.

Parastatals versus Private Initiative

As already discussed, governments in the region that accord wide-ranging regulatory support to parastatals (and, in Malaysia, to the privatized successor) do not provide a "level playing field" for domestic markets (Rashid, Gulati, and Cummings 2008). It is worth briefly recalling examples of such interventions during the 2007–08 food crisis:

• The establishment of what was effectively a minimum farmer price in Thailand that significantly exceeded prevailing market prices and the government's consequent reluctance to release accumulated stocks for export at a loss
• Setting minimum buying prices in Vietnam, backed up by minimum export prices and export licensing, together with favorable interest rates applied to state bodies
• The sale of rice by the parastatal in the Philippines at prices that the private sector found uncompetitive
• Interstate restrictions on the movement of paddy and rice in Malaysia

Such long-standing policies that skew competition in favor of state enterprises are summarized country by country in following text and given more extensive treatment in the case studies following the conclusion to this work. Box 4.1 presents the case of a market where governments have kept interventions to a minimum.

Financing Supply-Chain Modernization

If rice supply chains in the five ASEAN nations studied are to gain in efficiency, curb losses, and produce enough quality grain of diverse varieties to build a strong base for the growth of open regional trade, they will need new milling equipment, more modern storage technology and facilities, and more reliable transport. All of those necessary improvements will require financing, which is less likely to come from government programs than, under the right conditions, from private investors.

In all the countries studied, larger companies report having fewer problems in obtaining short-term credit to cover operating costs than smaller ones. Such companies as mini- and local millers face greater problems in accessing finance than larger ones. Normally paying cash for their purchases from farmers or paddy traders, they have the advantage of providing immediate payment and of being able, as well, to respond with agility to local conditions. Still, they often must wait 30 days or more for payment from their own customers, after milling has been completed and shipments made.

Box 4.1

The Status of Maize in the Region's Agriculture

Not a staple in traditional Asian diets, maize has become popular thanks to booming regional demand for livestock and poultry feed and energizing private sector investment. Beyond supplying important help in disseminating hybrid seeds and know-how to maize farmers, governments have kept interventions to a minimum. Private companies, national and foreign, have been the agents transforming the maize business by financing and managing modern, integrated supply chains.

Total maize output in the four producing countries (Malaysia is not a producer) expanded by 45 percent in the first decade of this century, compared to average annual growth rates of roughly 33 percent from the 1960s through the 1990s. Production more than doubled in Vietnam, where maize imports skyrocketed 14-fold (admittedly from very low beginnings and still only one seventh of production) as the country's meat, poultry, and aquaculture exports swelled. The annex to chapter 1 (table 1A.2 a and c) shows the growth in maize production and imports over the last half-century.

Private Sector Presence. In all the study countries, growth also mirrored rising domestic demand for pork, beef, fish, and chicken. Homegrown consumer appetites, to cite one example, were strong enough in Indonesia that consumption of chicken feed—one fourth of it coming from maize—increased at an annual rate of 8.3 percent between 2005 and 2009. In Malaysia, which imports most of the maize processed by about 70 animal feed companies, including U.S. and Thai multinational corporations, industry sales grew at an annual 14 percent rate from 2004 to 2009.

Vietnam's domestic consumption of meat and fish has increased greatly. Of the firms operating approximately 180 animal feed mills in Vietnam, 15 large multinationals—including Cargill (United States), Cheil Jedang Group (Korea), Charoen Pokphand (CP) Group (Thailand), New Hope (China), Proconco (France), and TTC (Taiwan, China)—together produce approximately 50 percent of the animal feed consumed in the country. So much new investment has entered the feed industry over the past three years that some participants are concerned that the industry may have overbuilt.

Domestic production in Thailand actually declined slightly over the decade as imports expanded more than fourfold to meet the needs of an industry with $4.5 billion in sales in 2008. One of the government's stated agri-industry

(continued next page)

Box 4.1 *(continued)*

development objectives is to make Thailand the center for the animal feed industry in Asia and the Pacific. Two giant Thai firms, CP and Betagro, are integrated backward and forward as chicken and pork farm franchisors and food retailers, with some 4 million tons of processing capacity shared almost equally between them. CP entered the animal feed business from the seed distribution business in the 1970s and now maintains a market presence all over the region. It has animal feed operations in Singapore and India; animal feed and livestock farming operations in Malaysia and Vietnam; and animal feed, livestock farming, shrimp farming, and integrated broiler operations in Indonesia. CP has also integrated forward into the food retailing business. Its subsidiary, CP Seven Eleven, is the largest convenience store operator in Thailand, with 4,030 stores. In addition, CP operates 79 Lotus Super Center supermarkets in China.

In the Philippines, as well, foreign companies are prominent among the top 10 (out of 70) animal feed businesses. The largest companies involved in the industry are San Miguel Corporation, the Philippines' largest corporation, with animal feed operations that account for 25 percent of production capacity. Among its competitors are Cargill Philippines (14 percent), Swift Foods (13 percent), General Milling Corporation (12 percent), and Vitarich (11 percent).

Representing fully 54 percent of the 6 million tons used for animal feed in the Philippines, maize has gained strategic importance for the government because of the larger, faster-growing, and higher value–generating livestock industry that it supports. More involved in the sector than their regional counterparts, Philippine authorities plan to offer enhanced incentives for private investment in aquaculture, poultry product processing, dairy, and other forms of meat production. By fostering long-term partnerships between chain integrators and farm-level organizations, the program would encourage processing facilities and distribution channel investments.

That level of public intervention in the maize industry is somewhat unusual in the region. According to data issued by the U.S. Department of Agriculture, no ASEAN country has undertaken domestic spending on maize above 5 percent of the value of production. Not only do Asian maize farmers generally have little political influence, but the need for market intervention, such as price supports, in the sector is also limited. Maize prices have been relatively stable and generally increasing, reflecting the increasing value of maize in the region to the rapidly growing livestock sectors.

(continued next page)

Box 4.1 *(continued)*

Weak Links. Although many grain collectors in Thailand contract with farmers for their maize crop, that stabilizing practice is not widespread in the other producing countries studied. In vertically integrated supply chains, some large feed companies manage their own commercial farming operations and even sell hybrid seed and fertilizer to farmers while marketing poultry and meat products.

At the lowest production level, however, the technology that could reduce physical and quality losses in the drying process and in protecting stored maize from insect and rodent attacks has not reached most smallholder farms. As a result, at a conservative estimate, the region may be losing 15 percent of the value of maize production.[a]

These losses result in lower returns to farmers, higher prices for consumers, and greater pressure on the environment because of lower production efficiencies. In this respect, if few others, ASEAN maize and rice supply share similar problems.

Source: Study Team.
Note: The maize market within the region is primarily related to the livestock sector. Yellow maize is a primary feedstock for animal products. Human consumption of white maize is marginal.
a. Food and Agriculture Organization (FAO) of the United Nations, Compendium on Post-Harvest Operations. http://www.fao.org/inpho/content/compend/text/ch23_03.htm.

Such a pattern of financing, however, weakens efforts to strengthen supply chains and can be counterproductive. In Vietnam, for instance, private companies expressed concern that SOEs enjoy preferential access to loans over private firms. In Indonesia, Malaysia, and Thailand, well-established private companies are generally able to secure loans from their banks, either solely on the basis of their reputations or, in the case of Indonesia and Thailand, by committing stocks held in their own ware-houses as collateral. In the Philippines, however, private companies in the rice trading and milling business have recently experienced difficulty in obtaining working capital loans. Small-scale millers and traders in the Philippines, for example, reportedly prefer to borrow working capital from moneylenders, despite higher interest rates, because these transactions avoid complicated paperwork (Dawe and others 2008).

As for the kind of investment capital needed to create or upgrade fixed assets, many companies prefer to use their own cash rather than bank loans for supply-chain infrastructure investments, arguing that returns do not compensate for the rates of interest that banks charge. In practice, that tendency limits the growth of fixed assets and poses a significant constraint to rice supply-chain development and consolidation. It reflects, in part, the risk that banks perceive to exist with long-term investment in the sector, as well as the low margins that prevail.

Financial resources and the responsiveness of the financial sector to the unique problems facing agribusinesses vary from country to country, as illustrated in summary form in the following pages.

In **Indonesia**, large rice mills are able to borrow short-term funds from banks for operating capital, but, as in other countries, banks are reluctant to lend and millers are unwilling to borrow for long-term investments. Millers prefer to use family or company resources for this purpose. According to one large miller, it would take 15 years to achieve a return on infrastructure investment at 2009 interest rates of around 13 percent. Although the millers' association has an active program to promote the use of improved equipment, such upgrading continues to be constrained by banks' reluctance to lend, by the small margins available from rice milling, and by millers' unwillingness to take financial risks.

Lacking collateral and therefore affordable credit, traders have to make do with smaller vehicles than the larger and more efficient ones that better borrowing conditions might let them acquire. Similarly, they are forced to buy and sell smaller lots. A general complaint within the private sector is that banks do not understand agricultural risk and, as a result, are reluctant to lend to that sector.[11]

With operating capital requirements generally higher than in the other countries, millers in **the Philippines** are frequently forced to sell rice quickly, rather than store it to guarantee throughput. To ensure continued operation during the off-season, however, they still need to build up stocks of palay (unmilled rice). In the past they could borrow operating capital with backing from the Quedan and Rural Credit Guarantee Corporation (QUEDANCOR), which also provided welcome risk management services. QUEDANCOR, though, ran into difficulties resulting from misguided loans, not to millers but, often, to politicians. Possibly as a consequence of the corporation's problems, banks reportedly stopped lending against stock to all but their most reliable customers. Previously they would lend up to 50 percent of the value of stored palay, in some cases even without the QUEDANCOR guarantee.

In spite of all these developments, established mills, even relatively small ones, can continue to secure finance for investment and operating capital. They are able to pledge other types of collateral. The main problem faced by the sector is that most of those involved are either not in a position to offer suitable collateral or are reluctant to do so because of the risks associated with their business.

In both **Malaysia** and **Thailand**, established private companies face few major obstacles to financing their operations. Malaysian companies involved in building integrated supply chains (linking wholesalers to millers and to collection centers and contract farmers), as well as companies doing business with BERNAS, are able to secure loans fairly easily and usually without putting up inventory as collateral for credit. Larger Thai exporters, similarly, can easily obtain export finance against letters of credit. Within domestic chains, on the other hand, the weakest participants can face working capital risks. Since supermarkets pay only after 90 days, for example, their suppliers are usually forced to hold three months of stock in order to realize scale economies in buying and milling. This means that they must effectively finance rice inventories for six months. Within the export marketing chain, where exporters and large traders pay their mill suppliers within 30 to 60 days, the latter are often cash-constrained as a result, paying cash to farmers and forced to extend credit to buyers.

In Vietnam, where SOEs enjoy a variety of advantages over the private sector, private traders and millers are at a disadvantage in seeking loans both for investment and operational purposes. As private exporters are subject to export quotas, and SOEs have priority where exporting is concerned, the former have difficulties using their rice stock as collateral for loans. The introduction of new milling equipment seems also to be severely constrained by a lack of credit. Leasing instruments have not been developed, and capital equipment suppliers do not have strong enough balance sheets to provide long-term financing to their potential customers.

To sum up, rice chains in all five study countries are cash-constrained, though to varying degrees, and loans for capital investments are consistently harder to obtain than credit for normal operations. Large-scale and more sophisticated trading companies experience fewer problems in securing external financing than do those that operate further down the chain. To be more precise, participants in rice marketing chains are more likely to seek loans for operating capital than for investment, and banks, which garner little sympathy over their own risk management concerns, are generally criticized for their reluctance to make inventory-secured loans and to price these loans affordably. Additional scope may exist for the development of warehousing and inventory credit programs, such as

QUEDANCOR. However, such programs first need to be investigated and assessed in the context of the particular financing needs of the participants in modernizing rice chains.

Coordinating the Public and Private Sectors

Where supply-chain modernization is the issue, an objective review of investment made in both the rice and maize sectors over the past decade reveals that the most beneficial undertakings have come from collaborative efforts combining the resources and comparative advantages of both the public and private sectors. Notable successes include hybrid maize seed research and its regionwide dissemination. Among the five countries included in this study, these simple lessons appear to be best understood and applied in Malaysia and Thailand, more recently in Vietnam, and more slowly in Indonesia and the Philippines. In assessing the enabling environments that support private sector investment, Malaysia and Thailand consistently outperform the other three countries in maize as well as in rice.

Most of the public-private coordination failures that directly affect food security exist in the rice sector, as already discussed in the analysis of government interventions in the rice market, and illustrated in preceding pages in the inquiry into the conduct of parastatal enterprises. After briefly noting some persistent and widespread, but mistaken, perceptions about the role of the private sector in contributing to food security, the following discussion deals first with the strengths and weaknesses of existing consultative mechanisms whose role, ideally, should be to coordinate the public and private sectors. Finally, the state of market institutions and the possible need to reform them are analyzed in an effort to ensure better coordination through price and delivery mechanisms.

Reconciling Conflicting Perceptions

Perceptions between public and private sector actors differ, and mechanisms for reconciling them have not proven to be effective, at least with respect to rice. Private sector representatives contacted in Indonesia, the Philippines, and Thailand all expressed concern that governments see development in terms of launching new "programs," rather than in terms of creating appropriate enabling environments in which the private sector can function effectively. They argue, with considerable justification, that programs focused on farmers and their organizations have not proved effective for a variety of reasons and that the most successful agricultural development impacts have been delivered by private companies. Selective cases are presented in following text.

Coming at such concerns from a very different angle, many governments question the value that private sector activity brings to food trading and, based on simplistic calculations of differences between buying and selling prices and of the risks involved, can feel that private firms need, at the least, to be carefully watched and probably reined in. Where officials, for instance, believe they detect unscrupulous speculation, rice traders respond by noting that when they assume the risk of storing grain in hopes of a profit, they are saving farmers or the public sector the costs of storage. Farmers are generally ill-equipped to carry out that function reliably, and government bodies generally have a poor track record of maintaining quality during storage. Thus, apart from anything else, storage by the private sector could be considered as making an important contribution to food security.

Still, public officials can move from suspecting speculation to accusing traders of hoarding when, for example, mills must maintain stocks of paddy to have access to raw material to keep operating and wholesalers need to keep large quantities of rice in stock to answer the demands of retailers in a timely, businesslike fashion. Ramos (2000) has found that whenever fluctuations in supplies and prices are noted, both civil society and governments seek to blame marketing agents. In 2008, the underlying suspicion of the private sector resurfaced in the Philippines when mills and wholesale and retail traders in the country were raided and investigated for "hoarding." Because of the raids, rice traders were afraid to carry large stocks, mills lost markets for their output, and farmers harvested palay for which no buyers appeared.

Clearly, it is important that politicians, and the officials who advise them, improve their understanding of the role and functions of the private sector. For their part, private investors might do well to join their sometimes adversarial regulators and competitors to consider creating trading mechanisms that could reduce risk and stabilize supply. Ideally, commodity futures exchanges could serve that dual purpose. Realistically, in the five study countries, opinion tends to run against such institutions.

Trading Mechanisms

Opinion could change. Officials and entrepreneurs could come to see new ways to improve the efficiency with which the rice and maize trade is currently conducted within the region. Substituting structured trade protocols for one-off protocols, for example, could reduce transaction costs.[12] So could relying on third parties to complete transactions and securitize traded inventories in lieu of the quid pro quo exchanges that currently dominate regional food trade. Improving the coverage, accuracy, and timeliness of market information would also significantly reduce uncertainties that breed risk in rice supply-chain operations.

One way to realize gains in all three of these areas simultaneously is by strengthening existing commodity exchanges or developing new futures exchanges. This direct approach to market institutional reform may be neither feasible not appropriate at this time. Other, more tactical approaches are worth considering, however.

At the top of this list should be the development of effective systems for collecting and disseminating real-time market information, which, as previously noted, farmers, rural paddy collectors, and smaller millers generally lack. Collecting and disseminating information is made easier by the fact that the largest volume of regional rice trade currently takes place among a limited number of participants: parastatals and relatively few large exporters.

Attempts by smaller mills in Thailand and emerging companies in Lao People's Democratic Republic, Myanmar, and Vietnam to compete in the export market have not been conspicuously successful in part because existing arrangements, while not monopolistic, keep smaller companies from learning trade and market information in real time. All companies contacted in the region, of whatever size, indicated a need for improved trade information, although there is more concern to get good crop forecasts, particularly concerning likely harvests in Vietnam, than up-to-date price information, which can usually be obtained through business partners. Maize is mainly traded by international companies, which have good access to trade information.

Commodity futures exchanges for rice. In order to operate, most commodity exchanges require generally agreed-upon standards that define commodity grades, terms of assured payment through intermediaries, and other accepted practices that are not currently part of the ASEAN national or regional rice trade. Although various grades are used in domestic markets, usually based on the percentage of brokens, these grades have not yet reached the requisite level of harmonization and sophistication to permit their use for trading without inspection of each sale lot. Even in Thailand, government tenders are based on visual inspection and quid pro quo transfers and not on agreed-upon grades and third-party intermediation.

Agreeing on a set of regional standards for both rice and maize trading would appear to be a priority objective if regional markets are to become better integrated in the near future. Realizing the objective of integration will not be easy when, for example, private exporters believe that governments' power to intervene at any time to influence the market price makes futures trade pointless. Further, the ethnic Chinese traders who carry out most rice business in ASEAN countries have developed good networks of contacts with one another both within countries and between countries. Understandably, they express little enthusiasm for alternative, more formal trading approaches to take the place of their well-established, if informal, practices.

Importantly, the creation of more formal or structured trade also typically requires the development of an institution that defines and enforces trading rules. Several market institutions operate within the region. However, none possesses the necessary qualifications and prerequisites to serve as a basis for rule setting within the regional market. Even the government-owned Agricultural Futures Exchange of Thailand (AFET), while it trades rice among other products, relies on rubber futures for the bulk of its business. The rice-trading protocols and contract terms that the exchange did adopt were premised on having suppliers bid to complete some of the government's tender sales and, after visual inspection and price negotiations, waiting two to three months for the actual transfers to occur. Exporters, however, had concerns over the quality of the rice they bought in this way, and despite AFET assurances, the exchange's involvement in rice futures seemed unlikely to continue once the Paddy Pledging Program discussed earlier wound down.

Buyers, moreover, generally see the rice-trading industry as a low-margin industry that survives based on rapid stock turnover in which AFET intervention would simply slow operations down. Traditionally reliant on a "gentlemen's agreement" to ensure trade security and transaction completion, they also viewed AFET operations as overly complex and involving too much paperwork.

Rice futures exchanges also appear to have dim prospects. In **Indonesia**, a commodity futures exchange does operate but mainly trades in rubber. When large-scale millers and traders discussed the possibility of trading rice on this exchange, however, they concluded there would be no benefit from such activity as long as Badan Urusan Logistik's active intervention precludes significant price fluctuations.

Similarly, in the Philippines, talk within the rice industry of creating a commodity exchange trade in rice or palay appeared to have sprung less from calculations of the broadly distributed benefits of such a market than from a defensive response to complaints by politicians and the media about high rice prices and a lack of transparency. Although some industry participants recognized the political value of an exchange where a clear national price could be set, they and others also acknowledged that the operation of an exchange would require quality and other standards on which agreement is hard to obtain.[13]

In the eyes of traders, issues related to quality, variety, and grade would also appear to inhibit the use of an exchange to promote regional trade. Rice is not traded on world markets as "rice" but as "rice with 5 percent brokens," "rice with 15 percent brokens," "rice with 30 percent brokens," and so on. A significant part of the world market, primarily involving trade with Africa, also involves parboiled rice. Even within the categories defined by the percentage of brokens, significant value differences exist. Thai exporters argue strongly that Thai rice with 15 percent brokens is not the same as Vietnamese rice with 15 percent brokens.

At an FAO-sponsored meeting on the Asian rice trade held in early 2011, a spokesman from the Singapore Mercantile Exchange announced plans to start trading in rice before the end of 2011. Participants at the meeting expressed interest in the possibility of such exchanges in the region. However, they noted that several important issues had yet to be resolved, in particular the issue of multiple grades. There was a need for a Basis Contract (probably Thai 5%), with other grades attracting premiums or discounts. However, some cautioned against having fixed premiums and discounts because they noted that market circumstances frequently changed and there were no fixed price relationships between grades. Others felt that there should be multiple Basis Contracts.

The difficulties that exporters raise with regard to the establishment of a commodity exchange or a futures exchange in the ASEAN region may be valid. At the same time, an element of protecting vested interests may also be at work. The very real difficulties associated with formulating agreed-upon standards may not be insurmountable, as is shown by the Chicago Board of Trade arrangements reported in box 4.2 (it should be noted that these are for "rough rice" or paddy, not white rice). As long as the current system is seen as working well for those now in it, while providing a barrier to new entrants into the trade, its beneficiaries would judge it against their interests to promote or support a new trading system based on structured trade.

Box 4.2

Chicago Board of Trade Contract Specifications for Deliverable Grades for Rice

Rice is traded on the Chicago Board of Trade (CBOT), but to a very limited extent. An average of only 2,000 trades take place each day, compared with 200,000 trades for maize. CBOT contract terms do not address the different qualities traded in the ASEAN area, but they do provide for quality differentiation. This may suggest a direction in which ASEAN could go.

The Chicago Board standard for U.S. No. 2 specifies the following:

U.S. No. 2 or better long grain rough rice with a total milling yield of not less than 65% including head rice of not less than 48%. Premiums and discounts are provided for each percent of head rice over or below 55%, and for each percent of broken rice over or below 15%. No heat-damaged kernels are permitted in a 500-gram sample and no stained kernels are permitted in a 500-gram sample. A maximum of 75 lightly discolored kernels are permitted in a 500-gram sample.

Source: Andrew Shepherd for this study.

In summary, the very tentative discussions within the rice private sector regarding the possible establishment of futures exchanges in the region seem not just premature but also fruitless. As long as government interventions can set prices and most traders are content with the informal status quo, the difficulty of setting clear standards is the icing on a cake that will not rise. For their part, officials are concerned about possible food security implications if rice futures were to attract too much speculative interest. Since progress depends on full consultation with private sector traders who can hardly be expected to greet enthusiastically new measures that might attract new competitors, the future of futures exchanges as a structured-trade mechanism is doubtful, to put it mildly.

Consultative Mechanisms

With commodity exchanges not in prospect, there may be a larger opening for consultation between concerned private and public entities about resetting government priorities and thus finding a joint approach to easing constraints on private investors. The private sectors of the Philippines and Thailand are particularly concerned about the way in which their governments tend to respond to food availability and price issues. They argue that instead of relying on the market to resolve difficulties, governments should provide funds for "development" projects, which the private sector judges to be rarely sustainable because they are both inconsistent with market realities and likely to promote both national and local rent seeking. There is a general recognition by those in the rice industry of the need to improve public-private communication, but that understanding has yet to prompt stronger private sector efforts to promote an improved dialogue.

Indonesia has a Food Security Council set up by a government regulation and within it working groups consisting of the private sector, technical experts (including academics), and civil society organizations. Although there has not been a thorough evaluation of the effectiveness of these working groups, they do play important roles in facilitating communication among stakeholders of the rice industry. According to respondents for this study, this had led to improved relations among stakeholders.

In *Malaysia*, consultation remains ad hoc. The Ministry of Agriculture and Agro-based Industry holds meetings irregularly with the associations of farmers, millers, and retailers at both the national and state levels. These take place whenever major policy changes are to be made that affect the industry or when crises arise. After the practice of flat-rate deductions at the time of farmer deliveries attracted much controversy, the Malaysian Institute of Economic Research (MIER) was commissioned by the government to study that issue and the crisis-period effectiveness of the government's National Food Security Policy of 2008. It organized focus group meetings to seek input. At separate sessions, farmers, seed producers and mechanization service providers, millers, wholesalers, and retailers aired their concerns, while government officials conferred apart at a different time. While there appears to be no formal multistakeholder body for the rice sector in Malaysia at this time, there was a previous proposal to form a Malaysian Rice Supply Chain Council involving both the public and private sectors and fashioned along the lines of the Malaysian Business Council, with a strong independent Secretariat. This proposal was being resuscitated in 2009 and built upon by the ongoing MIER study.

The Philippines rice industry tried to establish an association that embraced the entire chain, including farmer representatives. It was known as the Alliance of Grains Stakeholders of the Philippines and aimed to promote industry coordination, with a particular emphasis on increasing profitability for farmers. However, the rice millers' association did not join, and the embryonic association appears to have quickly folded.

The government of **Thailand** established a Rice Policy Committee, chaired by the prime minister. Industry stakeholders participate only in subcommittees, and the subcommittee chairs, who are politicians, sit on the main committees. The subcommittees cover production, marketing, paddy pledging, stock release, provincial matters, price guarantees, and auditing. The subcommittees were primarily designed to provide the government with advice on specific problems related to the Paddy Pledging Program and have not functioned as a general forum for discussion of industrywide issues. Members of the subcommittees are industry associations, including the exporters' association, said to be the oldest association of any type in Thailand; the millers' association; the rice packers' association; and representatives of farmers and traders. The millers' association has alleged that the associations representing large exporters and large domestic packers have dominated the discussions and that their own perspectives have not been fully considered. In any event, no formal ongoing consultative mechanism exists, and the proposals for government intervention announced in mid-2009 to replace the Paddy Pledging Program with a price insurance scheme were apparently implemented without industry consultation.

In conclusion, it appears clear that formal consultative arrangements between governments and their rice private sectors are conspicuous by their absence, not least because few mechanisms currently exist to allow the private sector to speak with one voice in its dealings with government. The consultations that do occur are carried out with each individual stage of the chain (millers, wholesalers, exporters) rather than with bodies representing the entire industry.

Conclusions and Recommendations

In the long run, efficient grain marketing and trade can be guaranteed only by having a strong private sector. In formulating policies, particularly for rice, governments therefore need to give greater attention to the impact of policy on the functioning of the private sector and on its ability to provide efficient, long-term services for both farmers and consumers.

For the present, the private sector sees government policies in a number of areas as binding constraints that prohibit their further investment in efficient supply chains, competitive markets, and improved sector productivity. Significantly, these constraints also correspond to areas where the private sector lacks capacity to act in its own interest or to implement changes without outside assistance.

The most significant of these constraints are the result either of the underinvestment of government funds in public goods or, conversely, the overinvestment of government funds in private goods that compete with those goods that private sector companies could and would provide in greater volume if appropriate incentives existed. A "zero-based" reexamination of the respective roles reserved for public and private investment and development of the rice sectors could begin the overdue process of reform. Coordinating development efforts, initially by strengthening institutions that can facilitate coordination, establish market rules, and disseminate market information, while now unlikely, should get some fresh impetus from such a thoroughgoing reconsideration of the status quo.

Transforming the policy discourse requires discussions with private sector companies about what they view as broken within existing chains and how best to go about fixing specific management problems with public, private, or combined public-private resources. For this, appropriate consultative mechanisms are required.

The fundamental need, though, is to engineer a shift away from traditional government rice sector policies that, if once pragmatic, have over time become ideological and politicized toward policies that focus on practical problems and that enlist for their solution the specialized competencies that only the private sector possesses. Such a shift could usefully begin by bringing rice sector stakeholders together in an open dialogue with the private sector participants responsible for creating efficient, precise, and adaptable maize supply chains in the region.

Notes

This report was prepared by the Study Team, drawing on preliminary studies and field research conducted by Francesco Goletti of Agrifood Consulting International, Inc. (ACI). It was based on two missions conducted by ACI to the five countries, a review of selected literature and data, and interviews with key informants. The study was conducted over a 60-day period between September 2009 and January 2010, including a first mission to Indonesia, Malaysia, the Philippines, Thailand, and Vietnam in September–October 2009 and a second mission in January 2010. Given the limited time and resources available for the study, only few key informants could be contacted in each country, and no systematic surveys could be undertaken. The second main source is a draft prepared by Andrew W. Shepherd, senior marketing officer, Market Linkages and Value Chains Group, the Food and Agriculture Organization (FAO) of the United Nations, Rome, as well as case studies prepared by Bustanul Arifin (Indonesia), Larry Wong (Malaysia), and ACI (Vietnam). Fieldwork was conducted in Thailand and the Philippines in July 2009 and in the remaining countries in September–October 2009. The assistance provided to Andrew Shepherd in Thailand by Juejan Tangtermthong and in Rome by Maja Rueegg is gratefully acknowledged. Comments received on earlier drafts from David Dawe of FAO and the case study authors proved very helpful.

1. Only 2,000 trades for rice occur daily, on average, on the Chicago Board of Trade, compared to 220,000 trades for maize.

2. ASEAN Trade in Goods Agreement. http://www.aseansec.org/22223.pdf.

3. More information is available at http://aseanfoodsecurity.wordpress.com/.

4. The Doing Business Project was launched in 2002. The first *Doing Business* report, published in 2003, covered 5 indicator sets and 133 economies. The 2010 report covers 11 indicator sets and 183 economies. http://www.doing business.org/about-us.

5. "An Enterprise Survey is a firm-level survey of a representative sample of an economy's private sector, covering a broad range of business environment topics including access to finance, corruption, infrastructure, crime, competition, and performance measures." https://rru.worldbank.org/ Methodology/.

6. BERNAS (Padi Beras Nasional Bhd.), a privatized firm since 1996 but still the government's partner in managing the rice sector, was due to lose its monopoly on rice imports at the beginning of 2011. Instead, the monopoly was extended until 2021. http://biz.thestar.com.my/news/story.asp?file=/ 2011/5/2/business/8582022&sec=business.

7. In addition to experiments in subcontracting and vertical realignment, joint ownership with farm cooperatives is even taking over milling facilities. Some mills, including ones owned at the municipal, provincial, and national levels, are being privatized.

8. Although an estimated 10 percent of mills have been upgraded to a reasonable standard, the equipment in the remainder is said to be antiquated.

9. This having been said, it is true that rice still represents less than 1 percent of supermarket throughput.

10. The annex to chapter 1 (table 1A.1 b, c, and d) shows how both imports and exports have grown in the region over the last half-century and, notably, how patterns shifted in the food crisis years of 2007–08 and 2008–09.

11. Such views are not unique to Indonesia. The usual response of banks is that a high proportion of bad debts originate in the agricultural sector.

12. *Structured trade* refers to rule-based trading in which the terms of sales agreements, collateral transport service contacts, and trade financial contracts are compatible with one another and are all based on terms and conditions that are generally agreed-upon within a trade or sector. Structured trade implies the creation and operation of an authority such as a regional commodity exchange that traders would recognize as the appropriate authority for setting rules covering each and every transaction.

13. Unless the exchange is based on samples, such as that in Mandalay, Myanmar, standard setting is unlikely to be practical in most places.

References and Other Sources

ASEAN (Association of Southeast Asian Nations). 2009. *ASEAN Trade in Goods Agreement.* http://www.aseansec.org/22223.pdf.

Christy, Ralph, Edward Mabaya, Norbert Wilson, Emelly Mutambatsere, and Nomathemba Mhlanga. 2009. "Enabling Environments for Competitive Agro-industries." In *Agro-industries for Development*, ed. Carlos Da Silva, Doyle Baker, Andrew W. Shepherd, Chakib Jenane, and Sergio Miranda-da-Cruz, 136–85. Wallingford, U.K.: Centre for Agricultural Bioscience International, in association with the Food and Agricultural Organization (FAO) of the United Nations and United Nations Industrial Development Organization (UNIDO). http://www.fao.org/docrep/013/i0157e/i0157e00.pdf.

Dawe, David C., Piedad F. Moya, Cheryll B. Casiwan, and Jesusa M. Cabling. 2008. "Rice Marketing Systems in the Philippines and Thailand: Do Large Numbers of Competitive Traders Ensure Good Performance?" *Food Policy* 33 (5): 455–63.

FAO (Food and Agriculture Organization of the United Nations). 1999. "Compendium on Post-harvest Operations—Rice." http://www.fao.org/inpho/content/compend/text/ch10-01.htm.

Kahn, Ely J. 1985. *The Staffs of Life.* Boston: Little, Brown.

Ramos, Charmaine G. 2000. *State Intervention and Private Sector Participation in Philippine Rice Marketing.* Quezon City, the Philippines: MODE (Management and Organizational Development for Empowerment) and Southeast Asian Council for Food Security and Fair Trade. http://www.mode.org/pdf/State%20intervention%20and%20private%20sector%20participation%20in%20philippine%20rice%20market.pdf.

Rashid, Shahidur, Ashok Gulati, and Ralph Cummings Jr. 2008. "Learning New Ways of Doing Business." In *From Parastatals to Private Trade*, ed. Shahidur

Rashid, Ashok Gulati, and Ralph Cummings Jr. Baltimore: International Food Policy Research Institute and John Hopkins University Press.

The Star Online. 2011. "Agreement on Monopoly of Rice Imports Extended amid Rising Food Prices." May 2. http://biz.thestar.com.my/news/story.asp?file=/2011/5/2/business/8582022&sec=business.

World Bank. 2010. *Doing Business 2010: Reforming through Difficult Times.* Washington, DC: World Bank. http://www.doingbusiness.org/reports/doing business/doing-business-2010.

CHAPTER 5

Conclusions and Recommendations

ASEAN . . . could marshal the still untapped potentials of this rich region through more substantial united action.

—Narciso Ramos, August 1967

Introduction

This book challenges policy makers who oversee the rice sector in the Association of Southeast Asian Nations (ASEAN) region to reexamine deep-rooted precepts about their responsibilities. As an essential first step, it calls on them to redefine food security. Fixating on national self-sufficiency has been costly and counterproductive. In its stead, coordination and cooperation can both improve rice production at home and structure expanding regional trade.

To enhance regional food security through quantitative and qualitative gains in rice production, policy makers cannot rely on government programs. They need to enlist private investors both as entrepreneurs and as partners who can bring capital, energy, modern technology, and experienced management into sustained efforts to reduce losses and heighten efficiency in supply chains.

The study's findings make it clear that current rice sector policies are not achieving the desired goals. Its examination of the 2007–08 food crisis found, in fact, that government policies and panicky responses were the primary factors behind soaring (and later diminishing) rice prices at the time. Those policies vary, but they share a common premise: food security depends, first of all, on self-sufficiency in rice. That premise has driven government intervention for decades, and unpredictable government intervention, in turn, has helped make the rice sector too risky to attract significant private investment.

Rice is a thinly traded commodity, a reality that also heightens risk, but the volatility of rice prices stems from misguided government responses to both real and, in 2007–08, only apparent shortages. In such circumstances, private entrepreneurs naturally limit their involvement in order to minimize risk.

Domestic and foreign private companies that have modernized maize supply chains in the ASEAN region could, in theory, bring their focus on efficiency and capacity for innovation to the growing, processing, and marketing of rice. In practice, they stay on the sidelines of the rice industry.

This book has explained why. This concluding chapter suggests measures that could encourage private investors to reconsider that reluctance.

Following a summary of the study's conclusions, the chapter examines steps that governments could take to better the investment environment for rice production and distribution. Among the proposals are specific, new forms of public-private partnership (PPP) and measures to advance trade coordination. The final section recommends potential roles for ASEAN and for multilateral development partners in strengthening regional food markets. A detailed Agenda for Action in improving the investment environment, strengthening supply-chain links, and promoting regional trade coordination is presented after the notes to this chapter.

Summary of Conclusions

Lessons of the Food Crisis

During the food crisis of 2007–08, traditional food security programs dictated the actions that the major rice-importing and rice-exporting countries either took or failed to take. Originally designed to pursue multiple and sometimes conflicting objectives, none of these programs emphasized strengthening farm-to-market supply chains. Some, originating in the Green Revolution era, did work to help farmers improve production. Others, which subsidized rice distribution to poor households, drew heavily on public revenues and allowed grain to be diverted to the non-poor. Few worked to stimulate private participants in the supply chains—collectors, millers, transporters, warehouse personnel, or traders—to make sustained investments in raising the efficiency with which they coordinated their chain-linked efforts.

Most of the programs, instead, were designed to counter short-term changes in market prices, to respond to food demand pressures induced by rapid price changes, or to position parastatal and other government-managed food security organizations to profit or recoup losses in times of market volatility. Rooted in commitments to national self-sufficiency in rice, internal political priorities within individual countries helped form these programs and ensured their retention in spite of unanticipated side effects, such as those accentuated by the recent crisis.

Among the side effects are high costs. The Philippines' food security program, for example, has become financially unsustainable. Its overhead alone requires a fiscal subsidy of about 1.5 billion pesos a year, and the effective cost of its rice subsidy activities more than tripled from 2007 to 2008 to reach 68.5 billion pesos.[1] Its monopoly hold over imports meant that its plan to bring 2.5–3.0 million metric tons of rice into the country in 2010 would create an inventory financing requirement of $1.5–1.8 billion.

During the food crisis, the government of Thailand also concentrated rice stocks in its hands, a plus for the public sector when international prices were high, as in the first half of 2008. However, when prices fell sharply over the next six months, the government was forced to absorb losses as the value of its rice inventory fell. Responding to petitions from rice farmers, moreover, the government raised the minimum prices it paid (Forssell 2009).

In Indonesia, where Badan Urusan Logistik (BULOG) policies did spare consumers from a price shock that would have greatly harmed the poor during the April–August 2008 price hike, government programs entailed longer-term costs. Domestic rice prices were much higher—$232 a ton higher on average—than international ones in the 2005–07 period. A recent World Bank public expenditure review (Armas, Gomez Osorio, and Moreno-Dodson 2010) also found that while public spending on overall agricultural development increased by 12 percent per year in real terms from 2001 to 2009, agricultural productivity remained relatively flat. The flow of public investment in Indonesia was strong; the apparent weakness lay in the kinds of investments the government chose to make.

The crisis also highlighted two structural weak spots: the low level of private investment, already noted, and the absence of regional policies or institutions empowered to coordinate rice policies among trading partners during periods of high market stress, or capable, at a minimum, of providing timely and accurate information regarding the location, status, and availability of tradable inventories within the region.

In the short term, the problem is not insufficient stocks of rice in the region, but rather that the efficient transfer of food staples from locations where surpluses are produced to locations where they are consumed has not developed. Rice production in each of the five study countries actually increased from 2006–07 to 2007–08, rising on a collective average by 0.5 percent and at a slower rate from 2007–08 to 2008–09. Their combined stocks of milled rice in 2008–09 were, in fact, significantly larger than in any other year of the decade.

Nor did underlying demand change; consumers in the region— although their numbers increased—did not suddenly start eating more rice. In fact, per capita consumption had been declining in the 1990s in Indonesia, Malaysia, and Thailand.[2]

One benefit of the food crisis has been the rise among ASEAN's leaders and their senior advisers of interest in understanding both the short-term causes of the emergency and the shortcomings it highlighted in traditional rice sector policies. Of these, the easiest to analyze, if not quickly remedy, are the factors that deter private investment in key links of rice supply chains.

Wanted: Private Investment and Expertise

It might be tempting to think that by patterning itself on the model of the maize industry, the region's rice sector could attract new firms or the same private firms that have brought to maize such crucial advances as modern storage technologies, effective risk management, and economies of scale and specialization. The appendix describes that dynamism at length. It also makes clear, however, how profound the differences are between maize and rice as crops and as markets.

The maize industry has registered remarkable growth with and because of minimal government interference. For private investors to approach the rice sector with comparable enthusiasm, policy makers will need to modify existing trade and subsidy policies resolutely, invest more in carefully targeted support and modernization programs, and explore new ways to cooperate with domestic and foreign companies.

Given the political and dietary importance of rice, governments in the region still need to implement policies that protect farmers and keep rice prices stable and affordable. At the same time, it is necessary to provide incentives for private traders to manage inventories of tradable rice effectively and to invest in technology and farm business models that hold out the best prospect of improving productivity and thus increasing the future rice supply.

To begin the needed transition in rice sector policies, priorities must change. At a fundamental level, governments in the region must switch their policy focus from producing rice to supporting efforts by the private sector to procure, process, and trade it efficiently—from raising output to strengthening the supply chains in which as much as 15 percent of the harvested grain now goes to waste.

Successful market development in the rice industry in Southeast Asia, as in other fields all over the world, depends basically on the willingness of individual entrepreneurs to invest in new business models and thus to improve the efficiency with which markets serve consumers. Therefore, when formulating food security policies, ASEAN governments need to give greater attention to the incentives or obstacles their policies create for private initiative. The goal should be to stimulate private sector investments in supply-chain modernization so as to increase production of farm outputs generated from enhanced input use, add value to basic farm commodities, and provide efficient distribution services to link farmers and consumers.

In the case of regional rice market development, this will entail a strenuous uphill effort. Moreover, instead of intervening directly in rice markets, governments in the region must develop ways to offer incentives and create regulatory systems that stimulate private sector activities. While a 180-degree turn from direct to indirect policy interventions in rice markets is arguably the best direction for future policy, it would seem unrealistic to expect this revolution in the short term.

Supply-chain partnerships. Another feasible early reform could address the lack of accurate information that farmers and small millers, among others, need when deciding whether to sell their product or—if they can—to hold it back from the market for a time. By insisting on standard and transparent contractual arrangements along the supply chain, reformed public procurement policies could make it easier for supply chain participants to share risks specific to small-farm agriculture.

Currently, most small rice farmers have trouble supplying grain in a consistent and standardized manner. They lack up-to-date technology and capital to finance inputs and technology improvement. In return for entering price and delivery agreements under contract farming arrangements, they could gain both credit to use in upgrading their operations and the promise of reliable payment in often volatile markets. Grain collectors and processors, in turn, could improve supply reliability by working more closely with farmers and could reduce their risk exposure by building similar partnerships with distributors or directly with wholesalers, perhaps even retailers, who are willing to forgo price-arbitraging freedom for reliable supply.

To expand such private sector opportunities, governments have a variety of options. Start-up programs could include education and training for local farmers, better-targeted government-led extension services, and efforts to develop product standards and certification procedures. Financial aid and model contracts[3] might help jump-start experimentation. Matchmaking services might even aid in connecting actors in supply chains with one another. Policies that support the spread of farmer organizations could lead to collective bargaining agreements with large, chain-linked buyers.

Among the latter, once such an environment begins to function, foreign investors such as the multinational corporations active in the maize sector could help local industries to develop modern supply-chain management discipline. Over the past two decades in many developing countries, private companies have developed new technologies and methods for managing the flow of food products from farms to markets. Increasingly adopted as practical operational methods through which chains function the world over, both supermarket chains and processors and traders have been particularly adept in applying supply-chain management methods to the flow of food staples.

Supermarkets, for instance, have refined and extended management methods for pulling food products through farm-to-market chains from the demand end, while grain millers and merchandisers have developed their own advanced management methods, which they typically apply from the center of farm-to-market chains. Both sets of methods have the effect of improving farm production and postharvest processing and, downstream, of assembly, storage, transport, and processing practices.

Public Sector Policy Reform

Regarding the general environment for doing business in the five study countries, private firms cite few difficulties that they believe cannot be remedied. A more widespread and deeper concern that keeps them on the sidelines of the rice sector is the range of interventionist government policies they face.

Each of the five study countries continues to deploy a wide array of protective mechanisms that distort national and regional rice markets. Among them, since 2009, programs designed to increase national self-sufficiency in rice have moved to the forefront and have become quite costly in both budgetary and real terms. Reversing this trend is the way forward with respect to improving the investment environment in the rice sector.

Traditionally, governments in the region have found themselves juggling conflicting goals as they develop and implement food security policy. On the one hand, they try to encourage production by ensuring a reasonable return for farmers; on the other, they try to ensure that prices are affordable for poor consumers. Exporting countries consider potential benefits to their economies resulting from increased export income, while importing countries assess whether food security considerations are best served by spending scarce resources on food imports or on promoting domestic production. Recent policies of the two rice-exporting countries, Thailand and Vietnam, have introduced significant additional risk in rice trading, as far as the private sector is concerned.

Moreover, in the current environment, traditional mechanisms designed into food security programs may no longer be appropriate for achieving their stated objectives. McCulloch and Timmer (2008) have suggested that access to input credits and to fertilizer is no longer the primary constraint that prevents farmers in the region from improving their incomes, diversifying their livelihood options, or accumulating productive agricultural assets rapidly. Government expenditures need to shift from supplying what are essentially private goods at discounted prices to providing public goods and to solving the coordination and information asymmetry problems that the private sector cannot effectively address on its own.

Parastatals are inherently inefficient—despite their mandate to operate as commercial entities and to remain financially independent. They do not pursue profit maximization objectives, and their management is frequently unable to make them financially self-sustaining. Exacerbating this condition, parastatals frequently capture economic rents, exert monopoly rights, and deploy anticompetitive tactics that put private companies at a disadvantage. In these ways, as well, they distort underlying markets and discourage private investment. While in some countries, like China, less distorting income support payment programs have replaced programs that support rice market prices, most of the countries included in this study continue to intervene directly in the rice market.[4]

In Indonesia, the Philippines, and Vietnam, private sector involvement in rice trading is restricted by the involvement of government bodies. Evidence presented by McCulloch and Timmer (2008), however, suggests that public procurement and government-managed distribution systems can be extremely costly, inefficient, and, indeed, ultimately ineffective in stabilizing prices. Poor targeting and inefficient distribution are particularly conspicuous in the rice procurement systems that continue to operate in Indonesia and the Philippines. While social protection programs may be laudable from a social security perspective and imperative from a political perspective, governments in the region need to weigh the costs of inefficient business as usual against the benefits of adopting alternative, less costly methods to attain the same goals.

In Vietnam, private exporters face considerable uncertainties and cannot maximize export returns, while millers find the obligation to stock beyond their immediate requirements a costly undertaking. In Thailand, government intervention in the market pushed up prices and withdrew rice supplies that could have earned export revenue. At the end of 2009, it appeared that revisions to the Thai government's market intervention policy were causing confusion and involving the Bank for Agriculture and Agricultural Cooperatives in noncommercial activities. Problems with the export management policy of Vietnam similarly remained unresolved.

Another kind of confusion—call it suspicion—revealed itself in 2007–08 as a strong, but not universal, tendency of governments in the region to look for scapegoats, "speculators," and "hoarders," in particular. They should have been looking closer to home at their own policies and the actions of some of their agencies in fueling the food crisis. Again, defining food security policy primarily in terms of the availability of rice supply, governments undervalue the sustained, efficient operation of markets and the development of efficient supply chains. The policies that Indonesia, Malaysia, and the Philippines have implemented in efforts to attain self-sufficiency, for example, are exclusively supply oriented and most often carried out through input subsidies (such as seeds, chemicals, and fertilizer). This kind of intervention is costly for government, diverts funding from more strategic investments with more sustained impacts such as irrigation and research and development, and undermines private sector participation in input subsectors.

It also feeds the mistaken perception that private sector misconduct, not government action and inaction, bears the primary blame for spiraling and gyrating rice prices in 2007–08. Box 5.1 is a summary damage report on those interventions.

Box 5.1

The High Cost of Price Volatility and Uncertainty for Farmers, Exporters, Consumers, and Governments

The initial reaction among politicians, government officials, and the population at large in 2007–08 was that the price rises afforded opportunities to the private sector for windfall profits. The assumption that the private sector was gearing itself up to make such profits may have been behind police raids on millers and traders in the Philippines and Indonesia, for example. However, in the Philippines, such raids had the opposite effect to that which the authorities desired. Traders and millers became frightened to hold stocks and reduced their purchases, resulting in less rice being available on the market and, as a consequence, a reduction in purchases from farmers by the mills, which experienced cash flow constraints. Far from making excessive profits, by mid-2009, it had become clear that many rice and maize intermediaries lost money in 2007–08. While some businesspersons may have benefited, it is likely that any such gains would have been fairly short term. If anything, the main beneficiaries of the price rises were farmers—but, again, these benefits were transient because farmers were faced with significantly higher input costs for subsequent harvests, for which they received lower prices.

There were two main reasons for the losses experienced by the private sector. Some traders and millers lost money when the market was on the way up because prices rose after they had signed contracts. Others lost money when the market was on the way down because they bought supplies at the top of the market and then had to sell at a loss. In the case of rice exporters in Thailand, traders had agreed to export contracts without having the required rice in stock. When prices did rise dramatically, exporters were unable to obtain supplies at prices that would have given them a profit; in some cases, they were unable to obtain rice at

(continued next page)

Box 5.1 *(continued)*

any price at all, as farmers preferred to sell to the government at the inflated Paddy Pledging Program prices. Exporters either had to take losses on export transactions or, where rice was unavailable, negotiate to pay compensation to their buyers. Maize traders in Vietnam and rice millers and traders in the Philippines and Vietnam, among others, faced an opposite problem, when a sudden fall-back in prices left them with expensive stock that could not be sold except at a loss.

The conclusion is clear. Significant price volatility causes just as many problems for the private sector as it does for consumers and their governments. Traders and mills have fixed and other investments that need to be profitably used, and the way to do this is to maximize capacity utilization. The same applies to operating capital: if traders or millers borrow money for a period of, say, six months, they want to rotate the money as frequently as possible to get the best use of it and be able to pay the interest. If a mill can buy paddy and sell rice once a month or more often, it is usually much more profitable than using the same money to buy paddy and sell rice once every six months, even if the price rises significantly over that period. Further, employees need to be kept working, which they will not be if all that the miller or trader is doing is stockholding.

Volatile prices introduce unnecessary uncertainty into the business of maximizing resource utilization. Exporters cannot be sure that they will be able to meet contracts; since 2008, they have been increasingly reluctant to sign contracts without the stocks to back them up. Processors cannot be sure that if they pay a high price for raw materials they will be able to sell the processed product before prices collapse. Market uncertainty is further exacerbated by policy uncertainty. Reducing risk by addressing both types of uncertainty in a way that is consistent with the operation of rice and maize markets in ASEAN countries would definitely find favor with the private sector.

Source: Authors.

Studies undertaken in the region have repeatedly found that agricultural marketing is extremely competitive. Governments and their officials, however, continue to see much private conduct in the market as part of an "evil middleman" syndrome. Misunderstanding the inherent necessity to keep operations profitable, they also seem not to appreciate the potential benefits of private sector stockholding for food security. "What we've got here," as a famous film character said, "is failure to communicate" (*Cool Hand Luke*, 1967).

Part of the problem in the nondialogue lies with the private partici-pants in both the rice and maize value chains. Individual associations in these chains (miller associations, exporter associations, and others) could improve communication if they were able to organize them-selves into industry associations of the entire chain in order to provide a focal point for discussions with governments (Shepherd, Cadilhon, and Gálvez 2009). However, the different sectors of the industries do not always see eye-to-eye.

Food security relies not only on the state of rice supply but also on the sustained, efficient operation of markets and the development of efficient supply chains. However, the policies that Indonesia, Malaysia, and the Philippines have implemented in their efforts to attain self-sufficiency are costly, exclusively supply oriented, and most often carried out through input subsidies (such as seeds, chemicals, and fertilizer).

Public-Private Partnerships

As discussed earlier, numerous opportunities exist to implement ASEAN governments' food security agendas by involving the private sector more deeply. Among them, PPPs present a particularly attractive way to create social dividends based on private investments. Partnerships can assume many forms, including private companies' delivery of services as specified by performance contracts, the application of new technologies to new uses requested in public grant offers, or the buildout of fixed assets under build-operate-transfer, concession, or joint-venture agreements.

For example, PPPs might be undertaken involving rice markets that would demonstrate the technical feasibility and financial viability of either a demand-pull or supply-push supply-chain organization. Under such an arrangement, public financing could assist in starting up a private sector proposal of a viable supply-chain model. Assets in the form of supply-chain infrastructure might be sold via auction once the chain had proved its viability and the proceeds used to pay back the private investor before reverting to the public treasury. In this instance and other similar ones, a PPP could be used to create commercial knowledge and to reduce, instead of increase, private sector investment risks.

Many of these "win-win" opportunities are neither ideological nor high risk. There is little disagreement with respect to their merits, and they involve actions that can be taken relatively easily and quickly. The remainder of this section discusses areas of possible productivity enhance-ment in the rice sector that are ripe for PPP.

Reducing Postharvest Losses, Upgrading Quality

One of the major factors affecting food availability and hence food prices and their fluctuations is the level of physical losses such as those that occur during rice harvesting and as a result of poor threshing, drying, and milling. Government policies that have led to excessive long-term storage have also had the ironic effect of increasing physical losses for rice in several of the countries studied.

Significant efforts and millions of dollars have been allocated to programs to reduce losses at the farmer level—in many cases, with limited success. Part of the reason may be that interventions have tended to concentrate on farmers rather than on the entire chain. Further efforts in this area are essential, but such efforts should adopt a value chain approach and work closely with the private sector to identify improvements that private partners judge workable and sustainable. Such improvements could include improved drying by mills and the introduction of more efficient milling equipment to overcome the existing low conversion rates in several countries.[5]

A related source of loss is the worsening quality of paddy that farmers and traders send to processors. The private sector may be partly to blame for deteriorating quality, as mills and traders often provide limited incentives for farmers to supply high-quality products, particularly from the standpoint of the moisture content, but the misdirected incentives of prevailing government policies also play an important part. In Malaysia, for example, a problem exists with mandated "flat-rate deductions" that effectively reward farmers who supply poor-quality rice. An additional concern for both quality and postharvest losses relates to the length of time a government agency—or, in the case of Malaysia, a private import monopoly—retains stocks, with the consequent danger of quality losses. As a first step, these adverse quality incentives need to be reversed.

While other countries have programs to promote improved quality, much more could be done by adopting a coherent, multistakeholder approach. Mills, for instance, could buy more wet paddy, thus reducing the need for on-farm drying and concomitant postharvest losses and quality deterioration. This action would require mills to invest in mechanical drying equipment, as some have already done in some of the study countries and as, with some additional incentives, others might do as well.

More an area for extension services, as noted earlier, the slow spread of contract farming could be accelerated through government technical assistance programs that help farmers and millers to understand contracts and that develop quality certification standards for the parties to fulfill.

The long-term potential for such developments, however, is currently constrained by arbitrary policy interventions that can jeopardize contract viability. Government purchases that drive up prices give farmers a powerful incentive to break contracts they might have concluded in a less distorted market.

Improving Logistics and Infrastructure

The ASEAN private sector trades internationally in only small quantities of rice, with the exception of exports from Thailand and Vietnam. From the private sector standpoint, therefore, port infrastructure is really a problem only in Vietnam, where the ports of Can Tho and Ho Chi Minh City, at least, require major upgrading to take large vessels and provide suitable storage.

A much more prevalent concern is the state of rural infrastructure, particularly roads in Indonesia and the Philippines. Clearly, this is an issue that affects more than the rice industry. The inefficiencies resulting from poor infrastructure have significant costs for parastatals and also for the private sector—and, by definition, for the region's economies as a whole. In choosing which public investments to make and where, officials should at least solicit private sector assistance in identifying the worst bottlenecks. Governments might also consider the value of toll roads as a way to get help in defraying some costs of improvements that benefit the private sector.

Improving Access to Market and Trade Information

Trade in rice, both within and outside the ASEAN region, tends to be dominated by the parastatals and by a relatively small number of large exporters. Attempts by smaller mills in Thailand, in particular, to compete in the export market have not been very successful. While existing arrangements are not monopolistic, greater access to trade and market information could help overcome some of the constraints that smaller companies currently face. All companies contacted in the region, of whatever size, indicated a need for improved trade information and crop forecasts, rather than more up-to-date price information, which can usually be obtained through business partners.

Providing Bank Finance for Supply Chains

Working capital for the rice chain is mainly provided by banks to large companies, by large companies to smaller ones, and, on occasion, by small companies and traders to farmers. In some countries, large companies are able to obtain loans on the basis of their own stocks without the need for formal warehouse receipts. Availability of operating capital is not considered a significant constraint by these larger companies, but it seems to limit the options of smaller mills and village-level paddy collectors.

Fixed investments in the rice sector are usually funded by company and family resources. Both small and large operators seem to use banks rarely for investment capital, with industry sources suggesting that returns are insufficient to pay existing interest rates. Lack of finance also appears to be a major factor constraining some consolidation of the rice-milling sector, in particular—the reportedly 100,000-plus mills in Indonesia and the approximately 300,000 in Vietnam. The fragmented and small-scale nature of rice milling leads to high costs and consequent inefficiency. Moreover, lack of investment in milling can be considered a significant cause of high postharvest losses and poor product quality.

The general view of those contacted for this research was that banks do not understand the needs of the agribusiness sector. At the same time, companies need to understand banks' need to make loans only for viable investments. Steps should be taken to bring banks and private sector representatives together to promote greater understanding.

Improving Warehousing and the Use of Warehouse Receipts

Storing rice or maize against warehouse receipts opens up two possibilities. First, depositors could approach banks to obtain loans using the warehouse receipt as collateral. Second, the use of warehouse receipts permits the operation of commodity exchanges (discussed below) that are able to trade the receipts. Both possibilities require reliable, certified, and insured warehouses, as well as a reliable system of grading that removes the need for visual inspection.

In southern Africa, attempts have been made to develop programs where maize and other crops are stored in independent registered warehouses and loans are made against warehouse receipts. The company taking out the loan has the option to sell the warehouse receipt, usually to a large-scale mill or feed company. In the case of the ASEAN rice chain, however, it is likely to be the mills that would seek credit, backed by inventory of paddy—rather than paddy traders, most of whom are very small.

To be viable, inventory credit must be carried out in an environment in which, under normal circumstances, seasonal price movements are greater than the cost of interest, storage, and any transport (Coulter and Shepherd 1995). Otherwise, there would be little incentive for mills to store; if they needed additional paddy, they could simply go out and buy it on the market. The necessary seasonal price fluctuations may not exist in the countries under study, both because of the management of the rice market by governments, particularly through parastatal and policy actions, and because of the fact that there is often double cropping and, increasingly, triple cropping. For mills, the attractiveness of inventory credit could be further jeopardized if they were required to incur storage and transport costs to store paddy away from their own premises. The Quedan and Rural Credit Guarantee Corporation (QUEDANCOR) program in the Philippines permitted storage at the mill (Coulter and Shepherd 1995).

In general, smaller companies seek to rotate their capital as quickly as possible and thus may have limited interest in long-term stockholding. Nevertheless, the scope for promotion of commercial inventory credit similar to that offered in the past by QUEDANCOR would appear to merit further, more detailed investigation. Such arrangements may assist more efficient mills in building up necessary stocks to permit greater capacity utilization.

Promoting Commodity and Futures Exchanges

Commodity exchanges require agreed-upon standards in order to operate, unless they function on the basis of visual inspection of samples. These standards do not currently exist in the ASEAN rice trade at a national level. Although various grades are used in domestic markets, usually based on the percentage of brokens, these have not yet reached the required level of sophistication. It is noteworthy, for example, that government tenders in Thailand are based on visual inspection and not on agreed-upon grades.

There have been some very tentative discussions among the rice and maize private sectors regarding the possible establishment of futures exchanges within the region. Trading in rice has been conducted by the Agricultural Futures Exchange of Thailand, although the exchange has tended to adapt its procedures to fit in with government policy implementation. In general, as far as rice is concerned, enthusiasm for the idea appears extremely limited among established rice companies.

Exporters in Thailand and Vietnam express four main reservations. First, the fact that domestic prices can be affected by policy interventions and by actions of state bodies makes the possibility of trading futures on the basis of market fundamentals almost impossible, and it also raises the possibility of rent-seeking trading by government officials who are privy to policy and administrative decisions, particularly in the case of national exchanges. Second, there is no clear understanding of any potential benefits of such trading in the context of existing marketing chains. Third, the wide variety of types and grades of rice makes the trade question whether an exchange could function for rice without the development of clear standards. Finally, there is concern about possible food security implications if rice futures attract too much speculative interest.

At the same time, it should be noted that the lack of enthusiasm of the private sector may reflect an element of self-interest in that it is clearly not in the interest of companies to support measures that may attract new competitors. The Singapore Mercantile Exchange has announced plans to open a regional rice exchange in the near future, and its experience needs to be closely monitored.

Progress toward structured regional trade might open the way for commodity exchanges. Those prospects are discussed in following text.

ATIGA and Rice Trade Reforms

Since the issuance of the ASEAN Integrated Food Security framework in 2008 and the further successful adoption of the ASEAN Trade in Goods Agreement (ATIGA) in 2009, the probability of affecting regional food policy reforms has greatly improved. With that said, it remains clear that rice deficit countries within the region would prefer to hang tenaciously on to their long-held goal of rice self-sufficiency.

At the 14th ASEAN Summit in Bangkok in February 2009, the heads of ASEAN member states signed the ATIGA to "achieve free flow of goods in ASEAN as one of the principal means to establish a single market and production base for the deeper economic integration of the region towards the realization of the AEC [ASEAN Economic Community] by 2015."[6] To facilitate private sector business transactions, the agreement codifies all trade-related agreements within ASEAN and clearly articulates the region's free trade rules, making them more transparent, predictable, and certain.

The agreement encompasses the key provisions of the ASEAN Free Trade Agreement (AFTA) on tariff liberalization, as well as its related rules on origin, nontariff measures, trade facilitation, customs, standards, technical regulations and conformity assessment procedures, sanitary and phytosanitary measures, and trade remedies. ATIGA enters into force with the deposit by member states of their respective instruments of ratification with the secretary-general of ASEAN. The process is envisioned "not [to] take more than one hundred and eighty (180) days after the signing of this Agreement."

Structuring Regional Trade

Even without the ATIGA formal framework, ASEAN states can move ahead with new structures for regional trade. A particularly attractive leverage point involves rice procurement policies and practices that are used by public sector entities to import food grains. Policy makers should be willing to explore the benefits of harmonizing these procurement practices and in the process setting regional rules for grain trading.

To make that sort of ambitious new approach possible, regional governments would need to establish workable standards for several important aspects, including (a) rice quality standards and controls; (b) technical capabilities of asset managers, warehouse personnel, and intermediary handlers; (c) liabilities of buyers and sellers under standard negotiable bills of sale; (d) clarity with respect to custodial responsibilities through the entire chain; (e) standard arrangements for the reassignment of ownership rights for products moving in transit; (f) standard securitized interests for third parties providing trade finance; and (g) carrier and port handling liability under standard bills of lading. Any such set of commercial rules would need to be updated and revised from time to time together with the private sector to reflect changes in technology and best business practices.

To this end, the National Food Authority (NFA) in the Philippines and BULOG in Indonesia might be tasked under ASEAN with formulating regionwide, rule-based procurement practices. These practices would include (a) setting standards for rice grades and quality levels; (b) establishing module lot sizes consistent with efficient transport and storage capacities within the region; (c) establishing trading terms consistent with International Commercial Terms (Incoterms®);[7] (d) defining the liabilities and responsibilities of all trading partners under negotiable contracts of sale; (e) establishing standard custodial responsibilities for third-party warehouse personnel and transporters; and (f) enabling third-party financial institutions to create secure interests in inventories that they have financed.

However, policy makers weighing the potential of such a trade structure will have to acknowledge the remaining bias in the region against full integration of individual national rice markets into either global or regional markets. An underlying assumption—which prevailing policies make self-fulfilling—is that the world rice market is not a dependable source of food supply because of its relatively small size and price volatility. However, good evidence exists that full liberalization of regional rice markets would allow ASEAN countries to realize benefits that would dwarf any costs associated with perpetuating existing policies (McCulloch and Timmer 2008). In any case, adjustment costs should not be the determining factor that deters full engagement in a more robust regional rice trade.

Grains Tariff and Related Reforms in ATIGA

The adoption of the ATIGA goals in 2009 has greatly improved the probability of bringing about regional food policy reforms. With that said, it remains clear that rice deficit countries within the region would prefer to hang tenaciously on to their long-held goal of rice self-sufficiency. One key test of progress will be the action that member states take to eliminate duties on all imported goods originating in ASEAN by 2010 for Brunei Darussalam, Indonesia, Malaysia, the Philippines, Singapore, and Thailand (ASEAN 6), and by 2015–18 for Cambodia, Lao People's Democratic Republic, Myanmar, and Vietnam. For rice and maize, import duties are to be reduced to 0–5 percent from the respective rates that will prevail at the time the agreement enters into force.

The new rates, referred to under the treaty as Common Effective Preferential Tariff (CEPT) rate levels, are legally binding. Although member states have committed not to increase their import duties above CEPT, Indonesia, Myanmar, and the Philippines have placed rice on their respective sensitive or highly sensitive lists and have "opted out" of the tariff reform. Indonesia has agreed to impose a 25 percent import duty as its final AFTA rate. Myanmar has until 2015 to adjust its import duty on rice. After its bilateral negotiation with Thailand, the Philippines will be imposing a preferential tariff rate of 35 percent on rice, with a possible earmarking of its imports from Thailand and Vietnam.

The result of continuing protectionist policies for rice—box 5.2 discusses others—is that apparently final AFTA rates on rice imports originating in ASEAN are far from those that might be expected in a free trade area. For instance, Malaysia, which has not nominated rice as a sensitive commodity, has committed to a final AFTA rate of 20 percent, down from its most-favored nation rate of 40 percent.[8] The importation of rice will apparently continue for some time to be significantly restricted by high tariffs.

However, tariffs are only one part of the problem. As discussed earlier in this chapter, the more important part is the continuing dominant role of parastatals in rice trading.

Box 5.2

Special Protocol for Rice

Article 24 of ATIGA creates an additional opening for protectionist practices. It gives member states a degree of freedom to opt out by requesting and receiving permission to raise import duties temporarily on rice or sugar in the case of underlying exceptional circumstances. This protocol provides that member states with export interests in rice and members granted the waiver must agree on ways to minimize adverse effects on the former and ensure continued market access for rice.

Given these arrangements at the time of this writing, it may be productive to put more structure into the decision-making process within ASEAN with respect to requests for waivers. Trade remedies under the World Trade Organization (WTO) passed through a similar development process. Contracting parties of the former General Agreement on Tariffs and Trade provided for opt-outs that conformed to rules and regulations ensuring that the variances from normal trade rules were minimized and that the conditions applicable to opt-outs were progressively diminished.

Although ATIGA requires member states to cease and desist from imposing prohibition or quantitative restriction on the exportation of goods destined for the region, it does not prevent member states from maintaining export restrictions in situations where the domestic price of an exportable product is held below the world price by the exporting member state in the interests of a price stabilization or when the product is in short supply, such as rice. The agreement, however, does emphasize the importance of lifting these restrictions if the conditions justifying them are no longer valid. As things stand at the time of this writing, qualifying provisions in ATIGA with respect to unilateral imposition of export restrictions may need to be elaborated further to remove any possible uncertainties that they may induce in the regional trade of rice.

Source: Authors.

Independent of ATIGA compliance, NFA's continued import monopoly complements the Philippine government's continuing restriction on private importation of rice to very limited quantities. Thailand's and Vietnam's demands to secure a larger annual volume commitment from the Philippines would perpetuate the same arrangement that has kept the flow of rice trade in the region as low as it has been to date because such arrangements would inevitably be government-to-government. Trade would have better prospects if the private sector on both sides of the market were legally enabled to participate. As of October 2011, NFA is permitting private sector imports. They have to be organized through tenders to NFA, however, and within quantity limits set by the government.

To end NFA's exclusive rice-importing privileges, however, the government of the Philippines would have to ask permission from its congress to amend the NFA charter. From the perspective of political viability, this would be difficult to accomplish not only in the short but even in the medium term. Legislative changes required to alter the NFA charter are in limbo, although in July 2010 the issues of overimportation and rotting rice stocks in NFA warehouses did encourage discussions on NFA reform.[9]

Rather than holding the entire ATIGA hostage because of this impasse, one possible step forward is for the Philippines to commit itself to amending the NFA charter within a workable but specifically defined time period.[10]

State Trading Enterprises

The example of the NFA illustrates a further obstacle to regional trade liberalization: the practice by many member states of operating through state trading enterprises (STEs) that have the authority to waive duties when they import rice, an option not extended to private traders. In effect, governments are telling the private sector not to import. To even out trading incentives, it is imperative that the private sector be accorded similar tax treatment as the parastatal when it imports or exports rice.

The ATIGA, however, is silent on the role of STEs and the preferential treatment that member states accord them at the expense of private firms. The worst situation exists when STEs exercise regulatory oversight. The resulting conflict of interest poses an even more significant disincentive for the private sector to invest in regional food chains. Furthermore, because of the advantages the NFA receives in fiscal subsidies and preferential access to commercial credit, no large private company has dared to enter the rice sector.

Without private sector dynamism, the sector will remain unreliable, inefficient, and a drain on many governments' budgets. Progressively limiting the participation of STEs in regional food staple markets is a reform on which ASEAN member states can agree as an overdue invitation to private sector participation in specific supply-chain development in the region.

Roles for ASEAN and for Multilateral Donors

Interviews, discussions, and correspondence conducted during the course of this study have made it clear that the private sector believes that external interventions are required to restructure the ASEAN rice sector to reduce the risks that deter private involvement and, through new commitments of private capital, improve competitiveness and productivity. There also appears to be general agreement among private companies that the regional market for rice needs to be reengineered into a more effective instrument to enhance growth and competitiveness. Regional trade policy, moreover, needs to focus more on allowing different economies to discover and exploit their unique sources of competitive advantage and less on increasing market access by surrendering national economic autonomy. In other words, regional rice trade policy needs to become more a "positive-sum, development-focused game" and less a "zero-sum, equity-focused game."

The private sector, however, lacks an effective starting point from which to influence policy reform in this new direction. What is missing is an institutional platform for advocates and advocacy of change. The private sector also lacks the requisite expertise in regional trade reform policy and the necessary capabilities to improve coordination among disparate governments, parastatal organizations, and various interest groups.

Arguably, the kind of fundamental industrial restructuring that this book envisions rarely takes place without a significant level of commitment from outside the industries and markets being restructured. To meet the challenge of reforming the regional rice sector, governments will need to correct deficiencies in the flow of business information, the coordination of businesses processes, and the setting of public policy.

Although the kinds of interventions required in each of these three areas differ in basic ways, a role exists in each for ASEAN as an organization and for development partners like the World Bank, the Asian Development Bank (ADB), and the Food and Agriculture Organization (FAO) of the United Nations.

A reasonable place to start on a multiparty initiative would be an open commercial learning process with the ongoing involvement of the private sector. In such a setting, commercial experiments could be deliberately undertaken, results studied, and findings regarding the creation of investor value disseminated to private sector stakeholders. The objective of the experiments would be to enhance productivity and competitiveness with new business processes, new control systems, and new technologies. The emphasis would be at the level of discrete business processes and technologies appropriate to them in farm-to-market chains, and not on rice sector reform per se. One example is specialized third-party logistics management services. Another is a regional commodity exchange.

PPPs can be particularly useful mechanisms for underwriting these commercial experiments as long as they are tested with the same set of criteria to ensure that (a) only technically and commercially qualified private partners are selected; (b) good value (in the form of new business information) is being realized for public monies committed; (c) risks are shared equitably and appropriately between public and private partners based on their ability to manage specific risks; (d) the processes for choosing strategic private partners are open, contestable, and subject to competition; and (e) the liabilities assumed by public parties are affordable and fall within the feasible range of budget projections.

Among various possible sponsors, ASEAN can serve as the coordinator and primary focal point for regional lending activities and as the primary disseminator of information concerning business process innovation among member countries. Individual ASEAN member countries can serve as sponsors of rice sector reform councils that bring together qualified and interested agribusinesses, technology providers, and providers of ancillary services to identify useful commercial experiments, evaluate their merits, and manage information dissemination once experiments have been completed. Multilateral development institutions like the World Bank and the ADB can serve as sources of financing and, together with FAO, as architects of project design and implementation.

If coordinated investments made in one activity within a farm to market chain they can result in significant productivity gains in subsequent activities. A second set of activities involves coordinating the activities of rice sector participants in order to capture the synergies which can be realized through improved efficiency, precision, and adaptability among synchronized chain processes. To modernize the ASEAN rice sector will require expertise which is currently missing within the industry's private sector, including expertise in industrial cluster development, process engineering which leads to enhanced competitiveness, and in all of the specialized ancillary services, and specialized managerial skills required to support a vibrant sector.

This set of industrial coordination activities entails investing in development forums in support of technical organizations like the International Rice Research Institute (IRRI).

Again, ASEAN can serve as the coordinator and primary focal point for this effort and as a facilitator for new business combinations that cross borders within the region. As suggested, individual member countries can sponsor rice sector reform councils composed of interested agribusinesses, academics, technology providers, and providers of ancillary services.

ASEAN has already begun a parallel set of efforts intended to focus on correcting policy weaknesses and creating an enabling business environment. This study is part of that process. The response that ASEAN and its member countries make to its conclusions and recommendations can signal a new beginning for efforts to remove policy obstacles to increased private sector participation and investment in regional rice markets.

The concluding Agenda for Action table incorporates the principles agreed upon at the Discussion Workshop on July 19–20, 2010, in Jakarta, Indonesia. The meeting was held to review a draft of the study and was attended by representatives of all five countries together with members of the Study Team.

Agenda for Action

Policy Reforms, Private Investment in Food Supply Chains, and Cross-Border Trade Facilitation

Action	Role of private sector	Role of public sector	Role of ASEAN	Time frame	Outcome
		Improving the Investment Environment			
1. Encourage greater private sector participation in food import and distribution programs currently carried out mainly by parastatals.	Organize and offer competitive tenders and develop management skills needed to respond to opportunities.	Outsource to private firms specific functions of parastatals responsible for food security. Open rice import market opportunities to private traders, at the same duty level enjoyed by parastatals.	Explicitly recognize and reward best practices in public-private sector policy collaboration. Facilitate regional trade negotiations and help steer negotiations toward outcomes that afford long-term beneficial results.	Medium term	Increased market competition for component services that support food security supply-chain management. Increased access to the Philippine market for regional rice suppliers in the private sector.
2. Promote and facilitate private sector participation (investment or maintenance) in specialized food logistics systems (food product compatible ports, rural roads, multimodal transfer facilities, and the like).	Coordinate with project implementation authorities. Invest in specialized food supply-chain infrastructure.	Fund project implementation efforts. Formulate, offer, and coinvest in PPPs.	Promote best practice regionally. Encourage the coordinated development of specialized supply-chain infrastructure elements at opposite ends of regional food trade corridors.	Long term	Waiting time, lead time, and logistics costs reduced by 50 percent.

3. Ensure fair competition between private sector companies and state trading enterprises.	Lobby for a more open, competitive, and contestable rice trade at the regional level.	Agree to reforms proposed under ATIGA.	Facilitate regional trade negotiations and help steer negotiations toward outcomes that yield long-term beneficial results.	Short term	Improved incentives for the private sector to invest in regional food chains.
4. Improve access to working and investment capital for supply-chain development.	Experiment with new modes of supply-chain finance.	Facilitate exchange of information between banks and private sector. Facilitate the collateralization of payments made and secured within supply chains.	Monitor and track best practices within the region.	Medium term	Improve farm access to third-party finance ensured and collateralized within supply-chain structures.
5. Promote and facilitate the development of commodity and futures exchanges to deepen existing exchanges or create new ones.	Contribute to the feasibility of a futures exchange. Thai and Singapore Commodity Exchanges provide technical assistance.	Formulate enabling legislation and supportive policies for private investment. Fund project implementation efforts.	Encourage the emulation of best market development practices and policies regionwide. Facilitate cross-listing of commodity contracts and the development of regionwide modes and means of commodity mercerization and collateralization.	Medium term	Effective risk management mechanisms available to the public and private sectors.

(continued next page)

Policy Reforms, Private Investment in Food Supply Chains, and Cross-Border Trade Facilitation *(continued)*

Action	Role of private sector	Role of public sector	Role of ASEAN	Time frame	Outcome
		Strengthening Supply-Chain Links			
6. Promote modern supply-chain methods in regional food systems.	Form food supply-chain associations with appropriate expertise and sufficient market influence to enhance the efficient, precise, and adaptable operation of regional food chains.	Enlist private sector support in the development and implementation of efficient ordering and supply-replenishment systems.	Facilitate the adoption of protocols needed for structured trade.	Long term	An ASEAN-supported Efficient Consumer Response Program.
7. Promote associations in rice and maize trade across the entire chain (miller associations, exporter associations, and the like).	Develop associations within specific food sectors that can promote coordination.	Recognize such associations as valid partners in policy discussions.	Monitor the development of associations within national domains and facilitate coordination and cooperation among private associations at the regional level.	Medium term	Facilitate coordination and cooperation among potential private sector participants in national and regional supply chains for rice and maize.

Strengthen informal and formal farmer and producer organizations.	Provide information to and purchase from farmer organizations, as long as they meet minimum volume and quality requirements and standards.	Put in place enabling legislation. Use matching grants to encourage the formation of reliable, adaptable, and responsive farm-level organizations that make strong supply-chain partners.	Provide platform for information on good practice and disseminate results.	Short to medium term	Reduced supply-chain investment risk. Reduced risk for complementary private sector investment in systems, specialized equipment, land improvements, and human capital.
9. Provide chain integration services to help connect local farmers to domestic and foreign agribusiness investors.	Commit resources to form links and integrate into regional supply chains.	Award matching grants for demonstration projects to prove the commercial viability of new forms of business links. Establish export market access matching grants.	Monitor efforts at the country level to improve the agribusiness investment environment. Facilitate interregional investment, mergers, and food distribution network expansion.	Short to medium term	Improved investment environment for agribusiness. Improved conditions for private sector to invest further in equipment, land improvements, and human capital.

(continued next page)

Policy Reforms, Private Investment in Food Supply Chains, and Cross-Border Trade Facilitation *(continued)*

Action	Role of private sector	Role of public sector	Role of ASEAN	Time frame	Outcome
10. Disseminate and promote postharvest practices and projects that focus on the entire rice chain to improve yields, enhance product quality, and reduce losses.	Participate with government in defining and developing PPP project designs that reduce postharvest losses and ensure high-quality product delivery.	With technical assistance from the FAO, IRRI, and the private sector, design and fund PPP programs that encourage investment in modern postharvest processing and storage facilities.	Monitor PPPs across the region, and recognize and disseminate best practices. Facilitate cooperation among regional companies that successfully pioneer best postharvest technology dissemination.	Medium term	Improved postharvest technologies adopted. Lower physical and quality losses.
11. Support the development of commercially sustainable forms of contract farming, where appropriate.	Test alternative business models for sharing risks and applying appropriate technologies within farm-to-market chains for rice and maize.	Facilitate the adoption, dissemination, and broad application of business models that fairly and efficiently share risks and rewards between private supply-chain integrators and farm-level organizations.	Monitor PPPs across the region and recognize and disseminate best practices.	Medium term	Improved ability of farm-level organizations to participate as reliable partners in regional food supply chains.

12. Establish agricultural product standards and certification procedures.	Form associations with appropriate expertise and market influence to affect and maintain commercially relevant food standards.	Ensure that national GAP and regional standards are in place in consultation with the private sector. Set up GAP certification mechanisms.	Facilitate adoption of common product quality standards at the regional level.	Medium term	Reduced marketing risk. Improved conditions for complementary private sector investments in structured trade.
13. Strengthen sustainable regional market information services, including crop forecasts, stock positions, and price information.	Provide content and information to, or invest in, market information services, and provide market monitoring and tracking services. Provide primary data to public agencies when requested and share expert knowledge regarding regional market conditions.	Provide content and information. Manage coordination and consistency with respect to crop forecasts, demand forecasts, and inventory levels. Implement appropriate statistical estimating and forecasting methodologies. Share information with other regional governments.	Create a set of regional databases and data exchanges among regional ministries of agriculture. Monitor and track regional market developments and report periodically to national ministries of agriculture. Ensure sustainability of AFSIS and improve and expand it.	Short term	Increased access on a sustainable basis to reliable and accurate market information services at the regional level, including services that forecast crop production, demand for specific grains, and food stock positions.

(continued next page)

Policy Reforms, Private Investment in Food Supply Chains, and Cross-Border Trade Facilitation *(continued)*

Action	Role of private sector	Role of public sector	Role of ASEAN	Time frame	Outcome
14. Facilitate implementation of WRSs.	Local banks and investors provide investment or technical assistance, or both, and commercial banks accept stocks as collateral. Insurance companies to consider providing insurance for such stocks.	Conduct feasibility study in specific local contexts. Formulate and implement legislation and regulation for WRS. Improve enforcement of legal security held against and in farm commodities. Lead WRS roll-out efforts.	Recognize and reward best regional practices. Facilitate the transfer of knowledge concerning best-in-class program designs regionwide.	Medium term	Established dense network of regulated regional public warehouses, compliant with ISO standards.
Regional Trade Coordination					
15. Promote structured trade.	Develop through appropriate authorities standards and rules affecting cross-border trade in rice and maize, including standard terms of sale, product quality standards, standard custodial responsibilities, and standard documentation.	Facilitate the adoption of harmonized trade standards in all public procurement practices involving rice and grain	Work step by step toward the development of standardized regional rules for grain trading. Task NFA and BULOG with formulating regionwide, rule-based procurement practices.	Medium to long term	Lower transaction costs. Rules-based trading. Standardized negotiable sales contracts. Securitized trading and low-cost risk management within the regional rice trade.

16. For rice and maize trade, harmonize customs documentation and clearance process requirements region wide.	Participate in the design and implementation of cross-border food product management systems.	Adopt harmonized documentation and clearance process standards. Adopt standardized EDI methods.	Facilitate trade and harmonize customs processes within the region.	Medium term	Adopted EDI in rice trade and harmonization of custom declaration.
17. Introduce more structure into the decision-making process within ASEAN with respect to granting requests for waivers that temporarily allow raising import duties on rice.	Lobby for a more open, predictable, and rules-based rice trade at the regional level.	Agree to reforms proposed under ATIGA.	Facilitate regional trade negotiations and help steer negotiations toward outcomes that yield long-term beneficial results.	Short term	Increased certainty and predictability about rice trade policy for private traders.

Source: Authors and participants at Discussion Workshop July 19–20, 2010 in Jakarta, Indonesia.

Note: AFSIS = ASEAN Food Security Information System

ASEAN = Association of Southeast Asian Nations

ATIGA = ASEAN Trade in Goods Agreement

BULOG = Badan Urusan Logistik (Indonesian national logistics agency); Perum BULOG is a state-owned enterprise (BUMN) that was established through Government Regulation (PP) No. 7/2003 to replace the national food logistic agency (BULOG).

EDI = electronic data interchange

FAO = Food and Agriculture Organization of the United Nations

GAP = Good Agricultural Practice

IRRI = International Rice Research Institute

ISO = International Organization for Standardization

NFA = National Food Authority (the Philippines)

PPP = public-private partnership

WRS = warehouse receipts system

Notes

1. Please note that the Philippines moved to a system of conditional cash transfers at the beginning of 2011 and, as a result, the NFA is no longer responsible for subsidized distribution.

2. Abdullah, Ito, and Adhana 2005.

3. See the Food and Agriculture Organization (FAO) of the United Nations's Contract Farming Resource Centre. http://www.fao.org/ag/ags/contract-farming/en/.

4. Please note that since this report was completed, Thailand's new rice policy has proposed to buy unmilled rice at higher-than-market prices.

5. Investment in any link in a farm-to-market chain has systemic implications that need to be fully analyzed and internalized inside any transaction leading to a long-term PPP. In the case of drying facilities, provisions need to be designed and negotiated to ensure that farmers without alternatives continue to have their paddy milled.

6. ASEAN Trade in Goods Agreement. http://www.aseansec.org/22223.pdf.

7. "The Incoterms® rules are an internationally recognized standard and are used worldwide in international and domestic contracts for the sale of goods." http://www.iccwbo.org/incoterms/.

8. According to World Trade Organization agreements, WTO members cannot treat their trading partners differently. This principle is known as most-favored nation (MFN) treatment. http://www.wto.org/english/thewto_e/whatis_e/if_e /fact2_e.htm.

9. For more on the issues, see "Philippines to Review Rice Import Program Amid Excessive Supply," *Commodity News for Tomorrow*, July 27, 2010, and relevant articles under http://www.riceonline.com/home.shtml.

10. Adding to the complexity of the issue is the fact that while the president may lower the high import duty on rice in the context of AFTA, the congress can always restore it. Avoiding confrontation with the legislative body, previous presidents resorted to tax expenditures for the NFA, and occasionally for the few private sector importers that the NFA authorized to participate.

References and Other Sources

Abdullah, Alias B., Shoichi Ito, and Kelali Adhana. 2005. Quoted in *Estimate of Rice Consumption in Asian Countries and the World towards 2050*, ed. Sushil Pandey, Byerlee Derek, David Dawe, Achim Dobermann, Samarendu Mohanty, Scott Rozelle, and Bill Hardy. International Rice Research Institute, the Philippines. http://worldfood.apionet.or.jp/alias.pdf.

Armas, Enrique Blanca, Camilo Gomez Osorio, and Blanca Moreno-Dodson. 2010. "Agriculture Public Spending and Growth: The Example of Indonesia." Economic Premise 9 (April), Poverty Reduction and Economic Management Network, World Bank, Washington, DC.

ASEAN (Association of Southeast Asian Nations). 2009. *ASEAN Trade in Goods Agreement*. http://www.aseansec.org/22223.pdf.

Commodity News for Tomorrow. 2010. "Philippines to Review Rice Import Program amid Excessive Supply," July 27.

Coulter, Jonathan, and Andrew W. Shepherd. 1995. "Inventory Credit: An Approach to Developing Agricultural Markets." FAO Agricultural Services Bulletin 120, Rome. http://www.fao.org/docrep/v7470e/v7470e00.htm.

FAO (Food and Agriculture Organization of the United Nations). Contract Farming Resource Centre. http://www.fao.org/ag/ags/contract-farming/en/.

Forssell, Sara. 2009. "Rice Policy in Thailand: Policy Making and Recent Developments." Minor Field Study Series 189, Department of Economics, University of Lund.

Incoterms®. 2010. By the International Chamber of Commerce. http://www.iccwbo.org/incoterms/.

McCulloch, Neil, and C. Peter Timmer. 2008. "Rice Policy in Indonesia." *Bulletin of Indonesian Economic Studies* 44 (1): 33–44.

Shepherd, Andrew W., Jean-Joseph Cadilhon, and Eva Gálvez. 2009. "Commodity Associations: A Tool for Supply Chain Development?" Occasional Paper 24, Rural Infrastructure and Agro-Industries Division (AGS), Food and Agriculture Organization (FAO) of the United Nations, Rome. ftp://ftp.fao.org/docrep/fao/012/i0945e/i0945e00.pdf.

WTO (World Trade Organization). Principles of the Trading System. http://www.wto.org/english/thewto_e/whatis_e/tif_e/fact2_e.htm.

Rice and Maize Supply Chains by Country

This section of the study provides background information on specific aspects of the rice and maize industries in each of the five study countries. The purpose is to allow readers interested in a particular country to find material related to it in greater detail than is provided in the necessarily compressed main text.

Each country profile begins with an overview of farm-level rice production followed in most instances by data on milling and domestic marketing; imports and exports; logistics and infrastructure; physical and quality losses; and the roles of state enterprises, including national food security agencies, and the private sector in the supply chains.

Each profile concludes with a discussion of maize supply chains, the subject of the appendix following the country profiles.

Furthermore, a statistical annex in chapter 1 presents data on rice and maize production, processing, exports, imports, consumption, and stocks in the five countries, the Association of Southeast Asian Nations (ASEAN) region, and the world for the decades of the 1960s, 1970s, 1980s and 1990s as well as year-by-year data from 2000–01 through 2009–10.

Indonesia

The Rice Sector

Farm-level operations. Indonesia experienced a period of self-sufficiency in the mid-1980s, but annual rates of production growth then declined in part because of droughts caused by two El Niños and excessive rains caused by the following La Niña. In recent years there has been some recovery in production, although barely enough to keep pace with population growth. This production growth has been achieved through both area expansion and some increase in productivity, in part brought about by the use of fertilizer subsidies. Farmers typically get only 63 kilograms or less of commercial rice from 100 kilograms of unhusked rice from old mills, compared to 67 kilograms possible from new mills.

The rice-harvesting, postharvest, and milling structure varies significantly around the country. During and after harvest, losses are reportedly high. Threshing equipment, whether traditional or mechanical, is usually rented by the farmer or labor group, but there are also entrepreneurs who do contract threshing.

Indonesia has two harvests: the first between February and May in the rainy season, which accounts for around 60 percent of production, and the second from October onward. Normally farmers sell either wet or dry paddy to collector-traders. These typically handle between 5 tons and 10 tons weekly; they may work directly with particular mills, supply the mill that offers the best price, or themselves be mill owners. Collectors often lend money to farmers for inputs or for consumption purposes, with repayment often in the form of "revenue-sharing" arrangements. Rural cooperatives (Kooperasi Unit Desa) are also quite significant in the marketing chain, and Badan Urusan Logistik (BULOG) (see below) buys small quantities.

The country experienced a period of rice self-sufficiency in the mid-1980s, but annual rates of production growth then declined, in part due to droughts caused by two El Niños and excessive rains caused by the following La Niña. In 1998, 2002, and 2003, Indonesia imported 6 million tons, 3.1 million tons, and 2 million tons, respectively. In recent years, production has recovered somewhat, although barely enough to keep pace with population growth. This production growth has been achieved through both area expansion and some increase in productivity, in part brought about through the use of fertilizer subsidies.

Indonesia did not suffer from the recent rises in world market prices in part because production increases allowed it to be insulated from world markets. In 2008, there was virtually no change in either the producer or consumer price for rice. When Indonesia had to import significant quantities in the past, world prices were relatively low and such imports did not have an upwards effect on prices.

Milling and marketing. Most of the country's 80,000 small mills are family operations that work for the seven to eight months of the year when paddy is available. Typically, they have only one or two dehuskers and one polisher, and some have facilities only to remove the bran, subsequently selling the brown rice to larger, more commercial mills. Medium-size mills may be equipped with one large dehusker, a separator, two polishers, and a grader.

Large mills are also equipped with driers and additional polishing equipment. While overall there appears to be surplus milling capacity, there are reportedly shortages in some parts of the country. In addition, a network of public mills operates and competes on a subsidized basis with private mills. The government began to invest in upgrading the technology used in these mills in 2008.

Farmers may have paddy milled on a toll basis for their own consumption. The charge imposed by a mill to convert from paddy to white rice is often one sixth of the rice obtained, with the mill keeping the bran. Larger milling companies work as rice traders to supply wholesalers and retailers, often throughout the country, but also carry out a large amount of milling and final polishing. Such companies may also import, when permitted. Large milling and trading companies supply the high-end markets, including the hypermarkets, supermarkets, and modern chain stores. They buy some paddy from farmers or through brokers but make the bulk of their purchases from smaller mills.

While it is easier to assess quality when buying brown rice from other mills for final polishing, the eventual output is usually of lower quality than when paddy is purchased. This is because rice from the small mills has probably been poorly dried and poorly milled, whereas if larger mills purchase the paddy themselves, they are able to process it correctly. Rice purchased from small mills is described as unhygienic and full of stones (because of the practice of drying at the side of the road). Significant losses at farm level in Indonesia are exacerbated by losses during milling. The milling ratio (conversion factor) has reportedly declined significantly in recent years due to the use of aging equipment and of mobile operations. If true, this has major implications for the ability of Indonesia to feed itself, suggesting that resources may be better directed to reducing such losses rather than to increasing production of paddy that is going to be badly milled.[1]

To improve quality, particularly for special varieties, the largest mills undertake some contract farming operations. They also send staff into the growing areas to try to identify promising fields that could be purchased with a forward contract. Still, formal links between farmers and millers remain generally underdeveloped. While there are a few examples of contract farming, mainly for specialized varieties and qualities, paddy is primarily a commodity that is sold on the "spot" market—that is, farmers sell to whoever offers the best price.

Some such firms supply rice for repacking by supermarkets; others have their own brands. No reliable information could be obtained regarding the size of the modern retail market in Indonesia. However, estimates put the market for high-quality rice at around 10 percent, with sales of branded rice much less than this. There is considerable competition in the supermarket sector, and department stores have also moved into the business. Minimarkets and discount retailers are attracting lower- to middle-income consumers away from supermarkets and traditional outlets.

For the present, traditional methods of distribution remain dominant. Millers and traders supply wholesalers operating in large markets in the main cities. These, in turn, supply retailers and sometimes distribute to other regions. Distribution patterns are fairly standard across the country, with the source of supply being both the very large and high-tech milling companies that also supply supermarkets and smaller mills. These millers typically complete the milling process by polishing to white finished rice.

Importing. From the mid-1960s to the late 1990s, the Indonesian parastatal, BULOG, was dominant in defending floor and ceiling prices through monopoly control over international rice trading and through domestic procurement, drawing on an unlimited line of credit from the Bank of Indonesia (Timmer 2008). In the late 1990s, imports by the private sector were permitted, but then halted again in 2003. More recently, BULOG imported significant quantities in 2007, and private sector imports were again permitted in 2008, but only until June of that year. With production reportedly equaling or exceeding consumption in 2009, and with BULOG's warehouses reportedly well stocked,[2] the only imports permitted in 2009 were specialty rice, such as sticky rice, a variety for diabetics, and rice types needed for Indian and Japanese restaurants.

Smuggling, which is possible because of Indonesia's lengthy coastline and corruption at the smaller ports, has been occurring in Indonesia for many years. These days, smuggled rice is believed to be primarily Vietnamese rice transshipped through Singapore and Malaysia and reaching Sumatra on small boats that have a capacity of around 100 tons.[3] In 2009, however, smuggling must have been minimal because Vietnamese free on board prices of rice with 15 percent brokens were around $450 a ton, and the selling price of comparable rice by Indonesia's millers was around $520 a ton, providing little margin for smugglers.

Logistics and infrastructure. Improvements to Indonesia's transport infrastructure in the 1980s helped the country achieve rice self-sufficiency at that time. Since then, however, conditions have deteriorated, and Indonesia's roads and smaller island port facilities now present a significant constraint for both the purchase of paddy and the marketing of rice. Throughout the archipelago of some 10,000 islands, interisland transportation in small vessels is essential, but the piecemeal development of such transport poses numerous challenges for the timely assembly and delivery of economic lots of rice. These include shipment scheduling and the lack of appropriately designed vessels.[4]

Exports from Indonesia, when they do take place, are usually in small quantities of high-grade rice. In these rare instances, port infrastructure poses no constraint for the private sector. It may pose problems for the parastatal BULOG when importing because of the large size of its consignments. The limited frequency and small scale of private sector exports and imports ensures that all private trade takes place in International Organization for Standardization containers, and Jakarta affords good container-handling facilities.

Indonesia operates just 600 kilometers of toll roads, while officials estimate that 1,500 kilometers are needed on Java alone.[5] Larger millers are reluctant to procure in more remote areas because of the high costs of transport resulting from a combination of small vehicles, long transit times (due to slow roadway speeds and frequent stops), and excessive damage to vehicles caused by poor road conditions. Companies that sell milled rice throughout the country experience high distribution costs because of the relatively poor infrastructure. Policies to promote regional autonomy in Indonesia do not appear to have increased the amount of investment in road and other infrastructure. Indeed, rice companies argue that the opposite appears to have been the case.

Indonesia depends on transport by trucks from its major rice-producing areas to its major wholesale markets and distribution centers. The operating cost per kilometer for a 12.5-ton truck in Indonesia is about

U.S. 34 cents (3,100 rupiah) per kilometer, as compared with about 22 cents in other Asian countries. A combination of factors causes these relatively high trucking costs, including the poor state of truck maintenance and the extended age of the fleet, the overloading of trucks, poor road maintenance, congestion in cities, and delays at road checks and provincial levies (Asia Foundation 2008).

Role of the parastatal. Indonesia's rice policy, long predicated on the view that food security is synonymous with self-sufficiency and that farmers need to be supported and consumers need to be protected from high prices, is largely implemented by the country's parastatal, BULOG, which intervenes in the rice market in two ways. First, the parastatal is charged with distribution of rice to the poorest households (see below). Second, BULOG intervenes in the market when the price to farmers for paddy goes below a certain price (Rp 2,500 per kilogram in 2009).

While it does buy some paddy, BULOG intervenes primarily by buying rice (20 percent brokens) from millers (at Rp 4,600 per kilogram in 2009).[6] Given that BULOG apparently sets itself a procurement target every year and has limited resources, it is not clear how it would respond if prices fell beyond the ability of its procurement target to influence the market. In addition to buying rice, BULOG also owns 132 rice mills, each with a capacity of 3 tons an hour. This volume would appear to be excessive in light of the parastatal's current involvement in the market, although there is clearly a perceived need to ensure nationwide coverage.

Rice Distribution: In 1998, before shifting to its Beras Miskin (Raskin) program, Indonesia used a general rice consumption subsidy tied to stabilizing rice prices. However, at the height of the Asian financial crisis in 1997, the government launched a subsidy program that targeted poor households, making them eligible to receive 20 kilograms of rice per month at the price of Rp 1,000, roughly 35 percent of the 2004 market price. The program is large, delivering around 2.2 million metric tons of rice to about 9 million beneficiaries. According to Sidik (2004), the subsidy amounted to Rp 4.6 trillion in 2004.

Indonesia has since adjusted its Raskin program. Based on recent data, about 19.1 million poor households are eligible to receive 15 kilograms of subsidized rice monthly. The program now accounts for 90 percent of BULOG's market operations. It is carried out through about 50,000 Raskin distribution centers located in 15 regions throughout the country.

All of BULOG's 25 regional and 105 of its subregional offices manage the Raskin program. BULOG also provides supplies to the military and in times of disaster.

While the distribution of rice is of some benefit to the recipients, it must be noted that the costs of the exercise are extremely high. The overall benefit of supplying the poorest third or so of the population with just 10–20 percent of their needs (depending on household size) at a discount of approximately 35 percent may therefore be questioned, as this effectively reduces the household expenditure on rice by only 3.5–7.0 percent.

Even this calculation, however, may exaggerate benefits for individual families, since local authorities can intervene in their areas to reallocate the 15 kilograms into smaller parcels to benefit a greater number of households. There are also suggestions that a significant percentage does not reach the intended beneficiaries. One earlier estimate was that 18 percent went missing, on average, although the bulk of the disappearance was accounted for by a relatively small portion of villages (Olken 2006). In the near future, the challenge will be to improve the cost-effectiveness of the program, concentrate more on assistance to people in urban areas, tighten eligibility criteria and beneficiary reporting, and ensure that the program is placed on a financially sound footing.

Role of the private sector. The private sector in the rice industry not only faces competition from a powerful parastatal but also often has to pay additional taxes levied by the local authorities that have gained new regulatory responsibilities under Indonesia's policies promoting decentralization. The increased unpredictability has led to a general decline in business confidence. The private sector's main concern is that fiscal decentralization has not led to decentralized investments in projects that facilitate agricultural development.

Nonetheless, private firms in the rice industry have demonstrated continued interest in the development of stronger backward links. Again, though, continued government involvement in price setting jeopardizes such progress, since either artificially high or low official prices could encourage one or both partners to a contract to break their agreement.

The Maize Sector

Production and consumption. In 2009–10, production of maize in Indonesia reached 9 million tons. In spite of production increases, an additional 100,000 tons had to be imported in 2009–10—a marked decline from the 1.436 million tons needed in 2003–04—to meet the demands of the animal feed sector, which has been growing still more rapidly. Significant increases in domestic production have taken place since the 1980s as a result of increased fertilizer use and the introduction of improved varieties, particularly hybrids supplied by two or three major seed companies. Production increases would probably have been higher if all farmers had been able to finance the purchase of improved seeds and fertilizer (Swastika and others 2004). Still, because of seasonal mismatches between demand and supply, Indonesia is both an importer and an exporter of maize at different times in a typical year.

The country has experienced significant increases in yield as a result of more efficient plant management practices and the introduction of high-yield seed stock. In 2008, fully hybrid seed was used in 54 percent of total planted farmland. Maize production is concentrated in Java, which accounts for 61 percent of production. Maize has become the country's most important cash crop. Small-scale farmers produce most maize in Indonesia and sell through traditional multitiered market networks to feed processors.

Maize, the second most important cereal crop after rice, is grown in almost every part of the country, with Java accounting for 60 percent of total production. Most maize is grown in marginal areas with low productivity, on rain-fed lowlands, or on dry land areas where rainfall is erratic and soil fertility is low (Swastika 2008). Some millers work on a contract basis with farmers. Unlike with paddy, millers can afford to employ field staff to monitor compliance with contract terms, as maize is more profitable than rice.

As a commodity for human consumption, maize is considered to be an inferior product, which the poor consume in a disproportionately larger share. Increasing affluence has led to a significant decline in maize consumption in Indonesia. Unfortunately, up-to-date data are lacking. Per capita consumption is reported to have dropped from 19.45 kilograms in 1984 to 3.69 kilograms in 1996 (Suhariyanto 2008). Estimates by the Food and Agriculture Organization (FAO) of the United Nations put total maize consumption at just 7 percent of total food consumption in 2001 (Swastika 2008).

Public Sector Role: The country has realized notable success is adapting plant science technology to local conditions. The Central Research Institute for Crop Research had successfully collaborated with both international and domestic seed distribution companies in its efforts to progressively improve maize yield. Both the trade and input subsidy regimes in Indonesia have been liberalized, and private sector companies are able to compete in the maize input market on an equal basis with state-owned enterprises (SOEs). The government has undertaken cooperative efforts with several international plant science companies, including BISI, Monsanto, and Pioneer, to improve yields of hybrid varieties.

The government also hopes to increase the use of locally produced basic materials, which are lower in price, through a number of rural development initiatives. For the past 20 years, the government has been pursuing a variety of rural economic development strategies, all designed to benefit smallholder farmers and strengthen cooperatives. The programs have been uneven in their impact and erratic in their outcomes.

A series of initiatives have been pursued at both central and provincial government levels. Federal decentralization of decision making in Indonesia has not assisted program design and coordination, and many donor-funded projects have failed. The most recent high-profile program that has been launched is the Rural Agribusiness Development Program, which commenced operations in 2008 (Agriculture and Agri-food Canada 2009a). In contrast, investment projects undertaken in the private sector to develop farm-to-market links for maize and other inputs into animal feed production have proved much more successful in realizing positive rural development impacts.

Private Sector Role: Foreign investors dominate the animal feed industry. They rely on imports for basic materials, especially maize, which is imported mainly from the United States and Brazil. They also import processed components. The feed market accounts for 7 million tons of yellow maize consumption annually. This share has been growing as increasing affluence has enhanced demand for animal products.

Approximately 120 animal feed component mills operate in Indonesia, with a total production capacity of 9 million tons per year. Most of these mills are located in Java because this is where the majority of Indonesians live and thus where the livestock industry—particularly the poultry industry—is concentrated (PT Data Consultants 2008).

The so-called "Livestock Revolution" is well under way in Indonesia. The largest businesses involved in the feed production industry, either as integrated concerns or as independent producers, include the Thai company Charoen Pokphand (CP) (estimated at 25 percent of total production capacity), Japfa Comfeed (16 percent), CJ Feed (7 percent), and Sierad Produce (5 percent) (Agriculture and Agri-food Canada 2009a).

Additionally, the private sector–led chicken production industry has been a notable success in Indonesia and has helped to drive the nation's agricultural economy forward. The chicken feed subsector alone required 4.1 million tons of feed in 2008. Maize makes up 50 percent of the raw material used in poultry feed. Broiler meat consumption increased at a rate of 8.3 percent per year from 2005 to 2009. In spite of rising prices, consumption increased from 5.1 kilograms per capita in 2007 to 5.4 kilograms per capita in 2008. This level, however, remains low compared with the level of 7.1 kilograms per capita for all of ASEAN.

Feed-producing companies are permitted to import maize into Indonesia free of duty. The cost of producing animal feed declined around 2000 when new port facilities in Jakarta enabled larger ships to carry grain imports. At that time, significantly, Cargill signed agreements with Indonesian partners to help improve port grain handling.

The industry has grown rapidly since its start in the 1970s. It grew at a rate of 8.4 percent for five years until it fell backward in 2007 in response to the avian flu epidemic. Avian flu was reported in several parts of the country, and chicken sales fell by 50 percent in one year. However, chicken and related feed sales bounced back in 2008.

Recently the industry has concentrated into fewer, larger-scale operators. Companies like PT Japfa Comfeed Indonesia, which leads the industry in the country, have developed aggressively through mergers and acquisitions and internal growth to take a strong integrated position in the animal feed, poultry-processing, cattle feed lot, and related subsectors (PT Data Consultants 2008). PT Japfa Comfeed operates nine feed mills in Indonesia and has a processing capacity of 1.87 million tons. In 2008, the company operated at 81 percent of this capacity in producing mostly high-protein feed for chickens.

In addition to PT Japfa Comfeed, other vertically integrated companies in the chicken feed and breeder and commercial farming businesses include Cheil Jedang Feed Indonesia, which is a subsidiary of Cheil Jedang from Korea and is involved in pig, quail, and shrimp rearing as well as chicken production; CJ Feed; Gold Coin; Malindo Feedmill, which is owned by a Malaysian family; Sierad Profeed Tbk; and CP, which operates animal feed milling facilities with aggregate capacity for 2.2 million tons in a number of areas in Indonesia. The company owns six animal feed factories, one fish feed factory, two chicken meat–processing plants, one factory producing animal husbandry equipment, and maize drying and storage facilities.

Malaysia[7]

The Rice Sector

Farm-level operations. In the country's three distinct geographic parts—Peninsular Malaysia, Sabah, and Sarawak—marked differences characterize the ways in which an estimated 138,000 farmers grow rice. Development emphasis has tended to concentrate on Peninsular Malaysia, where the country's eight rice granaries, or large-scale irrigation schemes, produced around 1.725 million tons of paddy in 2007. These have all been provided with government support services, which permit double cropping and modern farming of paddy. The government is also providing incentives designed to encourage private investment and service provision. Land on some of these schemes has been consolidated, with some farmers renting land from the original tenants. The resulting larger plots have made more efficient farming and higher yields possible.

Most farmers in Sabah and Sarawak, where there are no private seed growers, plant subsidized seed produced by the Department of Agriculture (DOA) Seed Production Centers once every three to four years, using their own farm-saved seeds in between new issues. The two states produced around 200,000 tons of traditional paddy in 2007. The situation is very different in Peninsular Malaysia, where farmers are encouraged to use subsidized certified seeds produced by DOA as well as seed sold by an increasing number of 14 private seed companies (including farmers' associations), which are given annual quotas by the government to produce the country's total estimated seed requirements. The DOA is gradually privatizing its seed centers to focus increasingly on seed certification.

The rice industry in Malaysia is heavily regulated, with the aim of assisting farmers, who are mainly poor, through subsidies and income support. There have been significant improvements in productivity, but production in many parts of Peninsular Malaysia seems to have reached a plateau because of competition for land from housing and industrial development. Given constraints on further developing the rice sector and the fact that the nation has a large trading surplus, some have argued that the country should aim for self-reliance rather than self-sufficiency and should work to build up innovative sourcing and trading alliances rather than concentrate on production.

The practice of imposing flat-rate deductions[8] for presumed moisture content not only provides no incentive for farmers to improve the quality of paddy that they offer to millers and brokers but also seems to positively encourage them to deliver bad paddy. Paddy quality is now regarded as a major problem, with high moisture content and considerable adulteration.

Despite this major setback, technological development and investments at the milling and packaging levels have resulted in local rice of comparable quality to imported white rice in terms of both physical characteristics (mainly with 5 percent brokens) and taste. There is scope for further improvement with a proper system of grading and prices that reflect the quality delivered.

From time to time government announcements commit Malaysia to rice self-sufficiency. That determination was reemphasized in 2009 after the price rises of 2007–08.[9] However, its levels of self-sufficiency have fluctuated between 68 percent and 86 percent since the 1970s. The levels are much higher on Peninsular Malaysia (more than 80 percent) than in Sabah (30 percent) and Sarawak (50 percent). Rice consumption in Malaysia, however, is lower than in the other study countries. The level—an estimated 79 kilograms per capita—largely reflects the greater wealth of Malaysian consumers, allowing them to move away from dependence on the staple food.

Milling and marketing. Of the country's 231 mills, 174 are in Peninsular Malaysia, down from 274 in 1997. The majority of paddy in Peninsular Malaysia is sold to mills in bulk (because of the extent of combine harvesting) via collectors or purchasing agents (including local farmers' associations), which are often strategically aligned with the combine harvester operators. In Sabah and Sarawak, on the other hand, many farmers still sell paddy to mills in gunny sacks. Those planting traditional varieties in Sabah and Sarawak use mills that perform contract milling for a fee.

The 40 mills operated by Malaysia's partner in the domestic paddy and rice industry, the former parastatal Padi Beras Nasional Bhd. (BERNAS),[10] only produce medium-quality, 15 percent broken rice, part of which is sold to private wholesalers and retailers, including BERNAS joint ventures.

BERNAS, the largest single milling company in the country, purchases 400,000 tons of paddy annually, from which it produces 275,000 tons of finished rice. BERNAS buys around 42 percent of local production and accounts for 44 percent of wholesaling through a number of subsidiaries. Significantly as well, BERNAS operates the "Save More" retail outlets and supplies rice to its own chains and others under a number of brand names. Suppliers to the supermarkets tend to be the larger wholesalers, which are integrated backward to mills in Peninsular Malaysia, Sabah, and Sarawak. They supply both local and imported rice.

BERNAS does not supply any of the supermarket chains directly, but does so through its wholesaling joint ventures. Among other private sector rice merchandisers, significant consolidation has taken place in recent years, with the intention of forming stable supply chains from production to consumption. Wholesalers have been buying up millers, and vice versa. Wholesalers have also been attempting to develop long-term relationships with supermarkets and hypermarkets. A number of large trading groups have emerged.

Milled rice goes through 1,239 rice wholesalers,[11] who were supplying local and imported rice to 44,637 retail outlets as of 2007. The actual number of companies involved may be significantly lower, as wholesalers require a license in every state in which they operate, and thus some may be counted more than once. Supermarkets and hypermarkets are growing in importance as rice distributors. As a consequence, the number of traditional shops selling rice has declined, particularly in urban areas. In Peninsular Malaysia, about 20 percent of rice goes through hypermarkets and supermarkets, 40 percent through convenience stores, and the remainder through traditional outlets.

Role of the (former) parastatal. Privatized in 1996 with the government retaining a "Golden Share," BERNAS remains the primary agency of a Malaysian rice policy that has historically focused on rice production and repeated commitment to rice self-sufficiency.[12] That determination was reemphasized in 2009 after the price rises of 2007–08. However, its levels of self-sufficiency have fluctuated between 68 percent and 86 percent since the 1970s. The levels are much higher on Peninsular Malaysia (more than 80 percent) than in Sabah (30 percent) and Sarawak (50 percent).[13]

In the highly regulated milling industry, BERNAS is the primary instrument for implementing that regulation.[14] Its aim has traditionally been to assist farmers, who are predominately poor, with subsidies and income supports. Since the crisis of 2007–08, however, the government has refocused its attention on increasing production in an effort to make the country self-sufficient.

Additionally, BERNAS manages the country's rice stocks, which it obtains from local paddy procurement as well as from imports. However, unlike the agencies in Indonesia and the Philippines, BERNAS has no mandate to provide subsidies for rice to the country's poor. Under its 1996 contract with the government, it is also responsible for managing and maintaining national rice stockpiles to ensure that the country has a sufficient supply of rice at all times. This role entails more than an emergency or food security function. It is also a mechanism to stabilize supplies and prices of rice in the country. Following the rice crisis of 2008, the government increased the national stockpile level from 92,000 metric tons to 292,000 metric tons at any one time.

Further, BERNAS acts as the buyer of last resort for paddy farmers, manages the Bumiputera Rice Millers Scheme for the benefit of Malay Muslim rice millers, and distributes paddy price subsidies to farmers on behalf of the government. BERNAS currently controls about 24 percent of the nation's paddy market and 45 percent of the local rice market. Its monopoly on imports, scheduled to expire in January 2011, has been extended for 10 years.

As rice millers are required to produce 30 percent of their output at standard and premium quality, BERNAS is free to determine the price for its superior-quality rice, the profits from which are used to cross-subsidize the minimum production required in standard- and medium-quality rice. Although its responsibilities in many ways duplicate those of the NFA in the Philippines and BULOG in Indonesia, BERNAS is a private company traded on the Kuala Lumpur Stock Exchange.

Role of the private sector. The primary challenge facing the private milling sector in Malaysia is the evolving role of BERNAS and the ability of its management to steer a narrow course between regulator and competitor without tilting the competitive table too far in its own direction. Two examples of its practices illustrate the challenge it is seen to pose to private companies with no public sector affiliation or responsibilities.

The first is the quasi-parastatal role that BERNAS plays in subsidizing fertilizer and other farm-level inputs. BERNAS manages public subsidies to small farmers as part of its "social obligation." It allocates subsidies according to careful records of the net weight of paddy that individual farmers sell to mills. Although administratively complex, the system would appear to have the merit of minimally disrupting the workings of the market. The subsidies for fertilizer and similar inputs, however, do earn some criticism from private firms that are unable to compete in that market because of the below-cost supplies that farmer associations supplied by BERNAS can provide.

Second, since 1997 the rate of direct subsidies to farmers based on their paddy sales no longer reflects previously enforced deductions for excessive moisture, impurities, or damaged and unripe grains. Since paddy deliveries to mills contain a high (and increasingly higher) content of impurities and moisture, the costs of the mills' purchases, as well as of the federal price subsidy payments, have risen. Higher handling, drying, and operating costs, lower milling recovery, and reduced storage times all have the effect of discouraging private millers from investing in modernizing their operations.

The Maize Sector

Production and Consumption. Malaysia produces relatively little maize—90,000–100,000 tons—and instead depends on imports of raw material to produce animal feed. The country imported 2.6 million tons in 2009–10 and 2.0 million tons in 2008–09. No import restrictions prohibit the importation of maize. Meat and poultry consumption has been increasingly rapidly in Malaysia. However, the country still does not produce sufficient meat products to satisfy domestic demand. In 2007, meat and poultry imports were valued at $400 million. In recent years, they have been growing at about 5 percent per year.

The government has undertaken targeted efforts to boost domestic production of beef cattle, goats, and dairy cattle as part of larger efforts to improve the rural economy and—to an extent—find substitutes for high-value food imports. The government has not been involved directly in supporting the poultry, egg, or pig industries.

Malaysia's animal husbandry industry consumes 3 million tons of feed ingredients per year. Fully 80 percent of these are maize related, another 12 percent involve process wastes, and only 3 percent involve other grains. A strong preference exists among all segments of Malaysia's animal husbandry sector to consume maize (Agriculture and Agri-food Canada 2009b).

Malaysia's livestock industry is dominated by the poultry sector, which accounted for 83 percent of industry sales in 2005. The pig and cattle farming sectors are much smaller, with shares of 9 percent and 2 percent, respectively (Agriculture and Agri-food Canada 2009b). In recent years, the government has attempted to stimulate cattle rearing by integrating it with palm oil production on 80 commercial farms. Pig farming involves 800 family farms. For several reasons, including the Islamic orientation of the rural sector, periodic outbreaks of disease, and small initial scale, pork production has been slow to grow. The poultry sector, on the other hand, has been growing quite rapidly. The key difference between the poultry industry and the pig and cattle industries lies in the level of commercially oriented investment.

Public Sector Role: In 2008, the government passed an animal feeds act that authorized an Animal Feed Board to supervise the quality of animal feed through import, production, sale, and consumption controls. Significantly, the board would have the authority to certify halal standards. The Islamic cultural credibility of Malaysia and its certification process have attracted interest from foreign investors in developing fully integrated farm-to-freezer systems for poultry production.

The Philippines

The Rice Sector

Farm-level operations. The Philippines has been 85–90 percent self-sufficient in rice in recent years, on average. *Palay*—the Filipino term for unmilled rice—is produced at an annual average rate of approximately 16.24 million tons all over the country, but with a heavy concentration on the island of Luzon, in part because of climatic conditions and in part because of the proximity of the major market of Metro Manila. Double cropping is common there.

Smaller farmers generally do their own harvesting; larger farmers employ laborers. Threshing is generally mechanized. Palay drying is carried out on roads or other available hard surfaces, such as gravestones, but a large proportion is delivered directly to mills wet, particularly on Luzon. For their own consumption, farmers usually have palay milled at small local steel-huller mills, known as *kikisan*, whose operators usually take payment in the form of bran residues. These custom millers are usually also farmers. Traveling millers with portable mills can also be found.

Considerable competition exists for the available surplus palay (Hayami, Kikuchi, and Marciano 1999). Assembly traders or collectors visit farmers—or, more likely, live in the village and arrange supply for traders or mills. They may either take title to the palay or receive a commission from the eventual buyer, who could be a large trader or a miller. Some do both. Those who take title rely on visual inspection to assess moisture content. There are also actors known as *viajeros* who buy palay, have it milled, and then sell the rice.

Farmers often deliver directly to mills under arrangements made by agents. Traders may buy palay from farmers for sale to mills or may have palay toll-milled for subsequent sale to wholesalers. The industry is very much based on long-term relationships, which are sometimes secured through credit transactions, with mills lending funds to collectors.

Quality issues: Traders report that the current quality levels of rice are poor. Laboratory analysis, in fact, has demonstrated that 80 percent of the rice in large retail markets fails to comply fully with grading criteria. Only 2 percent of the samples met a nonmandatory standard above the lowest national grade.[15] As in Indonesia, there is a strong correlation between price and the degree of yellowness of the grain. Moisture meters are little used by farmers and even by mills in these two countries, partly because of their high cost.[16]

Price, rather than quality, remains the dominant factor in the rice market at all stages of the supply chain, from farmer to consumer. In particular, moisture levels are excessive. Although mills in Luzon are trying to address this problem by doing the drying themselves, farmers elsewhere seem to have little incentive to dry well because most mills offer no quality premium. Farmers are reportedly reluctant to sell to the parastatal National Food Authority (NFA) because it imposes more stringent quality standards (Ramos 2000). Mills, as well, have little incentive to dry well because wholesalers and retailers base their decisions on volume and availability, not quality.

Milling and marketing. The milling and distribution industry is fragmented; few dominant companies operate in the rice sector. All mills in the Philippines process to the white rice stage. In the last two decades, some limited consolidation of mills has occurred, and there are now approximately 10,000 mills in the country. The millers' association estimates that around 10 percent have been upgraded to a reasonable standard, but other milling equipment is said to be antiquated. Recovery rates using dried palay are as low as 62 percent, when 67–68 percent can be achieved with new technology. Wet palay recovery is said to be around 58 percent (Hayami, Kikuchi, and Marciano 1999). It could be argued that low recovery rates have a significant impact on the country's rice deficit and, consequently, on its need to import.

There are many rice varieties in the Philippines, and rice is usually marketed under the name of the variety. Mills often employ agents to carry out the rice marketing for them. Rice targeted at the upper end of the market, mainly through supermarkets, is chosen from selected varieties. Extensive treatment is required to add value for sales to supermarkets, involving color sorting to remove yellow rice and the removal of broken rice (brokens), with the high-level supermarket standard being 5 percent brokens. Broken rice so removed gets mixed in with other rice. Unlike the situation in other regional markets, there is no rice flour market that could absorb brokens, and using rice for feed is not only uneconomic but would also appear inappropriate in a rice deficit country.

Much of the rice trading is carried out at the Intercity Rice Market located just north of Manila. Here, a rice-processing and -trading cluster has emerged around the operation of 120 small millers, each with capacity of about 4 tons an hour. These millers and merchandisers buy dried palay from traders who bring truckloads down from producing areas in the north and also from farmers in the vicinity. Depending on seasonal factors, they may also buy palay and rice from outside Luzon. While many of these mills do only simple milling, others have become more specialized and add value to their product with the help of color separators or rice polishers.

These small mills sell to other millers and traders operating in the same market or to wholesalers and retailers who journey to them from the Intercity Rice Market to source product. Manila merchandisers sell either to retailers or direct to consumers. Millers also buy white rice from importers who are permitted to import specialized varieties such as "Hom Mali" jasmine rice from Thailand and glutinous rice from Vietnam. Importers generally include the larger millers or traders. However, smaller companies sometimes group together to undertake imports.

Commercial mills also mill palay purchased by the NFA, an activity that has given rise to frequent allegations of corrupt practices in the mills' handling of such palay. The corruption seems to stem primarily from rent-seeking activities of NFA staff (Ramos 2000).

While some mills supply the top end of the market directly, the standard method of distribution is through rice wholesalers, who are often also millers, and, below them, wholesalers and retailers, who carry out a dual function. Rice milled outside the Manila area is usually transported in large trucks to the Tondo area of Manila. Wholesalers have warehouses in this area and also on the outskirts of Manila. Sales used to be made to retailers straight from the trucks, although this practice is now less common.

Most mills do not supply retail stores directly, since they would have to transfer rice from larger trucks to smaller vehicles to complete retail store deliveries, and traffic congestion and vehicle cost mean that such direct deliveries to retailers are not cost-effective. There is some vertical integration in the rice trade, with millers either owning the wholesale company or working through a company owned by a relative (Ramos 2000).

Outside of Metro Manila, however, millers often supply retailers directly. They make considerable efforts to ensure regular demand from retailers, and sales of rice on credit are used to promote loyalty (Hayami, Kikuchi, and Marciano 1999). Rice is usually sold through specialized rice stores operating in town markets, but general retailers also sell it. More than in the other study countries, consumers are aware of several different varieties and are prepared to pay premiums for those they value most.

Supermarkets and the modern retailing sector (including the ubiquitous convenience stores) account for a growing percentage of rice sales. Some of the larger millers in the Manila area have the capacity to do retail packing and either sell their own brand to supermarkets or produce and pack a store's own brand. A recent trend has been for some supermarkets to sell in bulk out of 50-kilogram bags, thus competing directly with established rice retailers. This practice applies mainly to the chains aiming at buyers in the first- and second-quintile socioeconomic groups. There is also a distinct group of supermarkets that target second-, third-, and fourth-quintile customers. These tend to buy rice and pack it in-store in 1-kilogram or 5-kilogram packs, selling only three varieties. These chains eschew sales from large bags as too time-consuming and the source of stock control difficulties. Like the traditional market, these supermarkets are very much oriented toward low prices.

In 2008, supermarket chains were asked by NFA to sell subsidized "NFA" rice, which they did with some reluctance, partly because they were required to collect the rice from NFA stores rather than have it delivered. While initial supplies were of high quality, the condition of rice provided by the parastatal allegedly dropped rapidly.

Logistics and infrastructure. The state of Manila's congested port and most roads in the Philippines presents important infrastructure problems, with vehicle transport the most affected. Although entering and leaving the Port of Manila is almost always difficult, most private sector rice imports are of small quantity and arrive in single shipment lots, posing less of a problem than would regular, large consignments. The container terminal is said to function relatively well, at least for small-scale consignments. By contrast, congestion, both on terminal and off terminal, does affect the larger consignments of the NFA imports, which have recently been dispersed for delivery to various islands and other parts of the country, rather than first landing in and then transshipping from Manila. This change in policy has helped to relieve some congestion. The capacity of ports other than Manila poses less of a problem.

Additionally, though, exporters from Thailand complain that they cannot ship containers to the Philippines because to do so only adds demurrage[17] and container detention costs and increases time for offloading up to 14 days. To avoid these delays and extra costs, the Philippines NFA tender instructions explicitly stipulate that rice should be shipped as general cargo in 50-kilogram bags in vessels that are no larger than 10,000 metric tons. For minor ports, vessels are restricted to even lower capacity.

In general, the NFA does not assume responsibility for storing and tracing shipping line containers or for scheduling vessel deliveries around peak periods. The total logistics costs to the entire chain as a result of the NFA's unwillingness to assume this risk is significant, since continuing to ship rice in break bulk modes also increases order-to-delivery times, increases inventory holding requirements, and reduces chain flexibility.

More significant internal transport problems involve moving shipments of palay and milled rice from the major producing area north of Luzon to Manila, as well as from most major islands, along congested single-lane highways. For the most part, these roads pass through urban areas rather than around them, making the use of large, more cost-efficient trucks impractical. Significantly, rural roads are also inadequate in many remote parts of the Philippines and cannot effectively support rice and maize assembly and shipment to urban markets.

Indeed, these are the very areas that operate as the supply end of national food chains. Heavily loaded palay trucks have badly damaged the road that connects the intercity milling area outside Manila with the north-south highway between producing areas and Manila. Estimates from 1999 put the percentage of paved road for the Philippines at just 17 percent, compared with more than 75 percent for Malaysia and Thailand (Ramos 2000). In Luzon, at the demand end of national food supply chains, roads are inadequate for a different reason—urban congestion. The operating cost per kilometer of a 12.5-ton truck in the Philippines is US 4.7–6.7 cents (2.08–2.95 pesos) per ton-kilometer (Center for Food and Agribusiness 2009).

Interisland shipments in the Philippines pose a second category of constraint due to infrequent and irregular sailings. Customers on smaller islands can never be sure when their shipments will arrive. The major cyclones in 2009 provided an extreme example of the kinds of problems faced every year during monsoon months, when ships are unable to sail and many roads become impassable.

Role of the parastatal. In the Philippines, the domestic rice supply chain is somewhat complex, with numerous participants at different levels. It is further complicated by the involvement of the government, primarily through the NFA's interventions in the consumer market. NFA, the sole licensing authority for the palay and rice trade, uses imports to lower consumer prices in the lean season.[18]

In addition to its price-setting role, the NFA has a mandate to stabilize rice prices by selling the commodity directly to the general public when prices become unaffordable. This program normally comes into play during the third quarter of the year, which is considered to be the lean period for rice production. When natural calamities hit the country, seasonal low supply deteriorates even more rapidly, and the NFA is charged with ensuring that rice stocks are available to carry the country through the lean period, doing so by injecting mostly imported rice into the local market through its accredited rice retailers.

The agency's rice subsidy program to benefit the poor involves it in cooperation with the Department of Social Welfare and Development in distributing rice at below-market prices. A third program executed by the NFA is designed to address humanitarian emergencies. The NFA implements this program in coordination with the National Disaster Coordination Committee and is expected to move rice stocks to areas hit by natural calamities, where normal market operations have ceased. Fifteen days' consumption of rice stocks are stored in various strategic distribution centers for this purpose.

Role of the private sector. A major challenge facing the milling industry in the Philippines involves securing access to capital for upgrading milling facilities and accelerating the process of competitive shake-out so that economies of scale can begin to emerge in the sector.

Private sector participants report overcapacity in milling facilities. Private millers are faced with competition from the NFA, and millers cannot source sufficient rice in the neighborhood of their factories. In some places north of Manila, there appear to be too many small mills. Millers, who operate their facilities no more than eight hours per day, are very keen to win a contract from the NFA for milling NFA palay. This situation is likely to be aggravated in the near future because new and modern mills are under construction in the rice production areas at Luzon. Some millers have invested in modern milling equipment and steam polishers, but they cannot operate them profitably because of overcapacity and marginal cost pricing. However, the area under rice production and production levels per hectare are unlikely to increase soon, and this may assist the sector.

The mills in the Philippines all process to the white rice stage. Although there has been some limited consolidation of mills in the last two decades, the total number (10,000), their small scale, and their apparent overcapacity would appear to leave significant opportunity for further consolidation. Economies of scale are not being realized in the sector.

The quality of rice produced is uneven, and competition among millers remains primarily price based. Consumers willingly accept 15 percent broken rice as long as the price is low. The millers' association estimates that 10 percent of mills in the country have been upgraded to a reasonable standard. However, the remainder of the nation's milling equipment is said to be antiquated. Recovery rates starting with dried palay are as low as 62 percent, when 70 percent can be achieved with new technology. Wet palay recovery is said to be around 58 percent (Hayami, Kikuchi, and Marciano 1999). It could be argued that these low recovery rates have a significant impact on the country's rice deficit and thereby on its need to import.

Market segmentation is just beginning to impact the national market, with supermarkets and other high-end food outlets demanding higher product quality, such as 5 percent broken rice. However, millers require additional processing steps (such as sorting to remove broken and discolored rice) and better technology to achieve these product specifications. As a result, the high-end market is relatively undersupplied. Significantly, unlike in other countries in the region, no market exists in the Philippines for either rice flour or rice-based animal feed where millers might be able to sell the by-products of more demanding, high-quality milling.

The Maize Sector

Production and Consumption. The Philippines has come close to maize self-sufficiency, in large part because of the high level of protection that the government provides to domestic farmers. Indeed, the yellow maize market is more protected in the Philippines than in any other ASEAN study country. This protection tends to carry over to white maize prices as well, and thus benefits all maize farmers, who tend to be poorer than palay producers. However, maize protection pushes up costs for feed producers, and these increased costs eventually affect the incomes of both animal-processing companies and small farmers who are involved in animal rearing.

In 2007, around 10 percent of domestic requirements in the Philippines were imported, while imports fell back from this level in 2008. By mid-2009, imports had reached 200,000 tons, the maximum permitted that year under the maximum access volume (MAV) in-quota,[19] which qualified for duties at 35 percent rather than the 50 percent that applies to higher import volumes.

While poultry production is largely in the hands of large, integrated companies in the Philippines, hog production remains predominately a smallholder activity. Poultry production is growing at about 15 percent per year, while the pig industry has suffered from food safety problems, and recently from "swine flu" scares, which have led to reduced demand for pork. As a result of the decline in demand from the hog industry, no maize supply constraints existed in mid-2009.

Feed Mills: There are 376 registered feed mills in the Philippines. However, there may be other mills that remain unregistered. Almost three quarters of the registered companies are on the main island of Luzon. Only the largest 26 companies, however, are members of the Philippines Association of Feed Millers (PAFMI). These companies are estimated to account for more than 60 percent of total feed production.

These large companies operate feedlots, meat-processing facilities, and some food retail outlets. Each of them has adopted a somewhat different business model. However, the business activities in which they have decided to invest directly, as well as others with which they affiliate con-tractually, are connected, with the help of production scheduling and quality control systems. In some instances, chain integrators rear poultry and other animals; in others, they manage franchisee farmers who do their rearing under contract. At the other end of the spectrum, many mills have remained relatively small family operations. In still other instances, maize traders have decided to add value to their operations by also going into the feed-processing business.

The price of maize has a direct effect on the competitiveness of meat products because it accounts for the largest share of input costs. In 2006, the farm gate price for maize in the Philippines was 10 pesos per kilogram. This price rose to 13–14 pesos per kilogram in 2007 and remained at that level for much of 2008. In July 2009, the price fell back to 10.8 pesos, although the NFA was still intervening in the local market in an effort to drive prices up again by buying at 13 pesos. Indeed, this may be a more realistic price to sustain supply commit-ments from farmers. Industry informants suggested that 10.8 pesos per kilogram was not profitable. In January 2009, little maize remained in the national supply chain, and the farm price rose temporarily as high as 25 pesos per kilogram.

Importing: Imports of maize into the Philippines involve somewhat com-plicated arrangements. Imports are all technically handled through the

NFA, although most of the import preparation work is actually done by PAFMI. The association consolidates import requests of individual members into large tenders. Only a few companies have sufficient demand to justify purchases of shipload quantities. Consolidation into shipload quantities enables buyers to minimize shipping costs. NFA charges group buyers the 35 percent import tariff. However, it absorbs other administrative costs. Other than this administrative cost saving, the advantages of NFA involvement are unclear. Moreover, its involvement in maize procurement appears to slow down the import process.

The prevailing in-quota import duty rate of 35 percent provides considerable protection for Filipino farmers. It remains to be seen what will happen under the ASEAN Free Trade Agreement (AFTA). There is some concern that the country will be flooded with imports from Thailand, although the current level of production in Thailand and the demands of the Thai feed industry suggest that this fear may be unfounded. Moreover, the high prevailing import duty also creates incentives for smuggling. Reportedly, Indonesian maize is being smuggled into the southern provinces of the Philippines.

The seasonality of maize production in the Philippines seems to be less pronounced than in the past. This can be attributed to the fact that farmers are now staggering planting dates in response to climate change. Although farmers are protected by the in-quota rate, they are still exposed to competition from feed wheat, which is imported with a duty of just 7 percent.[20] Only the largest feed mills have access to imported wheat, however, with the result that smaller mills, which depend on local maize, have become less competitive (Costales 2008).

In 2009, some 1 million tons of feed wheat had been imported by September; as a result, maize prices fell significantly from January highs. Because of the higher prices of traditional animal feed ingredients, feed producers sought out other lower-cost ingredients; the result was large increases in palm oil cake imports and the use of residues from the food-processing and brewing industries. The consequences of these new feed formulations may have altered demand for feed ingredients permanently and thus may have had a sustained effect on demand for maize (Agriculture and Agri-food Canada 2009c). That possibility remains to be confirmed, however.

Although there has been some new investment, few traders have built modern drying facilities; like rice, most maize is still dried along the side of the road. The moisture content of traded maize frequently exceeds 13 percent. Roads are poor in rural areas, and as a result transport costs are high. Given the choice, many feed companies indicate that they would prefer to import from South America rather than buy locally because supply can be erratic during rainy seasons and quality can be spotty. Several government programs exist that are designed to promote more thorough maize drying.

If farmers continue to spread their cultivation activities over the entire annual cycle and move away from peak seasonality, traders may find it more profitable to make investments in processing and drying units, which can operate near full utilization on a year-round basis. At present, large feed companies such as San Miguel are starting to buy maize directly from farmers and dry it themselves, rather than relying on traders.

Transport Infrastructure: As with rice, transport infrastructure is poor and is a major handicap. Yellow maize production is in the north of Luzon, but most feed mills are around Manila, and there is only one significant road connecting the two areas. The main white maize–producing regions of Southern Mindanao, Central Mindanao, and the Autonomous Region have the smallest ratios of roads to harvested area of any regions in the country.

Average maize marketing costs in 2000 were as high as $60 per ton, compared to less than $20 per ton in Thailand (Costales 2008). Mindanao is also a major producing area for yellow maize. Maize has been shipped to Manila in barges that have a capacity of 7,000 tons. However, demand for such shipping from the south has decreased as new feed mills in Mindanao now take up most of the available supply. Companies consider Manila's port facilities and discharge rates to be adequate for large quantities of feed wheat, for example, as the available ports can handle ships of 50,000–60,000 tons.

Thailand

The Rice Sector[21]
Farm-level operations. Thailand produces around 20 million tons of rice annually, of which 4–5 million is "Hom Mali" jasmine rice. Exports have accounted for around 40–50 percent of this production, on average. About half of Thai exports usually go to Africa, with parboiled rice accounting for a major percentage of these exports.

Quality Concerns: The large export companies have been reporting declining rice quality for some time. These reports apply to both normal rice and to "Hom Mali," which is losing some of its aroma, exporters argue. Traders also express concern about the alleged lack of investment in research and development, particularly as it affects the quality of jasmine rice. Mills, for their part, dispute exporters' assessment of declining quality. They argue that quality can be affected by cold weather or drought, and thus one poor season should not be seen as indicative of a long-term decline. Thailand does not suffer the same level of moisture-related problems with paddy as do most of the other study countries, primarily because a much larger proportion of Thailand's paddy crop is dried mechanically by the mills.

Additionally, exporters constantly complain about farming practices, citing the amount of grass seed found mixed with the paddy. Allegedly, this indicates that weeding is not being done intensively. Some business executives also feel that the introduction of new varieties of rice is leading to declines in quality. Many farmers have produced five harvests in two years, even though the industry still talks of the "first" and "second" harvests. In 2008–09, those with access to irrigation tried to produce six crops in two years to take advantage of inflated prices.

New varieties permit paddy to reach maturity more rapidly. However, the industry argues that rapid maturation is achieved at the expense of lower quality. Another factor influencing quality was said by Thai exporters to be the shady practices of mills, which, until 2009, received paddy on behalf of the government under the Paddy Pledging Program (box 1). Having no real financial interest in the quality of what they procured, they were alleged to have paid too little attention to quality at the time of purchase. Exporters argue that there is a need for national paddy standards to be introduced.

Quality problems are not new. The trade in Thailand indicates that the first harvest of the year is usually of good quality and that the second crop is always less reliable, since paddy is then harvested in the rainy, hot season and becomes "parboiled" naturally in steamy weather. Thai exporters like to hold over stocks from the first crop until the second is available since they may have to blend the two to compensate for the poor quality of the second. In any case, export specifications usually cannot be met from the second crop alone. However, from 2007 on, these blending practices became difficult because of the way the government intervention program was operated. Then and subsequently, exporters could not guarantee that they would be able to purchase the rice required for blending.

When the Thai government issued tenders, information was provided on whether the rice was first or second harvest. But large rice traders

Box 1

Thailand's Paddy Pledging Program

Thailand's 30-year-old Paddy Pledging Program came into being to provide soft loans to farmers who gained a three-month-long delay in selling their crops. The farmers could use the crops as collateral for subsequent loans and could retain the option to keep the loan or repay it and sell the paddy for more than mills would have paid 90 days earlier (Poapongsakom 2008). The Thai model, which was refined after it started in 1981–82, has had a positive impact on the agricultural sectors of several developing and transition countries.

In the 21st century, however, the scheme has been increasingly used to stabilize prices and to promote farmer income. By 2009, fully half of the second, or dry season, harvest of 7 million tons—compared to a typical 10 percent level over the first 20 years—was pledged under the government program, a reflection of the fact that government lenders were paying significantly more for paddy than the prevailing market price. Farmers kept their loans; public warehouses accumulated inventories; and millers and traders ran into difficulty buying paddy or rice on the local market.

The government's slowness to sell its stocks—or rather, its unwillingness to sell at a loss—caused shortages, particularly for exporters. Furthermore, the scheme reportedly skewed private sector calculations by encouraging the construction of added mills primarily in order to profit from favorable rates for handling pledged rice and boosting returns for the warehouse owners that stored milled rice for the government.

In 2008 the conservatively estimated financial costs to the government stood at about $900 million,[a] and in November 2009, unsold rice in government storage was estimated at 6 million tons. Before the year ended, the government announced a new program that would guarantee farmers a minimum price, thus establishing a form of crop insurance that went beyond Paddy Pledging. It also alarmed farmers, who feared an eligibility standard requiring them to deliver paddy with a moisture content of 15 percent or less, and projected costs appeared very high.

Source: Authors.
a. Poapongsakorn 2008, quoting a "Public Warehouse Organization" source.

said they could not rely on this information because of mills' and warehouse operators' practice of sometimes blending rice from the two harvests, selling the blend, and substituting the stock with other rice of uncertain harvest. Some tendered rice was reportedly two years old. Exporters claimed to have been given inadequate time to check stocks before bidding for them. At the same time, exporters are also concerned about the quality of rice received through normal marketing channels from private mills. These mills often lend money to farmers and are thus in a difficult position when it comes to rejecting farmer deliveries for quality reasons.

If suitable rice is available, exporters and suppliers to the domestic market in Thailand have many options for reprocessing, whether they buy directly from mills or from government stocks. For example, they can buy 5 percent broken rice and remove the brokens from these stocks to achieve 100 percent head rice. Brokens so removed can then be added to 5 percent broken rice to make up 15 percent broken rice. An export market exists in Africa for 100 percent broken rice, and broken rice can also be converted to rice flour for use in rice noodles—and in animal feed, when competitive in price.

Thai consumers are generally unaware of rice varieties. Sticky, jasmine, and white rice are the basic categories, and little quality or price differentiation exists within the generic white rice category. The staple product is 5 percent broken rice, and strict labeling rules apply to rice products. Thailand's Quality Control Board collects samples from supermarkets. However, the board intervenes only in the case of "Hom Mali." Consumers generally consider price as the best indication of quality and pay accordingly.

Milling and marketing. Millers buy from farmers either directly at paddy assembly markets or indirectly through paddy traders, known as *young*. The existence of assembly or wholesale markets is one reason for the relative efficiency of the Thai rice chain (Dawe and others 2008). These assembly markets are particularly prevalent in the central areas of the country. All Thai millers carry out milling to the white rice stage and then sell to exporters or domestic traders, who may operate their own reprocessing facilities where they clean and further separate broken grains from head grains.

Relatively little contract farming is carried out in Thailand. However, some mills and exporters are beginning to contract directly with farmers so they can be certain of collecting the qualities and quantities that they require. Contract farming is becoming more prevalent, particularly with "Hom Mali" and other specialized varieties.

The millers' association states that 1,000 mills operate in the country, of which 700 are members of the association. Association members with less than 100-ton daily capacity account for around 30 percent of total mills; those with 100- to 300-ton capacity account for 50 percent; and those with over 300-ton capacity account for 20 percent. The biggest mill in Thailand has a capacity of 2,000 tons per day and produces parboiled rice for export to Africa. Further consolidation would appear likely to reduce competitiveness, given the need for mills to be located close to the producers.

Milling capacity in Thailand is considered to be of a generally high quality. Importantly, besides adding value to raw product, millers also provide a conduit for financing primary production. The scale of the industry appears to be well matched to the country's farm production base.

No toll milling takes place in Thailand,[22] so farmers who need rice for their own consumption must sell paddy and buy back milled rice. To address what is perceived to be a problem—the need for farmers to gain access to their own rice—the government recently introduced a scheme to provide small mills with a capacity of 5–10 tons per day to farmer cooperatives. However, as of mid-2009 no financial incentives existed for farmers to obtain these mills. Given the high buying prices being offered by government for paddy, no financing for public mills may soon be forthcoming. The millers' association also argues that the quality of milled rice produced by these small mills is not as good as commercially milled rice and may compromise Thailand's reputation for high quality.

Role of the private sector. Modern retail, including minisupermarkets and convenience stores, now accounts for 40–50 percent of the total rice market. The supermarket sector continues to grow, and competition has intensified in recent years among the leading companies. Supermarket chains in Thailand have had a significant impact on their suppliers and have generally raised the bar on supply channel management methods. The major merchandising issue in Thailand involves the power struggle between packagers through their association and emerging supermarket chains.

Supermarkets offer multiple product formats, such as stock-keeping units, each of which is keyed to the purchasing power, buying preferences, and tastes of the different consumer segments that they serve. Prepacked 5-kilogram bags are still the norm for rice packaging. However, chains also offer open, self-serve, pay-by-weight formats.

The interface between rice millers and packers and retailers in Thailand is managed through an intermediating industrial group, the Rice Packers

Association. This group represents its membership collectively in negotiations with individual chains.

The Rice Packers Association carries out several functions, including controlling the quality of packed rice. It also carries out negotiations with supermarket chains as a collective association. Almost all rice is sold ready-packed to supermarkets in 5-kilogram packs. However, some chains are beginning to display open sacks from which customers can serve themselves.

Most supermarkets pay their suppliers only 90 days after receiving shipments, and these suppliers usually hold three months of stock, meaning they effectively must finance rice inventory for six months. Different supermarkets, of course, follow different procurement practices. For example, Carrefour has centralized its buying operations for the region in Singapore, while TESCO buys on a country-by-country basis. TESCO buys its private brands for its Thailand outlets from up-country packers. What is constant among the chains, however, is their interest in stabilizing rice prices for their customers. In this respect, supply-chain integration under supermarket aegis is having an important impact on domestic rice markets.

The Maize Sector

Production and Consumption. Small-scale farmers in the upland areas, which are often quite remote, mainly grow maize. Yields have increased significantly with the introduction of hybrids. At the same time, output sustainability is threatened by the need for mechanized farm operations and high-priced farm inputs. These, in turn, cause increased soil erosion, particularly on sloping land (Ekasingh and others 2004). In irrigated areas, three crops of maize can be grown annually. In the country as a whole, the main harvest comes in July and August and accounts for around 80 percent of production. The second crop comes in December and January and accounts for around 15 percent. A small third crop is harvested between March and May.

Aflatoxin contamination has presented major problems for the Thai maize industry. Farmers who produce two crops harvest their main crop immediately after maturity in July, since they have little time to leave it in the field to dry because of the need to replant. Such maize can have a moisture content of 20–30 percent and needs to be sold immediately to traders with drying facilities (Ekasingh and others 2004). Crops left in the field to dry can normally be sold at an acceptable moisture level of around 15 percent.

Until two decades ago, Thailand exported most of its maize crop. However, with growing affluence leading to increased consumption of animal products and with the development of export industries for animal products, the country now consumes almost all of its production in feed mills.

Consumption of maize varies annually between 3.5 million and 4.5 million tons, depending on the cost of maize and the relative cost of potential substitutes in the animal feed mix. In recent years, maize has accounted for close to 40 percent of total feed ingredients. The principal domestic substitute is tapioca (cassava). Thirty percent of this crop is usually exported, so there is a ready supply when the maize-cassava price relationship turns in its favor. Current government policy is to promote the cassava industry and to reduce imports of other imported feed ingredients, such as soybean meal or cake and fishmeal.

Exporting: Thailand now exports around 600,000 tons of maize a year. The level of production is roughly equivalent to consumption, so it appears that the surplus for export is made up of cross-border imports from Cambodia, Lao People's Democratic Republic, and Myanmar, together with some official imports. Whether the new maize price insurance scheme will deter such unofficial imports or whether Thai farmers will be able to claim unofficial imports as their own production remains to be seen.

Public Sector Policy: In recent years, the Thai government has been supporting a program of production enhancement in neighboring countries through contract farming. This program applies to 10 commodities, including rice and maize, all of which can then be imported into Thailand duty free. The continuation of these programs for maize in 2010 and beyond may be in doubt, however, as under AFTA, duty on maize is supposed to be zeroed out. At least part of the current incentive will be removed for private sector investment in foreign production.

Starting in 2008, the government of Thailand implemented a pledging scheme for maize similar to the one that already applied to paddy. This program was introduced following farmer complaints in 2008 after high commodity prices fell. Under the previous program, maize was pledged to traders' warehouses. The pledging price in July 2009 was 8.50 baht per kilogram, compared with the then-prevailing market price of 7.00 baht per kilogram. When it became apparent that this scheme was financially unsustainable, the government announced an alternative program of price insurance for maize similar to that introduced for paddy at the end of

2009. This program aimed to provide a guaranteed price, equivalent to production cost plus 20 percent. According to private sector interviewees, the previous system caused problems, as the quality being stored was allowed to deteriorate. The implications for quality and other matters of the new program have not yet been determined.

Private Sector Role: Thailand's animal feed industry includes more than 1,000 manufacturers. Around 200 of these are medium to large businesses. The majority produce livestock feed. However, about 150 also specialize in aqua feed. The largest animal feed factories are those that are integrated into the poultry and pork businesses. Some of these large businesses, such as Betagro and CP, also market their feed products to a broad base of independent farmers.[23]

Animal feed users are very price sensitive, since feed can account for up to 70 percent of the production cost of meat, eggs, and poultry (Agriculture and Agri-food Canada 2009d). Prices for feed are controlled and monitored by the government as part of an effort to control the price of meat and poultry in the retail market. Such controls caused major issues between the feed industry and the government in 2007 and 2008, when official feed prices set in 2004 were liberalized in a one-off market liberalization initiative. The new lower prices that came into effect immediately conflicted with the higher prices already locked in place by local producers who held significant inventories of higher-priced inputs such as maize and thus caused the whole feed industry to realize a significant loss for some time.

Companies like the CP Group are disseminating their management processes across the region as they continue to invest and expand. In the process, they bring with them modes of procurement that involve buying maize wherever it is least expensive and moving it to where the company is processing animal feed. In this way, intracorporate transfers are helping to integrate maize markets regionally.

Most of the relationships between farmers and collectors or intermediaries are based on contract farming. Before each planting season, farmer and merchant agree on the varieties of maize that the merchant wants to buy, and the merchant delivers appropriate seed and other inputs to the farmer in time for planting. The merchant records all advances to the farmer and deducts money due from farmers from revenues payable to them at the end of the harvest season. Some merchants blend the maize they receive and sell mixed grades to feed mills. However, most insist on uniform-quality deliveries from each farmer and further sort and grade before selling to feed mills. For this value addition they receive higher prices.[24]

Vietnam

The Rice Sector

Farm-level operations. With just over 7 million hectares under rice cultivation, Vietnam produced around 36 million tons of rice in 2007. Of this total, more than half came from the Mekong River Delta, which also supplies more than 90 percent of rice exports. As in Thailand, the country can produce both wet- and dry-season crops in lowland areas. Triple cropping is practiced in some provinces.

Use of farmer-retained seed is common, and production of specific varieties is unusual. Production costs are generally less in Vietnam than in Thailand because of higher yields and lower labor costs, although labor shortages at harvesttime can limit production. While most rice continues to be harvested and processed manually, significant growth has taken place in the use of combines and threshers. Such equipment is owned by millers, well-off farmers who rent it out to their neighbors, or farmer groups.

As in other countries in the region, few large-scale, contract farming arrangements exist for the production of standard rice in Vietnam. However, one noteworthy program involves the production of japonica rice on 700 hectares. This production is targeted at the Japanese market.

On average, farmers sell about 70 percent of their production, retaining the rest for family consumption, animal feed, and seed. A growing proportion of paddy is supplied directly to modern mills, but about 85 percent of sales continue to be made to collectors who buy at the farm gate. This type of intermediation is particularly prevalent in the Mekong Delta, where traders often provide credit in either cash or inputs to farmers, and thus are limited to working in an area where they can monitor farmer transactions.[25] After sun drying, farmers sell to collectors, who then deliver to dehuskers. Transport is almost entirely by boat, at least in the Mekong Delta.

Milling and marketing. Dehusking (to produce brown rice) and polishing (to the white rice stage) are usually done by different mills. Reasons for this practice are partly traditional, but the larger companies indicate that first-stage millers lack the storage to hold paddy, brown rice, bran, and white rice. This fragmented chain is said to be a contributory factor to poor product quality and to high postharvest losses, estimated by Goletti (2002) to be at least 9 percent.

This two-stage practice supports small-scale operations in the paddy-rice supply chain, particularly that of the Mekong River Delta. However, it also contributes to transport and handling losses. Dehuskers typically operate outdated and poorly maintained equipment, which exacerbates the situation. The fragmented supply chain structure in the Mekong River Delta hampers the transformation into shorter and more modern rice chains, which have lower postharvest losses.

Serious quality problems also affect rice production. For example, the use of farmer-retained seed led one research team to identify numerous varieties in one 50-kilogram bag of seed. Millers complain about the high moisture content of paddy, but, as in other countries, there are few incentives for farmers to sell properly dried paddy.

Large-scale millers have their own laboratories where they test samples before buying from traders. Smaller buyers usually work on the basis of visual inspection. While they may lower the price paid for poorer quality, they will still accept almost everything offered to them. Attempts to promote flat-bed driers have not moved forward very quickly, in part because of high costs and the fact that utilization is high only during a few months of the year. Some millers argue that such driers can actually reduce quality when run by unskilled operators.

An important development in Vietnam in recent years has been the introduction of mechanical grain driers as part of integrated factories that carry out drying, milling, polishing, and packaging. There is a similar arrangement in Korea, for example, where "Rice Processing Complexes" have formed as public-private partnerships (PPPs) between the government and millers. The Philippines government also recently expressed an interest in collaborating with Korea to introduce such factories.[26] Mills in Indonesia would like to make similar investments. Widespread introduction of integrated factories in Vietnam and the Philippines, however, would appear to be constrained by the high cost (despite positive returns), credit constraints, and policy and institutional weaknesses discussed below.

Some confusion remains about the number of mills and polishers in Vietnam. According to some estimates, there are around 300,000 dehuskers in operation. If true, this implies an extremely small scale of operation, a fact that was confirmed during field visits. Most mills also carry out toll milling of small quantities for farmers for their own family consumption. Payment for milling is normally made by leaving the bran behind for the miller to sell. In the Mekong Delta there are some 350 large mills or polishers, mainly SOEs, with a capacity of up to 30 tons an hour, and 30,000 smaller plants. The dehuskers are all in the private sector. However, SOEs account for about 60 percent of the rice-polishing capacity, buying the dehusked rice from the dehuskers.

As a result of mandates received from the government, millers are frequently forced to build up stocks in excess of their normal requirements. Vietnamese millers and polishers often find themselves with excessive quantities of rice that they cannot easily sell. The high moisture levels absorbed by these stocks require that the rice be remilled and repolished every few months to remain saleable. This double processing contributes to millers' losses.

SOEs continue to handle an estimated 60 percent of domestic rice milling. Buying from dehuskers, sometimes directly, but usually through traders, they polish the rice and then sell it via wholesale markets. Private millers follow a similar pattern. The wholesale trade is entirely in private hands and involves a large number of participants who either have fixed assets and stable businesses or who exploit arbitrage opportunities. Retailers purchase rice at wholesale markets. Most specialize only in rice.

A typical retailer sells 20 different grades and types. Supermarkets are still relatively underdeveloped in Vietnam, and consumers generally prefer to buy rice from traditional outlets. Supermarkets sell prepacked rice in 5-kilogram bags, which are not available in other retail shops. Observations of retail food quality suggest that standards are generally higher in supermarkets. There has not been much retail branding of rice to date. However, in the north of the country, the Northern Food Corporation (VINAFOOD1), an SOE, is beginning to supply convenience stores and supermarkets with special quality, prepacked, and branded rice.

Exporting. SOEs also monopolized exporting until 2002, and the private sector still accounts for only an estimated 10 percent of exports (Goletti 2009). All other exports are carried out by SOEs, with the Southern Food Corporation (VINAFOOD2) accounting for 50 percent of the total. Unlike in Thailand, there is virtually no branding of rice for export, but Vietnam enforces minimum export prices and export licensing. Stop-go approval stems from changes in the minimum export prices.

VINAFOOD1 operates in the north of the country, while VINAFOOD2 operates in the south. VINAFOOD2 is responsible for about 50 percent of exports. It trades on its own account and also subcontracts private

companies to provide rice for export. Private companies are able to conclude export contracts, but these are subject to approval by the Vietnam
Food Association (VFA); where possible, the companies therefore prefer
to subcontract to VINAFOOD2.

There are no regionwide trade standards for rice, but at present traders do not consider this a problem. Although application of sanitary
and phytosanitary regulations may affect trade with some countries
outside the region, there is no evidence of such problems within the
ASEAN region.

Role of the public sector. Since the late 1980s, Vietnam has made
remarkable progress as it has converted from a closed command economy to an open market economy (Athukorala, Huong, and Thanh
2009). Key to this transition has been the implementation of agricultural reforms, including the transition from collective regimes to a system in which farmers can freely make production decisions and market
their produce.

When Vietnam abolished quantitative restrictions on rice exports in
2001, the initiative opened up international trade to private players. Rice-
exporting companies, however, were still required to preregister their
export contracts. Hence, the bulk of Vietnamese rice exports remain
highly regulated by the government through the VFA, a government body
that works in close collaboration with the state-owned VINAFOOD1
and VINAFOOD2.

Vietnam's Export-Import Management Mechanism for 2001–2005[27]
replaced the nation's export quota with regulation through minimum
export prices (MEPs). These regulated prices are intended to ensure that
sufficient rice is retained within the country to cover domestic needs. The
use of MEPs and the uncertainties caused by frequent changes in them
continue to distort the decisions of private traders. MEPs are supposedly
set so that farmers can realize at least a 30 percent return on rice farming.
It is ironic that, if they were enforced as they were designed, MEPs would
actually favor Vietnam's rice consumers rather than its rice farmers
because MEPs would be set above export market levels, thus increasing
supply to the domestic market.

On May 1, 2005, all Vietnamese companies holding a license to trade
in food or agricultural commodities were also permitted to participate in
rice exporting. Exportation of rice now falls under the direction of a management team led by a deputy minister of industry and trade. Other high-
level ministries that participate include the Ministry of Agriculture and

Rural Development, the Ministry of Finance, the Government Office, the Ministry of Planning and Investment, and the State Bank.

Through this mechanism, the government often imposes various temporary market intervention measures, such as pledging to purchase all rice in storage (at the peak of the harvest, when supply exceeds demand) in order to maintain stable prices. Another type of intervention involves the VFA, which may be directed from time to time to request enterprises to desist from exporting and stop signing further export contracts in order to stabilize domestic prices. Given that Vietnam is a surplus country, the continuing role of SOEs appears to be somewhat of an anachronism left from the days of state planning, when Vietnam had little or no surplus. It is here that the greatest scope exists for extending the role of the private sector.

In the first half of 2008, a series of disruptive policy interventions involved first setting export targets, then reducing them, advising private exporters not to open new export contracts, banning export sales outright, and canceling or changing minimum export prices (Slayton 2009). The purpose of these regulations was to keep rice within Vietnam's borders in order to safeguard local supply and keep it affordable. By raising the MEP, the government effectively signaled private traders not to procure paddy, since a high MEP set above market levels deprived them of a reasonable return in the export business.

At the same time, the government, through VINAFOOD2, continued to export rice to the Philippines based on a government-to-government agreement. This governmental direct dealing represented a clear conflict of interest vis-à-vis the private sector. Essentially, the government-owned exporter cornered available export contracts and drove the private traders out of the market.

Interestingly, local prices failed to decline in response to these initiatives undertaken in the name of food security. Indeed, by April 2008, rice prices in Ho Chi Minh City (HCM City) had doubled. Slayton suggests that when the head of the VFA projected that rice prices could reach $1,400 per ton, local traders expected further increases and increased their purchases. They held those stocks longer than they should have, however, and in the second half of 2008, these traders were caught with large volumes of rice when the price fell by half in just a matter of months. As a result of financial losses, private trading company procurement slowed, thus pulling down farm prices.

Frequent changes in regulations introduce a fair amount of uncertainty into the domestic rice market in Vietnam. This uncertainty typically induces speculation and ultimately results in financial losses to all players. In the end, those whom regulations were intended to help have also incurred significant losses. Farmers had to discount the value of their stocks in the summer harvest of 2008, and rice consumers were forced to adjust their consumption as well in response to rising prices. Private traders who changed their fundamental mode of operations in an effort to stay out in front of government maneuvers ultimately incurred losses as well.

Rice distribution: Although ensuring access to rice for low-income households is not a day-to-day concern for a major rice exporter like Vietnam, in 2008 concerns arose within the government that the local rice market, particularly in HCM City, might run out of supply at the same time that rice was being exported to the more lucrative overseas markets. This possibility prompted the VFA to ask its members to allocate more of their supply to the local market.

A top Ministry of Industry and Trade (MOIT) official attributed concerns like this to the underlying weakness of the local rice distribution system. While recognizing that the export supply chain is working smoothly, the MOIT official believed the Vietnamese food system needs larger food companies that are better able to organize the distribution of rice and other food efficiently and quickly, while at the same time having enough credibility and local market influence to stabilize domestic price fluctuations.

The role of the private sector. A great deal of consolidation and ownership restructuring is under way within the Vietnamese milling sector, including experiments in subcontracting, vertical realignment, joint ownership with farm coops taking over milling facilities, and privatization of mills—including ones owned at the municipal, provincial, and national levels of government. The future direction of industry restructuring poses the biggest challenge and the biggest opportunity for the industry.

While VFA's mandate is to coordinate and regulate the rice market in Vietnam on behalf of the government and to monitor food security in the country, it is also charged with being an impartial intermediary between the government and the private sector. It is supposed to protect the interest of farmers, although farmers are not members of the association, and VFA tends to be dominated by large traders, including, particularly, the SOEs. About 100 exporters or members are registered by VFA.

In Vietnam, the wholesale sector is entirely in private hands. Rice retailers tend to specialize only in rice rather than being general retailers. They purchase rice in wholesale markets and resell in local neighborhoods or villages. A typical retailer sells 20 different grades and varieties of rice. Supermarkets are relatively underdeveloped, and consumers generally prefer to buy rice from traditional outlets. Supermarkets sell prepacked rice in 5-kilogram bags, which are not available in other retail shops. Observations of retail food quality suggest that standards are generally higher in supermarkets. There has not been much retail branding of rice to date. However, in the north of the country, VINAFOOD1 is beginning to supply convenience stores and supermarkets with special quality prepacked and branded rice.

In general, private sector expansion comes second to the goal of assuring farmers the ability to realize a margin of 30 percent over their cost of production. Policing the buying prices paid by village collectors, however, is almost impossible, and a minimum farm price ignores the role many village traders play by providing credit to farmers who, at harvest, accept lower prices for paddy. Further, a minimum export price discourages exports, and a parallel requirement that mills purchase more stocks than they really require leads to inventory buildup, which, in turn, pushes prices down.

The Maize Sector

Production and Consumption. Increases in the production of maize in Vietnam in recent years can only be described as spectacular (Gulati and Dixon 2008). Between 1990 and 2006, maize production increased more than sevenfold to reach a current level of about 4 million tons. The country has multiple growing zones for maize, but a combination of government policies and market competition increasingly favors growing maize in upland areas and rice in lowlands. Maize competes primarily with rice, sweet potato, and cassava for land in Vietnam. It is the relative price of maize that determines from year to year what land is committed to which crop.

Maize also competes with these same commodities as an input into animal feeds. Since 2006, rapid growth in the animal feed market has been driven primarily by Vietnam's meat and aquaculture exports. However, domestic consumption of meat and fish has increased greatly as well. Pork accounts for 80 percent of meat consumption, followed by chicken (11–12 percent) and beef (3–4 percent). Feed accounts for 70 percent of the price of these animal products.

As a share of inputs into feed production, maize (24 percent) follows cassava (27 percent) and exceeds rice (18 percent). Broken rice and bran are both significant inputs in feed production. Most demand for maize comes from pig production. Most feed is mixed by farmers and is a combination of own-grown and purchased feed components. Maize accounts for 7 percent of pig feed and 31 percent of chicken feed. According to the Animal Feed Association, total demand for animal feed is around 17 million tons. Manufactured feed equates to around 7 million tons. The remainder is formulated on farm by small-scale farm operators from an array of inputs, including sweet potatoes, sugar residue, waste materials, fruits, and vegetables.

Feed mills: There are currently about 180 animal feed mills in Vietnam. These are scattered throughout the country. However, the largest mills are located in HCM City and Hanoi Province. Fifteen large multinationals—including Cargill (United States), Cheil Jedang Group (Korea), CP Group (Thailand), New Hope (China), Proconco (France), and TTC (Taiwan, China)—together produce approximately 50 percent of the animal feed consumed in the country. A number of large Vietnamese companies participate in the industry as well, including AFIMEX (An Giang), DABACO (Bac Ninh), Hoan Duong (Hanoi), Long Chau (Dong Nai), Ngoc Hoi Animal Feed Mill, NOPICO (An Khanh), Thanh Binh, VIC (Hai Phong), and VINA. The total capacity of Vietnam's animal feed mills is estimated at 5.4 million metric tons. A great deal of new investment has entered the feed industry over the past three years, and some participants are concerned that the industry may have overbuilt.

Many of the ingredients that go into feed mix are imported. Prices for these inputs are set in U.S. dollars. Vietnam imports fully 60 percent of the maize, soybean meal, fish meal, meat and bone meal, rice bran, wheat bran, premixes, and vitamins needed to produce animal feed locally. In total each year, the sector imports 40 percent of the maize that it uses, 80 percent of the soybean meal, and 50 percent of the fish meal required for feed production.

Private sector role: Unlike rice production, maize production has not been a primary focus of government policy. Indeed, only recently has government policy allowed the conversion of rice-producing land to other agricultural purposes. However, the government has greatly assisted with the increase in maize productivity through its hybrid seed promotion program. It launched this program through the national agriculture extension service, which includes the extension of input credits, technical support, and farmer advising all managed at the district level.

A parallel, private sector seed distribution system also operates in which farmer field technicians provide some of the same services as government agriculture extension agents. Private seeds, however, are typically more expensive than those provided by agriculture extension agents. Some of these programs have developed into PPPs of interesting sorts. For example, Southern Seed Company, one of the country's largest seed distributors, relies on its own sales force in the south and on government agents in the north. Both imported hybrids and locally developed ones are used in Vietnam. Although yields still remain 20–30 percent lower than in other developed countries, they are rising rapidly. The National Maize Research Institute developed a notably successful hybrid. Other seed companies, including Bioseed Genetics Vietnam, and CP Seeds, are active in Vietnam as well.

Notes

1. One extreme estimate puts the conversion rate as low as 0.57 in these mills, compared with a more normal rate of 0.63 and the possible rate of 0.67 or better that can be achieved with modern equipment.

2. According to private sector sources interviewed, there may be some doubts about the quality of rice in store, however.

3. From industry sources, based on interviews by Andrew Shepherd for this study.

4. See Inter Island Transport Project, Indonesia. 2005. http://www.adb.org/Documents/Environment/Ino/ino-interisland-port.pdf.

5. *Newsweek.* 2009. Asian Edition. July 20, 2009.

6. Broken rice is rice with kernels that are less than three quarters the length of the whole kernel (http://www.fao.org/WAICENT/FAOINFO/AGRICULT/AGP/AGPC/doc/riceinfo/Riceinfo.htm). The percentage of rice that is considered broken is a measure of the quality, or level of refinement, of rice. Brokens are the rice fragments produced during threshing and hulling. They are removed in the rice mill by screening at the end of processing and are usually further processed into rice flour or rice semolina.

7. Since Malaysia exports no rice, imports very little (0.75 million ton in 2007), and, except for the smallness of the Sabah and Sarawak ports, suffers from no significant infrastructure weaknesses, those issues are not discussed in this section.

8. Until the 1990s, on occasions when the moisture content exceeded 14 percent, buyers made subtractions from the total paddy weight to reflect this fact,

using a linear scale developed by the government. Deductions were also made for impurities and for damaged and unripe grains. However, by 1997, a new system became dominant under which all paddy sold by farmers to licensed mills has a standard rate of deduction predetermined by each state. Initially this was intended to represent the maximum rate, but it has effectively become a flat deduction rate.

9. Malaysia has almost always elected to be a net importer of rice, targeting about 86 percent rice self-sufficiency, according to Deputy Agriculture and Agro-Based Industries Minister Datuk Rohani Karim.

10. See http://www.bernas.com.my/.

11. As with the process of consolidation in the milling sector, the number of wholesalers has dropped from the 1997 level of 1800.

12. From 1931, when the Rice Cultivation Committee was formed, a succession of government organizations have been devoted to rice promotion, culminating in the formation of the Rice Board, or Lembaga Padi dan Beras Negara (LPN), in 1971. In 1974, LPN was given the sole import rights for rice. In 1994, it was corporatized into BERNAS, which was to take over all commercial and social functions. In 1996, BERNAS was fully privatized while still being charged with social obligations such as subsidy distribution to farmers and the function of being a buyer of last resort. It was also given sole import rights for 15 years.

13. See note 9.

14. See Athukorala and Loke (2009) for an enumeration of other specific roles of BERNAS besides importing.

15. A limited market exists in the Philippines for high-quality rice, mainly the market serviced by supermarkets. In general, the Philippines market is price sensitive, and suppliers are oriented toward low prices. Incentives for good-quality postharvest treatment are limited, and this situation results in poor-quality rice with a short shelf life being the main product available to consumers. Much rice is marketed with 35–40 percent brokens. This percentage is much higher than in, say, Thailand, where the corresponding percentage is 5 percent. In part, the high level of brokens can be attributed to the many stages in the marketing system and frequent handlings of the bags.

16. This remains the case even though the International Rice Research Institute has developed cheap meters in collaboration with a Chinese company. Whiteness meters are used only in large mills.

17. "The term demurrage refers to payment (due or charged) when [a] load is delayed/held-up/not loaded/off-loaded, etc. when agreed. [It] also applies if [the] vehicle/ship/rail wagon [is] delayed when empty." Chartered Institute of Transport & Logistics. http://log.logcluster.org/glossary/index.html.

18. The NFA's role, particularly in 2007–08, and the costs of the program are discussed at length in chapter 2.

19. MAV is the popular term in the Philippines for the in-quota volume, the amount of imports allowed to come in at a low volume under the third pillar of the Agreement on Agriculture (AoA). AoA is an international treaty of the World Trade Organization (WTO) aimed at reforming trade in the sector and encouraging market-friendly policies. AoA has three pillars: market access, domestic support, and export subsidies. Rules under market access envision tariffication of all nontariff barriers and progressive reduction in tariffs. The tariffication agenda included the provision for granting minimum access quotas for imported agricultural products at low tariff rates different from the normal rates that apply to import quantities. Checking with original author.

20. Feed wheat is wheat used for animal feed, not for human consumption.

21. Thailand does not import rice. Chapters 2 and 3, respectively, examine the role of Thai parastatals and aspects of the export sector not discussed below.

22. *Toll milling* is the practice of milling rice that belongs to other parties, usually farmers or small traders, for a fee, for residual bran and husks, for a share of processed grain, or for a combination of these.

23. In its 2009 annual report, the CP Group, the largest animal feed producer in the region, explains its maize procurement policy on page 14 as follows: "As agricultural products (maize and soybeans) are the major cost components in animal feed, accounting for 32% of total cost, the company has set up a central purchasing unit responsible for procurement of all ingredients used in livestock and aquatic feed. Our procurement policy is to purchase quality raw material meeting the nutritional requirements with priority given to domestic producers particularly those situated in close proximity to our feed mill plants. This is to support our local farmers as well as to minimize transport costs. Only when domestic supply is insufficient or has inferior quality will the Company resort to imports." http://www.cpfworldwide.com/elctfl/iranr/anrdwlen7.pdf.

24. Based on field surveys completed by the Agrifood Consulting International, Inc. team.

25. See Shepherd (2004) for a discussion on agricultural marketing financing in Asia.

26. See http://pinoybusiness.org/2009/05/31/korean-funded-rice-processing-centers-to-be-built-in-the-country/.

27. Decree No. 46/2001//QD-TTg.

References and Other Sources

Agriculture and Agri-food Canada. 2009a. "Characteristics of Indonesia's Market for Animal Feed." http://www.ats.agr.gc.ca/ase/4771-eng.htm.

———. 2009b. "Characteristics of Malaysia's Animal Feed Market." http://www.ats.agr.gc.ca/ase/5231-eng.htm.

———. 2009c. "Characteristics of the Philippines Market for Animal Feed." http://www.ats.agr.gc.ca/ase/4770-eng.htm.

———. 2009d. "Characteristics of Thailand's Market for Animal Feed." http://www.ats.agr.gc.ca/ase/4774-eng.htm.

———. 2009e. "Characteristics of Vietnam's Market for Animal Feed." http://www.ats.agr.gc.ca/ase/4776-eng.htm.

Asia Foundation. 2008. *The Cost of Moving Goods. Road Transportation, Regulations and Charges in Indonesia.* Jakarta: Asia Foundation.

Asian Development Bank (ADB). 2005. *Summary Environmental Impact Assessment: Inter Island Transport Project (Ports), Indonesia.* July. Manila, the Philippines: ADB. http://www.adb.org/Documents/Environment/Ino/ino-interisland-port.pdf.

Athukorala, Prema-Chandra, and Wai-Heng Loke. 2009. "Malaysia." In *Distortions to Agricultural Incentives in Asia,* ed. Kym Anderson and Will Martin, chapter 5, 197–221. Washington, DC: World Bank.

Athukorala, Prema-Chandra, Pham Lan Huong, and Vo Tri Thanh. 2009. "Vietnam." In *Distortions to Agricultural Incentives in Asia,* ed. Kym Anderson and Will Martin, chapter 8, 281–302. Washington, DC: World Bank.

BERNAS (Padi Beras Nasional Bhd). http://www.bernas.com.my/.

Center for Food and AgriBusiness. 2009. "The Maize Value Chain and Logistics Analysis in Mindanao." Draft final report, University of Asia and the Pacific.

Charoen Pokphand Group. 2009. "Annual Report." Bangkok, Thailand. http://www.cpfworldwide.com/elctfl/iranr/anrdwlen7.pdf.

Costales, Achilles C. 2008. "The Philippines: Maize Economy, Incentives and Policies." In *Maize in Asia: Changing Markets and Incentives,* ed. Ashok Gulati and John Dixon. New Delhi: Academic Foundation, in association with the International Maize and Wheat Improvement Center (CIMMYT), the International Food Policy Research Institute (IFPRI), and the International Fund for Agricultural Development (IFAD). http://www.academicfoundation.com/n_detail/maize.asp.

Dawe, D. C., Piedad F. Moya, Cheryll B. Casiwan, and Jesusa M. Cabling. 2008. "Rice Marketing Systems in the Philippines and Thailand: Do Large Numbers of Competitive Traders Ensure Good Performance?" *Food Policy* 33 (5, October): 455–63.

Ekasingh, B., Phrek Gypmantasiri, Kuson Thong-Ngam, and Pichet Grudloyma. 2004. *Maize in Thailand: Production Systems, Constraints, and Research Priorities.* Mexico City: International Maize and Wheat Improvement Center.

FAO (Food and Agriculture Organization of the United Nations). 1998. "Crop and Grasslands Service: International Rice Commission." http://www.fao.org/WAICENT/FAOINFO/AGRICULT/AGP/AGPC/doc/riceinfo/Riceinfo.htm.

Global Filipino Business and Investing Community. 2009. "Korean-Funded Rice Processing Centers to Be Built in the Country." May 31. http://pinoybusiness.org/2009/05/31/korean-funded-rice-processing-centers-to-be-built-in-the-country/.

Goletti, Francesco. 2002. "Rice Value Chain Study: Vietnam." Report prepared for the World Bank, Agrifood Consulting International/World Bank.

———. 2009. "Economic and Sector Analysis for Agriculture, Rural Development, and Natural Resources Management in Vietnam in 2009 and 2010 (Phase 1)." Internal Report by Agrifood Consulting International/World Bank.

Gulati, Ashok, and John Dixon, eds. 2008. *Maize in Asia: Changing Markets and Incentives*. New Delhi: Academic Foundation.

Hayami, Yujiro, Masao Kikuchi, and Esther B. Marciano. 1999. "Middlemen and Peasants in Rice Marketing in the Philippines." *Agricultural Economics* 20 (2): 79–93.

Logistics Cluster. Logistics Operational Guide. http://log.logcluster.org/glossary/index.html.

Olken, Benjamin A. 2006. "Corruption and the Costs of Redistribution: Micro Evidence from Indonesia." *Journal of Public Economics* 90: 853–70.

Poapongsakorn, Nipon. 2008. "Thailand's Rice Policies and Their Effects on the World Market." Paper presented to the FAO/AFMA International Workshop on Rice Policies and Food Security in Asia, Chiangmai, Thailand, February 10–12.

PT Data Consultants. 2008. "Market Intelligence Report on Animal Feed Industry in Indonesia." May. http://www.datacon.co.id/animal%20feed%20industry.html.

Ramos, Charmaine G. 2000. *State Intervention and Private Sector Participation in Philippine Rice Marketing*. Quezon City, Philippines: MODE (Management and Organizational Development for Empowerment) and Southeast Asian Council for Food Security and Fair Trade. http://www.mode.org/pdf/State%20intervention%20and%20private%20sector%20participation%20in%20philippine%20rice%20market.pdf.

Shepherd, Andrew W. 2004. "Financing of Agricultural Marketing: The Asian Experience." Occasional Paper No. 2, AGS/FAO, Rome. http://www.fao.org/ag/ags/subjects/en/agmarket/markfinance.pdf.

Sidik, Mulyo. 2004. "Indonesia Rice Policy in View of Trade Liberalization." Paper presented at the FAO Rice Conference, Rome, February 12–13.

Slayton, Tom. 2009. "Rice Crisis Forensics: How Asian Governments Carelessly Set the World Rice Market on Fire." Working Paper 163, Center for Global Development, Washington, DC.

Suhariyanto, Kecuk. 2008. "Indonesia: Maize Economy, Incentives and Policies." In *Maize in Asia: Changing Markets and Incentives,* ed. Ashok Gulati and John Dixon. New Delhi: Academic Foundation, in association with the International Maize and Wheat Improvement Center (CIMMYT), the International Food Policy Research Institute (IFPRI), and the International Fund for Agricultural Development (IFAD).

Swastika, Dewa K. S. 2008. "Developing Maize for Improving Poor Farmers' Income in Indonesia." CAPSA-ESCAP. http://www.uncapsa.org/Flash_Detail .asp?VJournalKey=31.

Swastika, Dewa K. S., Firdaus Kasim, Kecuk Suhariyanto, Wayan Sudana, Rachmat Hendayana, Roberta V. Gerpacio, and Prabhu. L. Pingali. 2004. *Maize in Indonesia: Production Systems, Constraints, and Research Priorities.* Mexico City: International Maize and Wheat Improvement Center (CIMMYT).

Timmer, C. Peter. 2008. "Postscript: The Debate over Food Security in 2006—An Update on the Role of BULOG." In *From Parastatals to Private Trade,* ed. Shahidur Rashid, Ashok Gulati, and Ralph Cummings Jr. Baltimore: IFPRI and John Hopkins University Press.

World Trade Organization (WTO). *Agriculture Fairer Markets for Farmers.* http:// www.wto.org/english/thewto_e/whatis_e/tif_e/agrm3_e.htm.

Supply Chains for Maize in the ASEAN Region

Introduction

This appendix assesses the strengths and weaknesses of the farm-to-market chains for maize in Indonesia, Malaysia, the Philippines, Thailand, and Vietnam and recommends means for strengthening them further. Because maize and rice crops and chains differ in a great many ways, particularly in the marginal role of the public sector and the dominance of private sector investment in maize, the authors have set the findings on maize apart from the main text, which concentrates on the role and problems of the rice sector in regional agriculture and trade.

Private investors, much more extensively than governments, are rapidly transforming supply chains for growing and processing maize used for animal feed in the Association of Southeast Asian Nations (ASEAN) region from "supply push" commodity chains to "demand pull" chains. Even though the development is in its early stages, maize chains, including those that handle imports of the grain, are increasingly being integrated into more sophisticated chicken, pork, and fish product chains, for which maize provides an essential feed stock. Several forms of integration have been tested within the region, including contract production connecting traders with farmers and vertical ownership and integrated control under a single corporate entity. It is in experimentation with different business models that maize chains differ most fundamentally from rice chains. The growing demand from producers of poultry, pork, eggs, and aquaculture for high-quality maize inputs at prices that are stable has created incentives for investment in stronger chains.

Modernization, however, has yet to transform the lowest level of the chain, the small-scale farmers who grow most of the maize in the region. As long as contracting with these numerous producers remains costly and affords few certain benefits to buyers, supply chains in the maize sector will remain underdeveloped and the opportunities to roll out the experiments that are under way will be limited. As discussed in this appendix, the pace of supply-chain transformation varies among individual countries in the region.

After describing country-specific developments in maize chains, the appendix analyzes activity costs associated with each link in a typical ASEAN maize-animal feed chain. Before reviewing the main conclusions and findings, the authors assess the primary weaknesses in existing maize chains, including physical losses and degradation in maize quality.

Country-Specific Developments in Maize Chains

The transformation of maize chains is reflected within the region generally in a marked shift in demand from white maize, usually a food for low-income households, to yellow maize, a key component of animal feed. One reference point is the Philippines. In the 1990s, white maize production declined by 4.4 percent annually, while yellow maize production increased by 3.3 percent annually (Costales 2008). By 2000, white maize consumption in the Philippines had fallen to 1.3 million tons. Meanwhile, consumption of yellow maize for animal feed was around 3.5 million tons (Costales 2008).

Yellow maize is not the only ingredient in animal feed and must compete with several other substitute inputs such as soya meal, feed wheat, and cassava, as well as other products that are high in complex carbohydrates. Farmers who sell into animal feed chains typically do so through trader intermediaries. However, the terms of these sales and their volumes have begun to influence the way in which maize is produced in the region, as described below. Although maize production is being integrated into large-scale animal feed chains all over the region, the pace of this integration and the conditions surrounding it vary from country to country.

In *Indonesia*, maize production was forecast to be 9.0 million tons in 2009, slightly higher than the estimated 8.7 million tons for 2008. However, data may be unreliable because production figures do not correlate well with maize usage information generated by the feed industry. Nevertheless, it is clear that significant increases have taken place in production since the 1980s, as noted in chapter 4, box 4.1. These increases have resulted from the introduction of improved varieties, particularly hybrids supplied by two or three major seed companies, as well as from increased use of fertilizer. Production increases would probably have been higher if all farmers had been able to finance the purchase of improved seeds and fertilizer (Swastika and others 2004).

Maize is grown in almost every part of the country, with Java accounting for 60 percent of total production. It is the second most important cereal crop after rice in Indonesia. Most maize is grown in marginal areas with low productivity, on rain-fed lowlands, or on dry land areas, where rainfall is erratic and soil fertility is low (Swastika 2008). Some millers work on a contract basis with farmers. Unlike with paddy, millers can afford to employ field staff to monitor compliance with contract terms, as maize is more profitable than rice.

As a commodity for human consumption, maize is considered to be an inferior product, which the poor consume in disproportionately larger share. Increasing affluence has led to a significant decline in human consumption in Indonesia. Unfortunately, up-to-date data are lacking. Per capita consumption is reported to have dropped from 19.45 kilograms in 1984 to 3.69 kilograms in 1996 (Suhariyanto 2008). Estimates by the Food and Agriculture Organization (FAO) of the United Nations put total maize consumption at just 7 percent of total food consumption in 2001 (Swastika 2008).

The feed market accounts for 7 million tons of yellow maize consumption annually, a share that has been growing as increasing affluence has enhanced demand for animal products. The so-called "Livestock Revolution" is well under way in Indonesia. The largest businesses involved in the feed production industry, either as integrated concerns or as independent producers, include the Thai company Charoen Pokphand (CP) (estimated at 25 percent of total production capacity), Japfa Comfeed (16 percent), CJ Feed (7 percent), and Sierad Produce (5 percent) (Agriculture and Agri-food Canada 2009a). Most of these businesses have some level of foreign ownership.

In *Malaysia*, the feed industry has been liberalized for a long time. There is little government involvement in the maize sector, although the government does control the price of chicken meat. The country imports almost all of its maize requirements, over 2 million tons of maize per year, mainly for chicken feed, pig feed, and, to a much lesser extent, for duck feed and aquaculture. In 2009, imports entered the country duty-free. Attempts to grow maize have proved unsuccessful, as farmers have found local production both uncompetitive with imports and less remunerative than alternative crops.

Such high import figures are a cause for some concern on the part of government officials. Under the Ninth Malaysia Plan, there are proposals to promote the alternative use of rice and other locally produced crops for feed. However, trade association sources interviewed during field visits for this study stressed that maize remained the preferred feed ingredient. The wisdom of using rice for feed when Malaysia is advocating rice self-sufficiency is also questionable.

The feed industry consists of multinationals, such as Cargill, as well as regional corporations like CP of Thailand and Leong Hup Holdings (a Malaysian group), which run integrated operations. They produce feed from maize they import, and they also sell maize to smaller-scale feed millers. Other companies include the Malayan Flour Mills group, Soon Soon, and Zeullig. Companies such as QL Resources and Kentucky Fried Chicken also operate integrated feed units, which are linked to their chicken production operations. Integrated companies import feed ingredients, operate feed mills, breed and rear parent chicken stock and rear broilers, and produce eggs. They both supply their own poultry industries and sell feed to other companies. Maize is the dominant feed ingredient for the chicken and egg industries, accounting for 80 percent of all ingredients in recent years (Agriculture and Agri-food Canada 2009b).

The Philippines has come close to maize self-sufficiency, in large part because of the high level of protection that the government provides to domestic farmers. Indeed, the yellow maize market is more protected in the Philippines than in any other ASEAN study country. This protection tends to carry over to white maize prices, as well, and thus benefits all maize farmers, who tend to be poorer than palay producers.[1] However, maize protection pushes up costs for feed producers, and these increased costs eventually affect the incomes of both animal-processing companies and small farmers who are involved in animal rearing.

In 2007, around 10 percent of domestic requirements in the Philippines were imported, while imports fell back from this level in 2008. By mid-2009, imports had reached 200,000 tons, the maximum permitted that year under the in-quota covering low-volume imports, which qualified for duties at 35 percent rather than the 50 percent that applies to higher import volumes.[2]

While poultry production is largely in the hands of large, integrated companies in the Philippines, hog production remains predominately a smallholder activity. Poultry production is growing at about 15 percent per year, while the pig industry has suffered from food safety problems and recently from "swine flu" scares, which have led to reduced demand for pork. As a result of the decline in demand from the hog industry, no maize supply constraints existed in mid-2009.

In 2008 there were 376 registered feed mills in the Philippines and perhaps others that are unregistered. Almost three quarters of the registered companies are on the main island of Luzon. Only the largest 26 companies, however, are members of the Philippines Association of Feed Millers (PAFMI). These companies are estimated to account for more than 60 percent of total feed production.

These large companies operate feedlots, meat-processing facilities, and in some cases, even food retail outlets. Each of them has adopted a somewhat different business model. However, the business activities in which they have decided to invest directly, as well as others with which they affiliate contractually, are connected, with the help of production scheduling and quality control systems. In some instances, chain integrators rear poultry and other animals; in others, they manage franchisee farmers who do their rearing under contract. At the other end of the spectrum, many mills have remained relatively small family operations. In still other instances, maize traders have decided to add value to their operations by also going into the feed-processing business.

The price of maize has a direct effect on the competitiveness of meat products because it accounts for the largest share of input costs. Rising maize prices in ASEAN countries have affected meat, egg, and poultry prices. In 2006, the farm gate price for maize in the Philippines was 10 pesos per kilogram. This price rose to 13–14 pesos per kilogram in 2007, and it remained at that level for much of 2008. In July 2009, the price fell back to 10.8 pesos, although the National Food Authority (NFA) was still intervening in the local market in an effort to drive prices up again by buying at 13 pesos. Indeed, this may be a more realistic price to sustain supply commitments from farmers. Industry informants suggested that 10.8 pesos per kilogram was not profitable. In January 2009, little maize remained in the national supply chain, and the farm price rose temporarily as high as 25 pesos per kilogram.

Imports of maize into the Philippines involve somewhat complicated arrangements. Imports are all technically handled through the NFA, although most of the import preparation work is actually done by PAFMI.

The association consolidates import requests of individual members into large tenders. Only a few companies have sufficient demand to justify purchases of shipload quantities. Consolidation into shipload quantities enables buyers to minimize shipping costs. NFA charges group buyers the 35 percent import tariff. However, it absorbs other administrative costs. Other than this administrative cost saving, the advantages of NFA involvement are unclear. Moreover, its involvement in maize procurement appears to slow down the import process. The prevailing in-quota import duty rate of 35 percent provides considerable protection for Filipino farmers. It remains to be seen what will happen under the ASEAN Free Trade Agreement (AFTA). There is some concern that the country will be flooded with imports from Thailand, although the current level of production in Thailand and the demands of the Thai feed industry suggest that this fear may be unfounded. Moreover, the high prevailing import duty also creates incentives for smuggling. Reportedly, Indonesian maize is being smuggled into the southern provinces of the Philippines.

The seasonality of maize production in the Philippines seems to be less pronounced than in the past as farmers are now staggering planting dates in response to climate change. Although farmers are protected by the in-quota rate, they are still exposed to competition from feed wheat, which is imported with a duty of just 7 percent.[3] Only the largest feed mills have access to imported wheat, however, with the result that smaller mills, which depend on local maize, have become less competitive (Costales 2008). By September 2009, some 1 million tons of feed wheat had been imported; as a result, maize prices fell significantly from January highs. Because of the higher prices of traditional animal feed ingredients, feed producers sought out other lower-cost ingredients. This substitution resulted in large increases in palm oil cake imports and the use of residues from the food-processing and brewing industries. The consequences of these new feed formulations may have altered demand for feed ingredients permanently. Any sustained effect on demand for maize remains to be confirmed, however (Agriculture and Agri-food Canada 2009c).

Thailand exported most of its maize crop two decades ago. However, with growing affluence leading to increased consumption of animal products and with the development of export industries for animal products, the country now consumes almost all of its production in feed mills. Consumption of maize varies annually between 3.5 million and 4.5 million tons, depending on its cost and the relative cost of potential substitutes in the animal feed mix. In recent years, maize has accounted for close to 40 percent of total feed ingredients. The principal domestic substitute is tapioca (cassava). Thirty percent of this crop is usually exported, so there is a ready supply when the maize-cassava price relationship turns in its favor. Current government policy is to promote the cassava industry and to reduce imports of other imported feed ingredients, such as soybean meal or cake and fishmeal.

Thailand's animal feed industry includes more than 1,000 manufacturers. Around 200 of these are medium to large businesses. The majority produce livestock feed. However, about 150 specialize in aquatic feed as well. The largest animal feed factories are those that are integrated into the poultry and pork businesses. Some of these large businesses, such as Betagro and CP, also market their feed products to a broad base of independent farmers.[4]

Animal feed users are very price sensitive, since feed can account for up to 70 percent of the production cost of meat, eggs, and poultry (Agriculture and Agri-food Canada 2009d). Prices for feed are controlled and monitored by the government as part of an effort to control the price of meat and poultry in the retail market. Such controls caused major issues between the feed industry and the government in 2007 and 2008, when official feed prices set in 2004 were liberalized in a one-off market liberalization initiative. The new lower prices, which came into effect immediately, conflicted with the higher prices already locked in place by local producers that were holding significant inventories of higher-priced inputs, and thus caused the whole feed industry to realize a significant loss for some time.

Small-scale farmers in the upland areas, which are often quite remote, mainly grow maize. Yields have increased significantly with the introduction of hybrids. At the same time, output sustainability is threatened by the need for mechanized farm operations and high-priced farm inputs. These, in turn, cause increased soil erosion, particularly on sloping land (Ekasingh and others 2004). In irrigated areas, three crops of maize can be grown annually. In the country as a whole, the main harvest comes in July and August and accounts for around 80 percent of production. The second crop comes in December and January and accounts for around 15 percent. A small third crop is harvested between March and May.

Companies like the CP Group are disseminating their management processes across the region as they continue to invest and expand. In the process, they bring with them modes of procurement that involve buying maize wherever it is least expensive and moving it to where the company is processing animal feed. In this way, intracorporate transfers are helping to integrate maize markets regionally.

The occurrence of contract farming is increasing as well. Collectors or intermediaries contract with specific maize seed producers to distribute specific types of maize seed to the farmers from whom they buy and with millers to deliver specific quantities and qualities of maize. An individual merchant may contract with more than one seed producer to satisfy the needs of various millers.

Most of the relationships between farmers and collectors or intermediaries are based on contract farming. Before each planting season, farmer and merchant agree on varieties of maize that the merchant wants to buy, and the merchant delivers appropriate seed and other inputs to the farmer in time for planting. The merchant records all advances to the farmer and deducts money due from farmers from revenues payable to them at the end of the harvest season. Some merchants blend the different varieties they receive and sell mixed grades to feed mills. However, most insist on uniform-quality deliveries from each farmer and further sort and grade before selling to feed mills. For this value addition they receive higher prices.[5]

In general, two standard grades are recognized for trading purposes in the country: Grades 1 and 2 (table A.1). In this way, Thailand has moved further toward the development of structured trade than any of the other countries included in this study. Some milling supply contracts may specify stricter standards for specific parameters than those that apply to the two standard grades.

In recent years, the Thai government has been supporting a program of production enhancement in neighboring countries through contract farming. This program applies to 10 commodities, including rice and maize, all of which can then be imported into Thailand duty

Table A.1   Maize Standard for Trading in Thailand

| | Weight (%) | |
Maize property	Grade 1	Grade 2
Average moisture content	14.5	15.5
Other colors kernel	1.0	3.0
Broken kernel and immature kernel	2.0	3.0
Partly broken kernel	4.0	6.0
Heavily damaged kernel	1.5	2.0
Weevilled kernel	2.0	3.0
Foreign material	1.5	2.0

Source: Ministry of Commerce 2001. "Notification Re: Prescribing MAIZE as a Standardized Commodity and the Standards of MAIZE (No.3), B.E.2544 (2001)" (unofficial translation). http://www.dft.moc.go.th/the_files/$$8/level4/Standard%20Maize.pdf.

free. The continuation of these programs for maize in 2010 and beyond may be in doubt, however, as under AFTA, duty on maize is supposed to be zeroed out. At least part of the current incentive will be removed for private sector investment in foreign production.

Starting in 2008, the government of Thailand implemented a pledging scheme for maize similar to the one that already applied to paddy. This program was introduced following farmer complaints in 2008 after high commodity prices fell. Under the previous program, maize was pledged to traders' warehouses at a price in July 2009 of 8.50 baht per kilogram, compared with the then-prevailing market price of 7.00 baht per kilogram. When it became apparent that this scheme was financially unsustainable, the government announced an alternative program of price insurance for maize, similar to that introduced for paddy at the end of 2009. This program aimed to provide a guaranteed price, equivalent to production cost plus 20 percent. According to private sector interviewees, the previous system caused problems, as the quality being stored was allowed to deteriorate. The implications for quality and other matters of the new program have not yet been determined.

Thailand now exports around 600,000 tons of maize a year. The level of production is roughly equivalent to consumption, so it appears that the surplus for export is made up of cross-border imports from Cambodia, Lao People's Democratic Republic, and Myanmar, together with some imports under the official contract farming schemes. Whether the new maize price insurance scheme will deter such unofficial imports or whether Thai farmers will be able to claim unofficial imports as their own production remains to be seen.

Vietnam produced about 4.6 million tons of maize in 2008, on 1.07 million hectares of arable land. This compares with around 1 million tons in the 1990s. Much of this growth has taken place in the upland areas, where maize has replaced upland rice. Maize is also grown extensively in irrigated areas in the Red River Delta and in the north-central coastal region. Yields have improved as the result of the use of improved open-pollinated varieties and of hybrids. However, the area planted to maize each year remains fairly unpredictable, as are the yields that farmers obtain. Farmers report major problems in obtaining credit to finance necessary inputs for maize (Dang and others 2004).

The rapid expansion in production over the longer term reflects income growth and a consequent change in food preferences within the country (Khiem and others 2008). More than 80 percent of maize production is used in the animal and fish feed industries. The remainder is used as cattle feed in the Highlands and as a substitute staple in the Highlands and mountains during times of rice shortage.

Feed mills buy from traders in lots of 300–500 tons. Traders, in turn, buy from collectors and farmers in rural areas, where there is reportedly considerable competition to purchase farm production (Thanh and others 2004). The research for this study did not identify any feed mills with their own buying stations. In early 2009, many smaller feed producers were experiencing problems, and some had temporarily closed their operations. This appears to have been the result of forward buying of high-priced feed inputs before market prices fell back in the second half of 2008. Other contributing factors included reduced demand for their products as a result of a slowdown in demand for Vietnamese fish and seafood exports, competition from imported poultry, and the general economic malaise, which led to a slowdown of growth in Vietnam (Agriculture and Agri-food Canada 2009e).

In addition to maize, feed industries in Vietnam use rice bran, broken rice, and some sweet potato and cassava. Imported feed wheat is also a major ingredient for the aquaculture industry. According to the Animal Feed Association, total demand in 2008 for animal feed was around 17 million tons. Manufactured feed supplies 7 million tons of this demand. The balance comes from feeds formulated on farms by small and medium-size farms from many inputs, including waste materials (Agriculture and Agri-food Canada 2009e).

Ambitious plans exist to expand the size of the feed industry, which implies that significant growth in maize production is likely. In the meantime, the government needs to facilitate imports to guarantee supply for the growing animal feed and animal husbandry industries. Consequently, in 2008 it reduced the import tariff from 5 percent to zero. In other respects, the government plays an insignificant role in the sector. Currently, around 20 percent of the maize that the feed industry requires is imported. Imports have been growing at around 20 percent annually. Approximately 250 feed mills operate in Vietnam, of which 60 percent are locally owned, 20 percent are foreign owned, and 20 percent are controlled by state-owned enterprises. Fifteen large companies, mainly multinationals, produce more than 50 percent of the country's animal and fish feed. These businesses include Cargill, CP, Proconco, Uni-President, ANT, Tomboy, and Grobest. Perhaps because of the involvement of such companies, the national distribution of animal and fish feed is well managed.

Cost Buildup along Maize Chains

The cost buildup illustrated in this section is based on a sample shipment of maize that originates in the upland areas of Thailand and moves to the area around Bangkok, where it is milled and blended into poultry feed suitable for use in the production of broilers. Broilers are then produced in Thailand, fast frozen, and shipped to the Philippines. A schematic diagram of the supply chain that supports this set of activities is presented in figure A.1.

Table A.2 breaks out the process costs for each activity in a typical maize farm-to-export animal feed–domestic poultry production chain. This chain represents relations among chain participants who are independent agents but whose commercial relations are integrated contractually. Other business models operate in Thailand in which stronger forms of joint ownership and joint control exist. The activities described in this particular chain are interconnected under the terms of contracts, which extend for at least one productive season.

Figure A.1   Cost Buildup along a Maize Chain from Upland Thailand to the Philippines

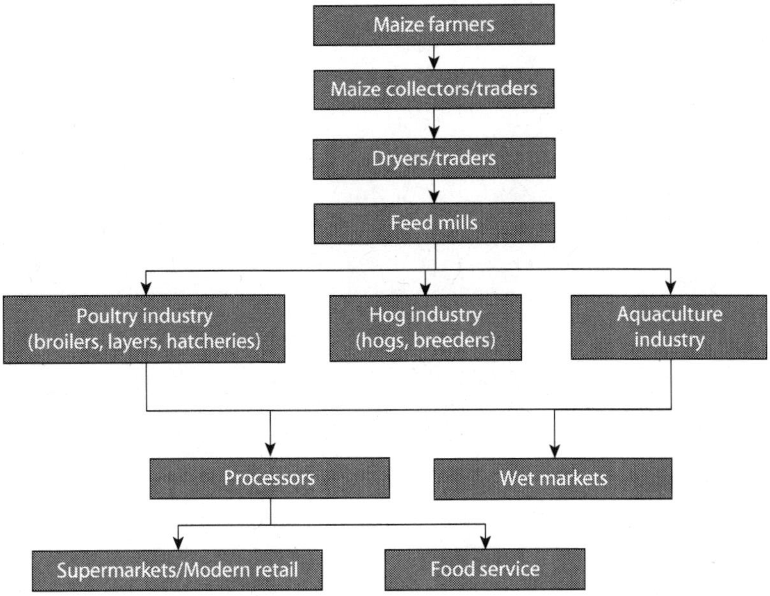

Source: Agrifood Consulting International, Inc. (ACI) team.

Table A.2 Activity Costs, Margins, Processing Time, and Prices within the Thai Maize Domestic Supply Chain

	Farm production	Collector or merchant	Sorter	Feed mill	Chicken producer
Activities and functions	Most of the farmers produce maize under some form of contract farming relationship with collectors or merchants. Typically, farmers receive inputs on credit in advance of crop delivery. The collectors or merchants deduct the cost of inputs and interest from the final sale price. Producers cultivate land and harvest products. Maize is transported to (contract) buyer(s).	Transport Materials: support seeds and all types of cultivation materials to grower (fertilizer, seed, herbicide) Temporary storage Bagging	Drying Sorting Temporary storage Bagging	Drying Sorting Export Grinding Feed mixing Feed packing Transport Feed recipe	Provide feed recipes to suppliers Purchase feed ingredients from suppliers
Specific activities within the supply chain		Sell to feed mill Transport by 6-wheel truck (7.5 tons) to CP Feed Mill, Ayuttaya[a]	Dry to 14.5% moisture content Sort to meet the quality standard required by feed mill	Dry to 14.5% moisture content; redry if stored grain absorbs higher moisture content Separate out bad kernels before the next process	Mix feed Prepare specialized feed recipe for each type of chicken Provide recipe for buyers that want to mix the feed themselves

	Grind and mill Mix with other feed ingredients Bag Export bagged animal feed		
Cost	4.05 baht/kg	Transport: 0.80 baht/kg Storage: 0.05 baht/kg Total = 0.85 baht/kg	2.00 baht/kg	Layer: 7.31 baht/kg Broiler: 9.57 baht/kg
Time	95–120 days	6 hours	1 day	1 day	2–3 days (Bangkok suburban)

Source: Background report on maize and animal feed chains in Thailand from local associate of Agrifood Consulting International, Inc. (ACI).

Note: kg = kilogram; km = kilometer; CP = Charoen Pokphand.

a. The distance from Wung Nam Kaew to Ayuttaya is ±500 km.

Competitive challenges exist at several key junctures within the chain, where prices inside the chain are determined through reference to market prices that suppliers outside the chain demand. Market reference prices, in lieu of prices negotiated and contractually agreed-upon in advance, create risks that need to be managed within the chain or priced and sold outside the chain. Various provisions to manage risks of this sort apply to different modes of contracting. With that said, the fact remains that the price of domestic maize may be constrained by import price parity. The price of frozen broilers may be constrained by the price of frozen broilers imported from Brazil and Poland. Competition in the processed meat business worldwide is increasingly based on the relative, end-to-end efficiency of competing supply chains. Increasingly, it is supply chains and not producers that compete with one another.

Several key points concerning the operation of this chain are worth underscoring. First, maize cultivation is input intensive. In this example, seed, fertilizer, and herbicide account for fully 35 percent of total cultivation and harvesting costs. Second, the elapsed time between when these costs are absorbed and when farm revenues are available to cover them is significant (95–120 days). During this time, the prices of animal feed, maize, and other cost factors can change. Hence mechanisms for risk sharing and for credit extension that bind the supply-chain partners are important to ensure continued investment in productivity-improving inputs and cultivation methods. Third, production relies significantly on labor hired to carry out plowing, sowing, harvesting, and threshing. Fourth, accountability for quality control—and, in particular, for minimizing moisture content—is woven into the set of interlocking contractual obligations to ensure that quality grain passes to the miller. Fifth and finally, chickens of different genetic designs require different feed formula. Millers thus must design their feed products to match the types of chicks that their clients are raising.

Weaknesses in Traditional Maize Chains

The weakest link in the study countries' maize supply chains is the first: the transfer of crops from farmer to trader or, in some cases, directly to feed producer. This is the stage in farm-to-market chains where traditional arms-length selling is still prevalent. Except in Thailand, few supply chains use contracts and other modes for sharing risk. Nor is it common to install systems that synchronize business processes and mutual support with respect to trade financing and information sharing. Unsurprisingly, it is also at this unmodernized entry point that the greatest losses in value occur, including physical and product quality losses.

Postharvest Losses: Quantity and Quality

Just as in the case of rice, after-harvest physical losses continue to be a defining feature of regional maize chains. Ideally, all chain participants should adopt cost-effective technologies that minimize physical and quality losses between harvesting and postharvest storage and drying and that complement one another for maximum effectiveness. Smallholder farmers, however, lack access to appropriate technologies, investment, or effective integration into supply-chain structures that afford adequate incentives. Table A.3 estimates the level of losses that are currently being absorbed in each link in a representative small-farm-to-market chain. It compares these losses with lesser potential losses available with best-in-class technology.

Postharvest handling methods for maize create product quality problems in most countries, as well as volume losses. The ASEAN countries studied here are no exception. Most maize quality problems relate to a failure to dry the grain adequately and to protect it appropriately from insect and rodent attacks.

In *the Philippines*, although there has been some new investment, few traders have built modern drying facilities; most maize is still dried along the side of the road. The moisture content of traded maize frequently exceeds 13 percent. Roads are poor in rural areas, and, as a result, transport costs are high. Given the choice, many feed companies indicate that they would prefer to import from South America rather than buy locally because supply can be erratic during rainy seasons and quality can be

Table A.3   Physical Losses in Representative Farm-to-Market Chains
percent

Supply-chain stage	Typical losses	Minimum estimated losses
Field drying	9	5
Transport	2	1
On-farm drying	5	3
Threshing	3	1
Storage	6	5
Total	23	15

Source: Food and Agriculture Organization (FAO) of the United Nations, Compendium on Post-harvest Operations. http://www.fao.org/inpho/content/compend/text/ch23_03.htm.

spotty. Several government programs exist that are designed to promote more thorough maize drying, and, at present, large feed companies such as San Miguel are starting to buy maize directly from farmers and dry it themselves, rather than relying on traders.

By contrast, in **Thailand**, most traders have access to drying facilities, because feed mills are generally very strict about moisture content and may reject consignments or pay a lower price when the moisture content is too high. Aflatoxin contamination has in the past presented major problems for the Thai maize industry. Farmers who produce two crops harvest their second crop immediately after maturity in July, since they have little time to leave it in the field to dry because of the need to replant. Such maize can have a moisture content of 20–30 percent and needs to be sold immediately to traders with drying facilities (Ekasingh and others 2004). Crops left in the field to dry can normally be sold at an acceptable moisture level of around 15 percent.

In **Vietnam**, storage of maize at the farm level is said to result in significant attacks from rodents and fungal disease, particularly when it is harvested during the rainy season. While various programs have promoted improved on-farm storage, farmers have not taken these up to any great extent. This may be because of the lack of suitable credit facilities, the need to make complementary investments in drying in order to realize a return, and the pressure on poor farmers to sell their crops immediately after harvest in order to raise cash.

A conservative estimate of postharvest losses puts them at 15 percent of the value of production. The result is lower returns to farmers, higher prices for consumers, and greater pressure on the environment because of lower production efficiencies. Smallholder farmers are the most affected by postharvest losses, since they often lack the knowledge, organization, and equipment to handle, process, and store grain safely. Experts[6] estimate these losses for the five countries in this study at a total of 6.4 million tons for the region, a very large number. Addressing the causes of the losses with the same energy and innovation that have modernized the later stages of the supply chains might even, over time, pay for itself by generating significant added amounts of higher-quality maize.

Key Findings

Increasingly, maize supply chains are becoming linked to supply chains for animal feed production in the region, not least due to the activities of large local and multinational firms involved not just in animal feed but in marketing poultry, meat, and fish products to regional and foreign consumers.

The level of direct foreign investment far exceeds the negligible level of the rice sector. Cargill appears to be the largest multinational corporation involved in the maize sector. Among ASEAN-based companies, the Thai firm CP has a major market share in all countries except for the Philippines, where it has recently made significant investments, many of which have gone into supply-chain strengthening.

Conversely, government intervention is more limited in the maize sector than in the rice sector. It has included controls over feed selling prices in Thailand, the Thai government's maize pledging scheme, and the continued involvement of NFA in the market in the Philippines. The level of protection provided by governments to maize producers varies considerably. The Philippines applies a tax of 35 percent on the first 200,000 tons per year and 50 percent thereafter. In Vietnam, on the other hand, import tariffs have been reduced to zero. Reliable access to maize at prices that are internationally competitive has become a prerequisite for the animal feed sector in order to competitively supply the rapidly growing poultry, meat, and egg industries.

Animal feed companies, which often also engage in husbandry of livestock, produce negligible quantities of their own maize requirements. Maize remains predominantly a smallholder crop in the region. However, production has also become increasingly a capital-intensive activity that relies on expensive agrochemical inputs and services provided by third parties to boost productivity. Little or no such intervention, public or private, however, addresses the inefficiencies of the small farmers whose drying practices, among others, cause production to fall significantly short of optimal levels of quantity and quality.

Although agribusinesses have spurred progress in integrating farm input-farm output-animal feed-animal production-meat processing chains, with trader/processors also selling hybrid maize seed, many small companies remain either processing maize into feed or using that feed for small- and medium-scale livestock production, but in both cases unable to provide much in the way of modernizing technology back the supply chain to farmers.

Significant problems continue to confront private sector developers of maize-anchored supply chains. In the Philippines and Vietnam, trade sources indicate that they would much prefer to import maize because of moisture problems with the local smallholder product. Significant problems with moisture have also been noted in Thailand.

More progress has been made in achieving economies of scale and of specialization in the maize sector than in the rice sector. Different development trajectories can be clearly discerned for both, with much strong backward and forward links developing in the maize sector, greater emphasis there on coordination in the achievement of chain-optimizing results, faster adoption of appropriate technologies, and much more rapid growth. The relatively low level of government intervention goes hand in hand with the vigor of the private sector. That relationship also reflects the fact that maize is not a staple of human diets and poultry and meat have yet to become issues for food security policy.

Notes

This report was prepared by the Study Team, drawing on preliminary studies and field research conducted by Francesco Goletti of Agrifood Consulting International, Inc. (ACI). It was based on two missions conducted by ACI to the five countries, a review of selected literature and data, and interviews with key informants. The study was conducted over a 60-day period between September 2009 and January 2010, including a first mission to Indonesia, Malaysia, the Philippines, Thailand, and Vietnam in September–October 2009 and a second mission in January 2010. Given the limited time and resources available for the study, only few key informants could be contacted in each country, and no systematic surveys could be undertaken. The second main source is a draft prepared by Andrew W. Shepherd, senior marketing officer, Market Linkages and Value Chains Group, the Food and Agriculture Organization (FAO) of the United Nations, Rome, as well as case studies prepared by Bustanul Arifin (Indonesia), Larry Wong (Malaysia), and ACI (Vietnam). Fieldwork was conducted in Thailand and the Philippines in July 2009 and in the remaining countries in September–October 2009. The assistance provided to Andrew Shepherd in Thailand by Juejan Tangtermthong and in Rome by Maja Rueegg is gratefully acknowledged. Comments received on earlier drafts from David Dawe of FAO and the case study authors proved very helpful.

1. *Palay* is the term used in the Philippines for unmilled rice.

2. The "in-quota" is shorthand for maximum access volumes negotiated under the third pillar of the Agreement on Agriculture, an international treaty of the World Trade Organization aimed at reforming trade in the sector and encouraging market-friendly policies. http://www.wto.org/english/thewto_e/whatis_e/tif_e/agrm3_e.htm.

3. Feed wheat is wheat used for animal feed, not for human consumption.

4. In its 2009 annual report, the CP Group, the largest animal feed producer in the region, explains its maize procurement policy as follows: "As agricultural

products (maize and soybeans) are the major cost components in animal feed, accounting for 32% of total cost, the company has set up a central purchasing unit responsible for procurement of all ingredients used in livestock and aquatic feed. Our procurement policy is to purchase quality raw material meeting the nutritional requirements with priority given to domestic producers particularly those situated in close proximity to our feed mill plants. This is to support our local farmers as well as to minimize transport costs. Only when domestic supply is insufficient or has inferior quality will the Company resort to imports." http://www.cpfworldwide.com/elctfl/iranr/anrdwlen7.pdf.

5. Based on field surveys completed by the ACI team.

6. Supporting data are from the ASEAN Food Security Information System (AFSIS); percentage of losses from FAO as reported in FAO, Compendium on Post-harvest Operations. http://www.fao.org/inpho/content/compend/text/ch23_03.htm.

References and Other Sources

AFSIS (ASEAN Food Security Information System). http://afsis.oae.go.th/.

Agriculture and Agri-food Canada. 2009a. "Characteristics of Indonesia's Market for Animal Feed." http://www.ats.agr.gc.ca/ase/4771-eng.htm.

———. 2009b. "Characteristics of Malaysia's Animal Feed Market." http://www.ats.agr.gc.ca/ase/5231-eng.htm.

———. 2009c. "Characteristics of the Philippines Market for Animal Feed." http://www.ats.agr.gc.ca/ase/4770-eng.htm.

———. 2009d. "Characteristics of Thailand's Market for Animal Feed." http://www.ats.agr.gc.ca/ase/4774-eng.htm.

———. 2009e. "Characteristics of Vietnam's Market for Animal Feed." http://www.ats.agr.gc.ca/ase/4776-eng.htm.

Charoen Pokphand Group. 2009. "Annual Report." Bangkok, Thailand. http://www.cpfworldwide.com/elctfl/iranr/anrdwlen7.pdf.

Costales, Achilles C. 2008. "The Philippines: Maize Economy, Incentives and Policies." In Maize in Asia: Changing Markets and Incentives, ed. Ashok Gulati and John Dixon. New Delhi: Academic Foundation, in association with the International Maize and Wheat Improvement Center (CIMMYT), the International Food Policy Research Institute (IFPRI), and the International Fund for Agricultural Development (IFAD).

Dang, Thanh Hat, Tran Dinh Thao, Nguyen Tri Khiem, Mai Xuan Trieu, Roberta V. Gerpacio, and Prabhu L. Pingali. 2004. Maize in Vietnam: Production Systems, Constraints, and Research Priorities. Mexico City: International Maize and Wheat Improvement Center (CIMMYT).

Ekasingh, Benchaphun, Phrek Gypmantasiri, Kuson Thong-Ngam, and Pichet Grudloyma. 2004. *Maize in Thailand: Production Systems, Constraints, and Research Priorities*. Mexico City: International Maize and Wheat Improvement Center (CIMMYT).

FAO (Food and Agriculture Organization of the United Nations). "Compendium on Post-harvest Operations." http://www.fao.org/inpho/content/compend/text/ch23_03.htm.

Gerpacio, R. V., J. Jocelyn D. Labios, Romeo V. Labios, and Emma I. Diangkinay. 2004. *Maize in the Philippines: Production Systems, Constraints, and Research Priorities*. Mexico City: International Maize and Wheat Improvement Center (CIMMYT).

Khiem, N. T., Mai Xuan Trieu, Tran Dinh Thao, and Dang Thanh Ha. 2008. "Vietnam: Maize Economy, Incentives and Policies." In *Maize in Asia: Changing Markets and Incentives*, ed. Ashok Gulati and John Dixon. New Delhi: Academic Foundation, in association with the International Maize and Wheat Improvement Center (CIMMYT), the International Food Policy Research Institute (IFPRI), and the International Fund for Agricultural Development (IFAD).

Ministry of Commerce, Thailand. 2001. "Notification Re: Prescribing MAIZE as a Standardized Commodity and the Standards of MAIZE (No.3), B.E.2544" (unofficial translation). http://www.dft.moc.go.th/the_files/$$8/level4/Standard%20Maize.pdf.

Suhariyanto, Kecnk. 2008. "Indonesia: Maize Economy, Incentives and Policies." In *Maize in Asia: Changing Markets and Incentives*, ed. Ashok Gulati and John Dixon. New Delhi: Academic Foundation, in association with the International Maize and Wheat Improvement Center (CIMMYT), the International Food Policy Research Institute (IFPRI), and the International Fund for Agricultural Development (IFAD).

Swastika, Dewa K. S. 2008. "Developing Maize for Improving Poor Farmers' Income in Indonesia." CAPSA-ESCAP. http://www.uncapsa.org/Flash_Detail.asp?VJournalKey=31.

Swastika, Dewa K. S., Firdaus Kasim, Kecuk Suhariyanto, Wayan Sudana, Rachmat Hendayana, Roberta V. Gerpacio, and Prabhu L. Pingali. 2004. *Maize in Indonesia: Production Systems, Constraints, and Research Priorities*. Mexico City: International Maize and Wheat Improvement Center (CIMMYT).

World Trade Organization (WTO). "Agriculture Fairer Markets for Farmers." http://www.wto.org/english/thewto_e/whatis_e/tif_e/agrm3_e.htm.